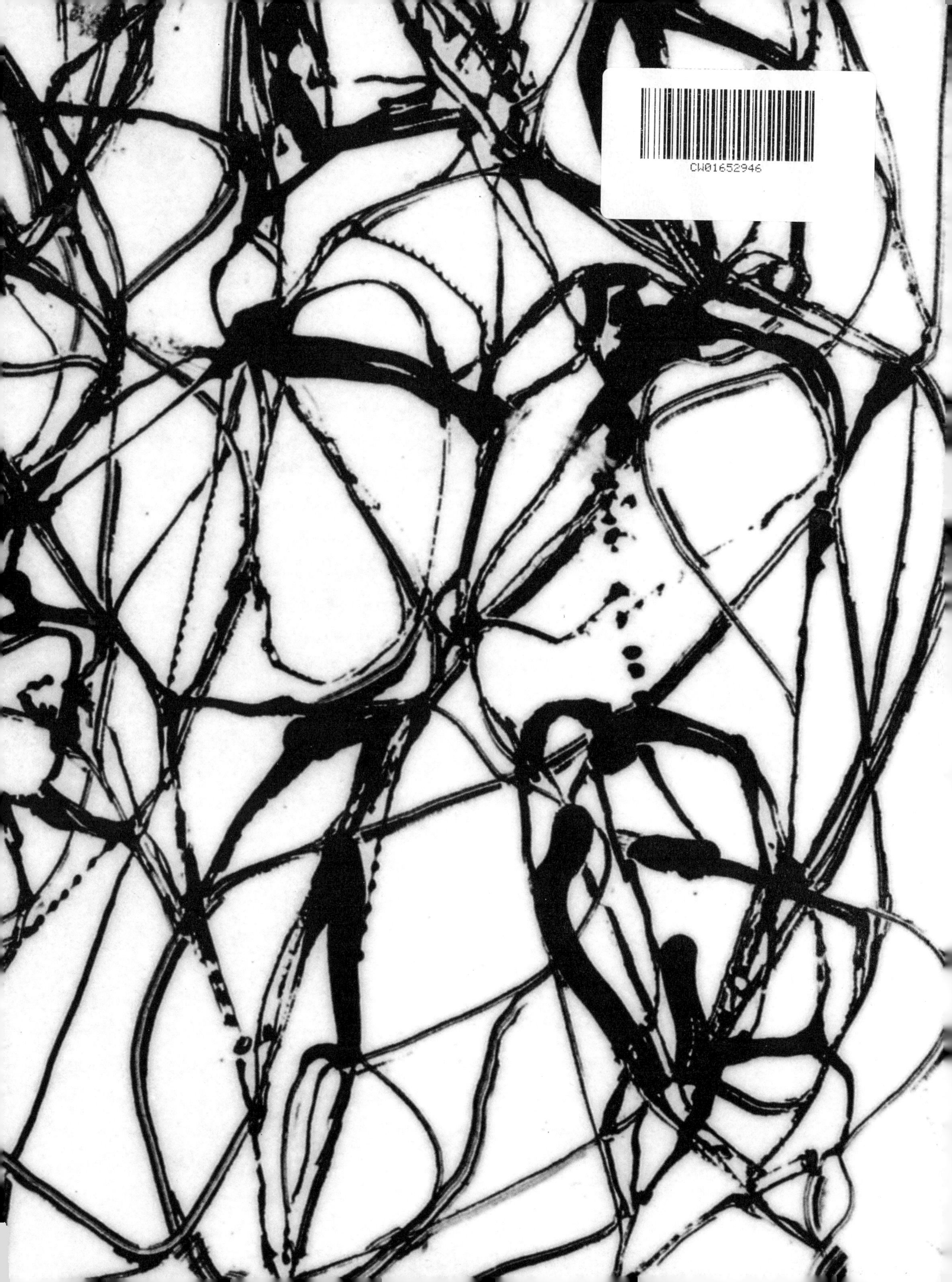

Brice Marden *Prints 1961-1991*

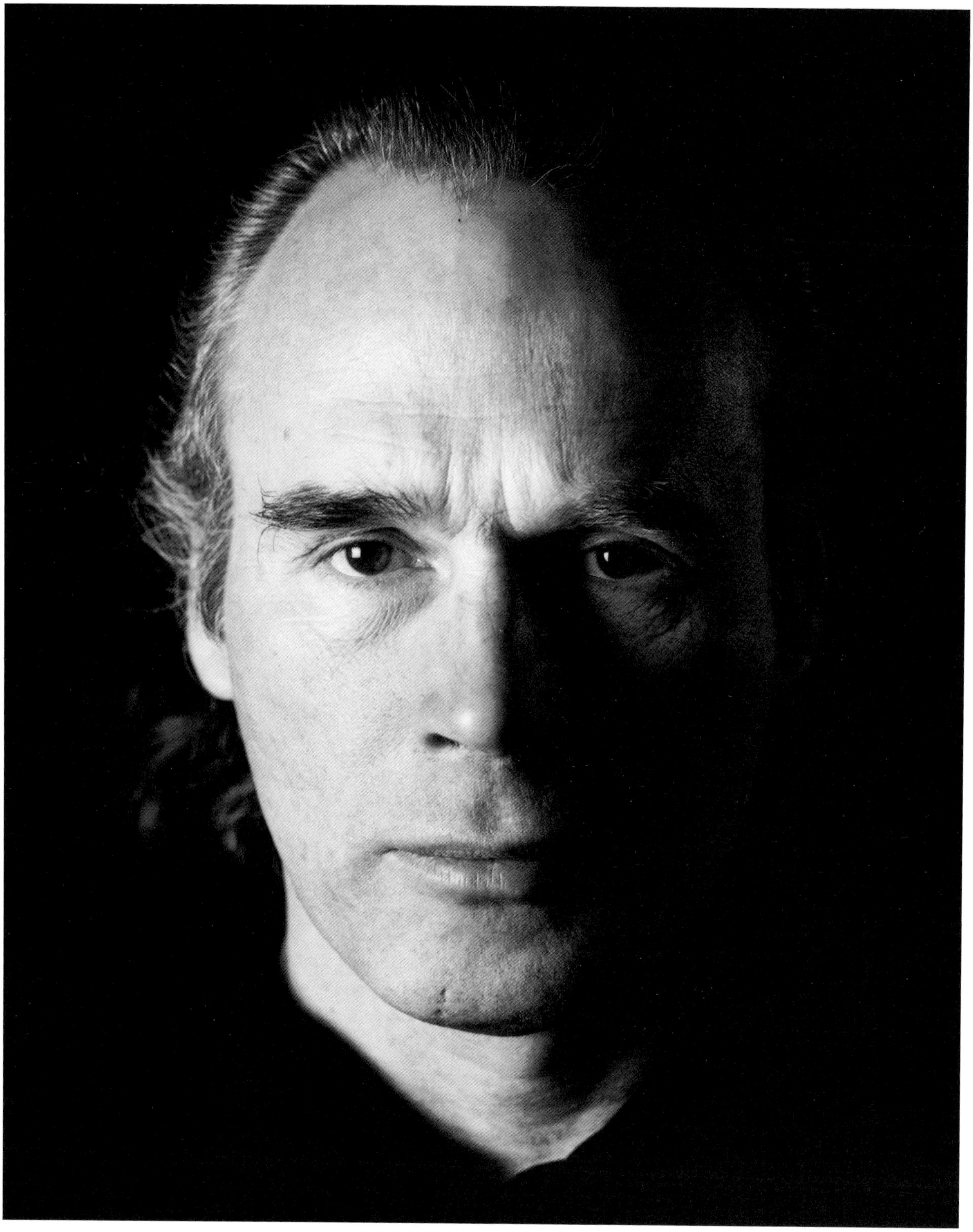

JEREMY LEWISON

Brice Marden *Prints 1961-1991*

A CATALOGUE RAISONNÉ

Tate Gallery

Cover
Etchings to Rexroth 1986 (no.40, print 16)

Frontispiece
Brice Marden © David Seidner 1991

Endpaper
Cold Mountain Series, Zen Study 1 1991 (no.43, detail actual size)

Photographic Credits
Mary Boone Gallery, New York; British Museum Photographs; Leo Castelli Gallery; Krzysztof Cieszkowski; Crown Point Press; D. James Dee; Bill Jacobson; Matthew Marks Inc.; Museum of Modern Art, New York; Documentation Photographique des Collections du Musée National d'Art Moderne, Centre Georges Pompidou; Saatchi Collection; David Seidner; Stedelijk Museum, Amsterdam; Tate Gallery Photographic Department; National Gallery of Art, Washington

ISBN 1 85437 091 X paper
ISBN 1 85437 092 8 cloth

Published by order of the Trustees 1992
For the exhibition at the
Tate Gallery: 26 February – 21 June 1992
and then touring to
Musée d'art moderne de la ville de Paris: 6 July – 4 October 1992
The Baltimore Museum of Art: 25 October 1992 – 3 January 1993

Published by Tate Gallery Publications, Millbank, London SW1P 4RG
Designed by Caroline Johnston
Duotones and colour separations of all exhibited works have been produced directly from the originals
Typeset in Photina by Status Graphics, London
Printed in Great Britain by Westerham Press, Edenbridge, Kent on Parilux Matt 150gsm

Seventy-five copies of the hardback edition are accompanied by an etching by Brice Marden titled 'Han Shan Exit 1' 1992, the details of which are as follows:

Etching, sugarlift aquatint and aquatint on Twinrocker handmade paper
Image size: 14 × 19 (5½ × 7½) Paper size: 19 × 25.4 (7½ × 10)
Colour: black 1 copper plate
Printed by Patricia Branstead at Branstead Studio, New York
and published by Tate Gallery Publications
Edition: 75 plus 15 APs, 3 PPs and 1 BAT
Inscribed below image b.r. and numbered below image b.l.; printer's stamp b.r.

Contents

Foreword

Brice Marden is one of the leading painter-printmakers of the second half of this century and it is fitting that the Tate Gallery, a keen collector of his prints, should present the first retrospective of his graphic oeuvre. Few artists in recent years have worked so sensitively with the intaglio medium and even fewer can have invested such apparently minimal images with so much meaning. Most of Marden's prints appear to be black and white but, like the 'artists of the night' whom he most admires, Velázquez, Goya and Zurbarán, Marden creates such subtle variations of tone that black is perceived as one of the richest of all colours.

The Tate Gallery has long admired Brice Marden's prints and acquired the portfolio 'Five Plates' in 1975, two years after its publication, as a gift of the Contemporary Art Society. Since then it has purchased three further portfolios. This exhibition is one in a series devoted to works on paper and manifests our continuing interest in Marden's work, which in recent years has undergone such radical change.

The exhibition has been selected by Jeremy Lewison, Deputy Keeper of the Modern Collection at the Tate Gallery, who has also written the accompanying catalogue. His own acknowledgments follow. I am delighted that the exhibition is to be seen at the Musée d'art moderne de la ville de Paris and The Baltimore Museum of Art as well as in London.

We are most grateful to Mirabelle Marden, Arnold and Mildred Glimcher, Richard Brown Baker, Crown Point Press and other private collectors, all of whom have lent unique works to this exhibition. The organisation of this show could not have taken place without the help of Matthew Marks, to whom I express our appreciation. Brice Marden's personal interest in the project has been essential and we are grateful to him not only for that, but for providing such a beautiful print to accompany the deluxe hardback edition of the catalogue.

Nicholas Serota *Director*

Acknowledgments

The writing of a catalogue raisonné is a fascinating but frustrating experience because the result can never be perfect. New information always comes to light after publication. This catalogue will be no exception. I can make no claims for it as a definitive work but merely as representing the latest state of my knowledge of Brice Marden's prints. In the early days of his printmaking activity he kept no records and therefore I have relied heavily on his memory. Even a professional organisation like Crown Point Press has only sketchy records of its early productions. More recently accurate notes have been kept which have greatly facilitated my work.

In the compiling of details I have been enormously helped by Matthew Marks and the staff of his gallery, particularly Elisabeth Ivers. I am grateful to them all for their time and patience. I also enjoyed a fleeting visit to San Francisco to talk with Kathan Brown who, more than anyone, has been responsible for the extraordinary quality of Marden's production. The information she provided has been invaluable in writing this catalogue. In New York, discussions with Jennifer Melby proved equally useful and Bob Feldman of Parasol Press was, as ever, genial and helpful. My visits to New York were greatly assisted by Peter and Laurie Rippon, Rebecca Smith and Peter Stevens and Jodie and Ian Wilkie, to all of whom I offer warm thanks. I am also grateful to Riva Castleman and Wendy Weitman of the Museum of Modern Art, New York for some vital last minute information and Mary Boone Gallery for help with photographs.

At the Tate Gallery I would particularly like to thank the staff of the Exhibitions, Registrar's and Publications departments for their constant support for the project, often in the most trying of circumstances, Krzysztof Cieszkowski and Beth Houghton of the Library and Jo Firth, Julia Gardiner and Fiona Robertson of the Modern Collection.

Finally, I am particularly grateful to Brice Marden with whom I spent many fascinating hours talking about prints. Without his support, co-operation and patience this exhibition could not have taken place.

Jeremy Lewison

The Discipline of Feeling
The Prints of Brice Marden

Brice Marden's studio above the Bowery is like a haven. To a visitor to New York the Bowery appears to be one of New York's noisiest and messiest streets, with customised trucks rumbling up and down, nose to tail, the frequent brain-damaging wail of police sirens, the constantly intrusive automobile horns, the sounds of ghetto blasters blaring out and its hardware shops whose contents of boilers, sinks and garbage cans spill out onto the pavements. In the midst of all this chaos Marden's studio is a place of order and, to the visitor at least, never an arena of activity. He never sees Marden at work. Crossing the threshhold he is immediately struck by an astonishing collection of shells with the most exquisite markings, arranged precisely in columns according to types and sizes. In the middle of the table lies a magnifying glass, placed so as not to disturb the grid. Two steps further in and he observes paintings in progress leaning against the wall, drawings in progress either pinned to the wall, flat on a table or leaning at an angle on a drawing board, a collection of sinuous sticks of various lengths and thicknesses standing in a jar, a small branch hung on the wall, a trolley normally used as a palette but without any paint, brushes large and small upright in another pot, containers of pigment and bottles of ink, postcards of paintings by Paul Cézanne and Jackson Pollock and books of oriental poetry and calligraphy, some open and some closed, often with passages underlined in pencil. There is very little paint on the floor and little sense of the arduous task of making a painting. The noise of the street is intrusive and, in the summer, the heat and humidity of this studio under the roof is crippling. But this is the studio of an artist for whom discipline, equanimity, equilibrium and control are key. The studio is a private world for a private activity.

Student Years

Marden was born in the New York City suburb of Bronxville on 15 October 1938 but was brought up in Briarcliff Manor in the county of Westchester. After spending a year at Florida Southern College, Lakeland in 1957–8 he moved to Boston University's School of Fine and Applied Arts where he was awarded a BFA in 1961.

His family did little to encourage his interest in art and had expected him to pursue a career in hotel management. However, his time at Boston was formative not only through the teaching he received but also through the art he encountered at first hand in the Museum of Fine Arts, and the Busch-Reisinger Museum and the Fogg Art Museum in Cambridge. Marden principally pursued studies in painting and remembers Reed Kay, a Boston painter, as having been a good teacher; he also took courses in printmaking, under the direction of Karl Fortess, with whom he learnt to make woodcuts and etchings. None of the former has survived. He recalls taking only one or two terms of printmaking classes and that at that time it did not appeal to him much. Most of his work was figurative and based on life drawing but, away from class, he was beginning to be a little more experimental, looking at Cézanne and Cubism. These interests are manifested in his earliest etchings (nos.1–4) which are respectively variations of the Cézannesque bathing theme, the fractured, Cubist bust, the synthesised landscape and still life.

Marden made the first three etchings at Boston University. Already these prints display some of the characteristics of his mature work, such as a tendency towards shallow depth, an emphasis on the plane, an interest in diagonal marks to divide the rectangle, extensive cross-hatching and, in 'Untitled' (no.1), both the division of the image into three discrete but linked sections and the joining of vertical forms. Furthermore, although Marden's oeuvre is renowned for its abstractness he considers his work to be closely related to landscape and the figure. Again these abiding themes, albeit treated in a relatively literal manner, are announced in the earliest works.

Spending the summer of 1961 at Yale Summer School of Music and Art in Norfolk, Connecticut, Marden found that his training had been much more academic than that of most of his fellow students. He felt that they had been 'taught out of *Artforum* and just had no grounding'.[1] He had appreciated his own Boston training for its immediacy: 'We had a model and you painted your painting and it was talked about in relation to the model', whereas students at other universities had been taught 'the look of art and it was all very second hand'. Nevertheless, when he was at Boston Marden already knew that he would not pursue a career as a painter from life, in the sense of making direct representations of objects before him, because he was already very interested in Abstract Expressionism, particularly the works of Franz Kline.

In addition to painting at Yale Norfolk, he studied etching with Richard Zieman who in turn had studied under Gabor Peterdi, a printmaker in the tradition of S.W. Hayter. Marden was still 'trying to figure out what Cubism was … this whole thing about front and back, simultaneous viewings. You read all these people trying to explain what Cubism is and you still don't really understand it so you have to try it out visually'.

Yale Norfolk was considered to be a trial ground for students intending to go on to study for the MFA at Yale University's School of Art and Architecture, where Marden enrolled in the autumn of 1961. Among his tutors at Yale University were Esteban Vicente, Alex Katz, whose teaching Marden valued very highly and, in printmaking, Gabor Peterdi with whom he studied etching exclusively. Peterdi's own approach to printmaking had little impact on Marden, who rejected his tutor's devotion to colour printing and his interest in Surrealistic abstraction, but the printmaking course was compulsory and he was able to learn from Peterdi a considerable amount of technical knowledge and sophistication. He would spend on average one day per week in the printmaking studio along with his fellow students Chuck Close, Richard Serra, Robert Mangold and Nancy Graves. Under the direction of Josef Albers, Yale was undoubtedly the pre-eminent art school in the early sixties.

Marden recalls that in his first year he was put into

> an advanced painting situation ... They put me into a more independent study group where I went in and had my own studio and my own space and I just painted. I had two visiting critics who came up from New York, John Schueler and Alex Katz. Schueler was a romantic and Katz was a real classicist. I also took drawing classes with Bernard Chaet and Bill Bailey but I quit, because basically there had been a lot of emphasis on drawing at Boston University, and I figured out I could draw from the model as well as I wanted to. At Yale they just wanted me to draw the same thing in a different style. The style in Boston was very painterly and we drew in the planes using heavy charcoal lines whereas at Yale it was very much related to Ingres. And I just said 'you are just trying to teach me a different style'. So in the second semester I told them I was not going to attend the class any more, and at that point I started to do a lot of abstract drawing in my studio and they accepted that. The next year Philip Pearlstein came to teach drawing and he used to set up one pose and we would draw it for six hours. It was a different kind of discipline and I took that. I did not mind that.

Disciplined practice was already highly attractive to Marden.

Printmaking was less structured and students could make any kind of image they liked. Marden remembers that many of his fellow students would make prints influenced by Mauricio Lasansky, where figures would 'disappear into a lot of marks ... I remember that there was a big thing about marks and that any mark was okay. It didn't make any difference how you made the mark. You could use any kind of mark.' Lasansky was influenced by S.W. Hayter and Picasso and his prints of the early fifties were characterised by strong *chiaroscuro* and a very active surface.

The emphasis on the mark was of critical importance to Marden, who henceforth was to exploit accidental and random mark-making in etching in direct contrast to highly controlled composition. He was less keen on the lengths that some of his colleagues would go to make marks; they had a tendency to use all kinds of unconventional instruments. Marden was and remains wedded to relatively traditional methods and media.

His continued interest in Abstract Expressionism was fuelled by regular visits to New York City. He remembers being impressed by exhibitions of Kline's work over the years (Kline died in 1962) while Willem de Kooning was also highly visible in exhibitions at Sidney Janis Gallery and Allan Stone Gallery in March and October 1962 respectively. Paintings by Jackson Pollock were scarcer, Pollock having died in the previous decade. Marden was also attracted to the work of Alfred Leslie and Ralph Humphrey and, while he was already aware of Jasper Johns and Robert Rauschenberg, he 'did not agree with their aesthetic. It was Pop Art and I was much more into Abstract Expressionism.' In spite of the fact that Johns's work used many of the strategies of Abstract Expressionism Marden read it in the way it was presented by 'the media ... kind of jokey.' He had read up on Duchamp but rejected his 'elegance' in preference for the expressiveness of Kline.

Although Abstract Expressionism still held sway in New York there was already a strong groundswell of critical reaction against its fundamental tenets, as evidenced in the work of Johns and Rauschenberg, Kenneth Noland and Ellsworth Kelly, Carl Andre and Frank Stella and Andy Warhol and Roy Lichtenstein. Barnett Newman and Ad Reinhardt were the models for a new generation of artists who admired the ambition of the Abstract Expressionists but rejected their idealism, heroic posture and angst-ridden outpourings. Marden had seen exhibitions of paintings by Newman as early as 1959 when Newman showed at French and Co. but he failed to appreciate them. He was more interested in the intimacy of easel painting favoured by Kline and de Kooning, although he must have been struck by Newman's emphasis on clear structure. The influence of Kline is evident in 'Untitled' 1961 (no.5) with its sweeping, slashing aquatint lines, some of which tail off into brush-like marks. As interesting as the influence of Kline, however, is the way in which this print anticipates Marden's later interest in oriental calligraphy. Kline himself strenuously denied such an influence on his own work, and Marden was yet to appreciate Far Eastern art, but there is no doubting his early interest in looping, intersecting lines, crisscrossing in energetic motion. These prints also show that Marden was beginning to come to terms with the gamut of etching techniques. He has

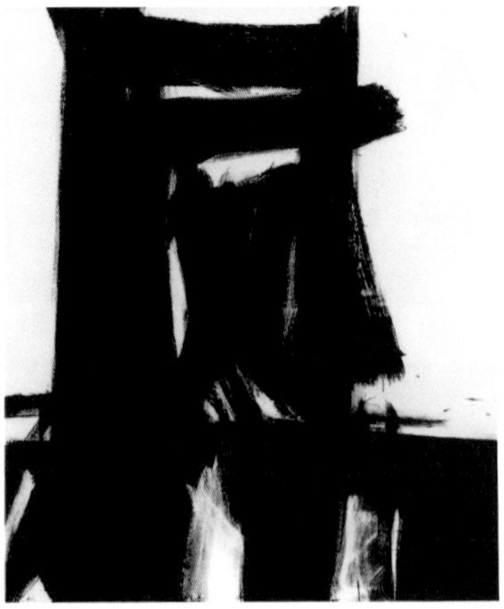

Franz Kline **Meryon** 1960–1 Oil on canvas 235.9 × 195.6 (92⅞ × 77) *Tate Gallery. Purchased 1969*

employed hardground etching, drypoint, sugarlift, foul biting and burnishing. He was also keen to exploit the potential in etching for varying the density of the ink by biting the plate in different areas for different lengths of time.

In two other prints (no.6 and a later state of it) Marden emulated some of de Kooning's mannerisms in paintings of the late fifties: the V shapes, the subdivision of the image into blocks of tone and the use of slashing, broad bands of black. Marden describes de Kooning as having had a 'huge influence' on him and remembers seeing de Kooning's etching 'Revenge' 1960[2] 'which really blew me away'. Paintings such as de Kooning's 'Bolton Landing' 1957 and 'Suburb in Havana' 1958[3] must also have had an enormous impact on Marden. The later of the two states of no.6 foreshadows Marden's predilection for horizontally divided formats contrasting light and dark tones, which was to become a hallmark of his work in all media. One other print of 1961 (no.8) suggests that he was also fascinated by de Kooning's black and white paintings and drawings of the late forties. Printed in small editions by Marden himself, most of these sheets were given to friends as presents or, in the case of Chuck Close, gambled away at pool.

By the end of his first year at Yale, Marden began to make paintings in which he divided a rectangular field horizontally and vertically by two lines intersecting at right angles, creating four quadrants. This format was repeated in two further prints surviving from the Yale period, 'Untitled' *c.*1963 (no.9) and 'Untitled' *c.*1963 (no.10). Both relate to a painting 'Untitled' 1962–3[4] in which two black and two grey rectangles, arranged in a chequerboard fashion, fill, or almost fill, a rectangular format. The grey and black rectangles do not quite meet along the central axes however. In the squarer of the two prints (no.9) Marden reverses the equation, so that the axial lines which bisect the field are rich in tone whereas the areas they border are blank save for some foul biting. The rough marks in the other print find their equivalent in Marden's emphasis on texture in the painting as well as in many drawings of this period. The division of the rectangle vertically and horizontally echoes the edges of the canvas or the paper, thereby emphasising its planar quality.

The division of the field by two lines intersecting at right angles, particularly in 'Untitled' *c.*1963 (no.9), indicates that Marden was interested in the paintings of Mondrian, although the former's nervous line and the impurity of his use of foul biting are distinctively different. Marden eschews the grand gestural marks of Abstract Expressionism in favour of a tighter, more controlled stroke. This finds its full expression in 'Watsonville' 1963 (no.11) which Marden made following his summer visit to Carmel, where he stayed with the folk singer, Joan Baez, his sister-in-law.[5]

Watsonville, north Monterey, according to Marden, is 'the artichoke capital of the world'. He remembers 'driving through there at dusk. They have these low rolling hills of artichoke plants like vines sprawling on the ground. There would be these plants going off over the hills. It is like being in a Rothko. I remember saying that.' The association with Rothko was related to the light more than to the configuration of lines. The resulting print, which he made on his return to Yale, is almost perspectival in the convergence of diagonal lines in the bottom two sections and is an abstract equivalent to the receding rows of artichoke plants. The upper rectangle relates to these sections like sky to land. The overall composition anticipates Marden's later interest in the post and lintel format.

The bisection of the bottom section of the print into two vertical panels echoes the configuration of drawings and paintings which Marden was now making, notably 'Dylan Study I' 1963 and 'Dylan Study II' 1963, named after the folk singer, Bob Dylan, who was in the crowd with whom Marden mixed. The 'Dylan' paintings were among the first works painted in what was to become Marden's signature format, although at this time the surface still consisted entirely of oil paint. It was not until 1966 that he began to combine oil paint with wax to make smoother, opaque surfaces.

Dylan Study 1 1963 Oil on canvas 106.5 × 127 (42 × 50) *Asher Edelman, Lausanne, Switzerland*

Marden relates how he began to arrive at the rectangular configuration of these works:

> I remember working at the Munson Gallery while I was at Yale. I got lots of rectangular mat boards which I would use as backing for the collages I did. At one point I did a lot of collages. One winter there was an iced-over sidewalk in front of the gallery and I spent a lot of time getting the ice off the sidewalk and I got this huge blister on my hand. I couldn't paint for about three weeks. So I made these collages which were a big help and sort of began to define this kind of rectangular situation.

The paintings were made in close tones of grey, green and blue and manifest Marden's desire to distance himself from the colourful paintings of the Abstract Expressionists. His teachers had criticised him for producing work too dependent on these models and his answer was to reduce his means. Marden had already unsuccessfully encountered Albers's colour theory while at Boston but now that he was at Yale, he felt bewildered and intimidated by it so he eliminated strong colour. 'What I used as my colour reference was my academic training where you observed the colours on a figure and you would play with them. It came out of that.'

Marden's restricted palette and his particular passion for blacks and greys also derived from his admiration of Manet and Zurbarán, whose work he had discovered while at Boston. In Manet he observed an emphasis on the brush stroke within broadly defined areas of black (see, for example, the black trousers of the firing squad in Manet's 'Execution of the Emperor Maximilien' 1867 in the Museum of Fine Arts, Boston),[6] and in Zurbarán he admired the object quality conveyed by the paint surface itself. 'A drapery could look like a coat. It had a weight to it that it would not have as silk but it still looked like silk'.[7] Marden's paintings at this time emit a sense of lightness while also conveying an impression of density. He was interested in these painters from an abstract point of view, analysing the work in terms of passages of paint. 'You could squint and it could look like a Kline', he remarked.

New York – Paris – New York

Marden left Yale in the summer of 1963 and by the autumn had set up in New York City in a small apartment on the Lower East Side. To support himself and his family he took a job as a uniformed guard at the Jewish Museum which, at that time, under the directorship of Alan Solomon, had one of the liveliest programmes of exhibitions of contemporary art in New

York. Among the shows which Marden helped to guard was the first retrospective of Jasper Johns.[8] He was stationed in a room which had early paintings including targets as well as 'Construction with a Piano' 1954.[9] 'That was a big deal for me. That realism related very much to the kind of realism, the sort of obsessiveness that was in Zurbarán'. The way Johns hijacked the painterly, broken surface for non-expressive purposes, to describe mundane objects in a deadpan way, particularly impressed Marden and encouraged him to continue on his own track. The emphasis on a disrupted surface of brush strokes in Johns's paintings far exceeded Marden's but found its equivalent in some of the latter's drawings. Marden was also interested in the relation of the motif to the plane in Johns's painting. 'It was right up'. Johns's use of grey must also have acted as an encouragement to Marden for he could see that, within these restricted means, Johns could achieve considerable variety and inflection.

Among other exhibitions which Marden remembers at the Jewish Museum was the *Black and White* exhibition,[10] where he admired the paintings of, among others, Ellsworth Kelly and Myron Stout. The exhibition also included works by Newman, Pollock, de Kooning, Kline, Johns, Rauschenberg and Stella among others, all of whom would have interested him. The very fact that the exhibition focused on restricted colour must have been pertinent to his reductive pursuits.

Marden quit the Jewish Museum in the summer of 1964 when he and his family were invited by his parents-in-law to spend a few months in Paris. His father-in-law, Albert Baez, who worked for UNESCO, was currently stationed there. The *chambre de bonne* of his sixth *arrondissement* house became Marden's studio. His regular routine was to work in the studio in the mornings and to visit exhibitions and galleries in the afternoon. He frequently went to the Louvre, obtaining a free pass for artists, and saw important exhibitions by Jean Fautrier and Kline at the Musée national d'art moderne. He visited small commercial galleries 'where they would have a little Giacometti or Balthus, a little this, a little that. Every gallery had a little bit of everything.' He already knew the work of many of these artists 'but this really familiarised me with them.' He also saw the work of fellow Americans Warhol and Rauschenberg, as well as of the European *informel* artists such as Wols. In addition he remembers the monochrome paintings of Yves Klein. But the most important artistic influence on him was Giacometti.

Marden had seen Giacometti exhibitions in New York before he came to Paris. He particularly admired Giacometti's use of restricted but nevertheless glowing colour and the way a frame drawn around the image, inside the edges of the canvas, would define space by creating a front plane and establishing a scale of distance relative to it. Marden used this device in his later etchings. The encrusted surfaces of Giacometti's sculptures (along with the roughened surfaces of Fautrier's '*Otage*' paintings, which Marden discovered for the first time in Paris) also struck a sympathetic chord, for they were both expressive and descriptive in a disciplined way.

Marden's stay in Paris coincided with a massive architectural cleaning programme instigated by de Gaulle in the aftermath of the Algerian crisis. 'They were restuccoing and repainting walls and I used to watch them. There would be all these drips at the bottom and my paintings at the time had these sorts of areas with drips at the bottom and I really related to that.' Marden was attracted to the physical surface of the walls which was dense, flat but with considerable depth, a real life equivalent to his own paintings. At home in his studio he would make *frottages* of tiles in the kitchen and these led to a series of grid drawings of dense, graphite surfaces.

First Screenprints

While in Paris, Marden succumbed to family pressure to apply for teaching posts back in the USA but continually failed to gain acceptance. Eventually his wife realised his heart was not in it and, finding their lifestyles incompatible, on their return they separated. In order to survive he took up employment in a frame shop in New York but he was soon asked to leave after breaking one sheet of glass too many. His next job, in 1965, was at Chiron Press, then exclusively a silk screen shop, which printed posters for the *Paris Review* and prints by Robert Motherwell, Saul Steinberg, Alex Katz, Helen Frankenthaler, Ellsworth Kelly and Ernst Trova among others. He shortly moved into the loft which became available above the shop.

Marden never cut any screens but he mixed inks and helped to print. He describes how 'we would print the first colour and I would print a few extra ones on this good paper. I would get a big rectangle and I would take it upstairs and draw over it.' At that point he was drawing monochromatic rectangles. The coloured surface felt less intimidating than the blank sheet and its greasy quality was particularly attractive to Marden.

Before moving to the loft above Chiron Press and while still living on Avenue C, Marden had started to make monochromatic paintings which he describes as 'having grown out of the involvement with those walls in Paris, and thinking about Giacometti.' He recalls that the painting 'Pair' 1965,[11] a monochromatic diptych, 'started out as a little homage to Giacometti. It had a frame all around the outside which eventually got painted out.' Printing monochromatic proofs obviously would have appealed to his sensibility at this time, and working on them helped him

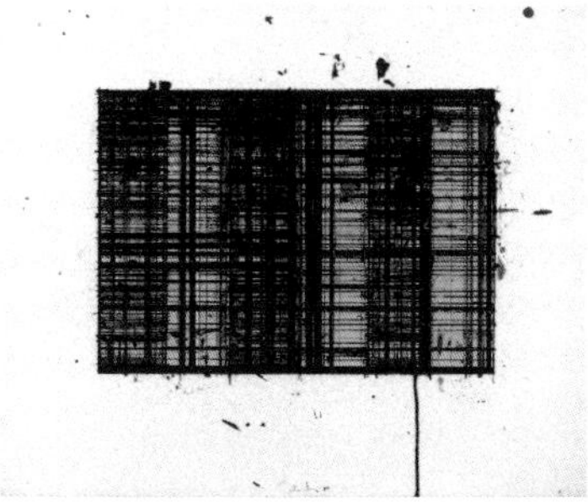

Painting Study 1 1980 Ink over screenprint on paper 49.9 × 60.3 (19 11/16 × 23 3/4) *Private Collection*

overcome the feeling of intimidation which occurred when he moved into the large loft above Chiron Press.[12] In drawing over other artists' stage proofs Marden anticipated his later practice of using his own screenprints and etchings as a base, giving him images to work against and on which to elaborate, as well as providing interesting and varied surfaces (for example 'Painting Study 1', 1980).

Marden describes his drawings over other artist's proofs as a lot of 'rectangles and squares. I was doing things that were really like three rectangles and sort of Judd-like in appearance. They were ideas for paintings which were never executed.' His first screenprint, 'Four' 1966 (no.12), was a variation on this theme.

Each of the three printed tones – dark grey, intermediate grey and light grey – is identifiable by drips in the band at the bottom of the print. This mimics the device he employed in his paintings from 1964 onwards. He derived it partly from his observation of the dribbles at the bottom of the stucco walls in Paris, and used it to narrate the history of the act of painting, or in the case of 'Four', of making the print. The border was also an indication of the scale of the mark and the overall image. The unpainted border had been a feature of a number of Johns's grey paintings of the late fifties which Marden knew well.

The build up of tones in 'Four' was exactly paralleled in the paintings of this period. Each layer, according to Marden, is like a 'veil of feeling ... Each layer was a colour, a feeling ... a concentration of feelings in layers. The drips memorialized the feelings, the layers, the colours.'[13] It was this concentration, the ability to transcend the object and invest it with feeling and mysticism which he particularly admired in Zurbarán. As for Johns, 'He took an absolute reality – a flag, a target – and made painting out of it. That really fascinated me.'[14]

The format of the print extends Marden's interest in the diptych consisting of separated panels first announced in 'Pair', while the elongated vertical shape of each block was adumbrated in 'Decorative Painting' 1964–5,[15] which is itself a painting of grey superimposed on grey. The smooth but slightly streaked surface was a new feature of Marden's art and echoes his use of beeswax combined with paint on the canvases, beginning with 'Wax I' 1966.

Comparison has often been made between Marden's use of wax and Johns's use of encaustic, but their material look is entirely different. Johns's paintings have hardened drips and a plastic-like surface. The encaustic is bound by wax. At times it can seem like brittle glue. Marden's surface is soft, smooth and malleable and is bound by oil. He had found that oil paint on its own created a reflective surface which disturbed the depth of colour. By combining it with wax he flattened and deadened it, asserting the

Decorative Painting 1964–5 Oil on canvas 105.4 × 45 (41½ × 17¾)
Herbert and Lenore Schorr, New York

primacy of the plane while at the same time building up a physical depth of medium. Keeping it warm on a hot plate, Marden applied it with brushes and smoothed it over with a spatula or a palette knife, invariably leaving the marks of the brush somewhat visible beneath the surface. These marks were not repeated in 'Four' but in 'Lana', 'Lana 2' and 'Lana 3' 1966 (nos.13–15), made around the same time, Marden parodies this process.

The 'Lana' series consists of three states. 'Lana 2' and 'Lana 3' combine the two screens of 'Lana' with one further screen. In 'Lana' Marden drew onto the screen with a crayon, emphasised the strokes, and printed it black. He then printed a flat grey-blue. The hatching on the first screen is sufficiently dense to break through the flat colour whose edge is subverted by the crayon marks which spill over the border along the bottom. The texture of this print is almost a screenprinted equivalent to the painting 'Last Dylan Study' 1964–6. Marden states that he did not cut any screens and thinks that he must either have drawn the edges or have taped them. In 'Lana 2' he added a flat, warm grey screen, which in 'Lana 3' he printed pink. The crayon marks which overlap the border indicate the progressive stages of the print and to that extent the passage of time. However, because of the transparency of the ink each layer retains a ghostly presence in the main body of the final state. Marden was not interested in the perfect finish achieved by a number of his contemporaries, such as Kelly, but retained evidence of the autographic mark, associated with Abstract Expressionism, as a transmitter of feeling. He states that in creating the border in the prints he 'was much more self-conscious because of the scale but it was also pretty self-conscious in the big paintings' in which the drips and dribbles of previous layers of paint were allowed to remain.

The use of grey-pink was consistent with a number of paintings of this period, for example '4:1 (For David Novros)' 1966,[16] while the landscape format of the 'Lana' prints is broadly similar to that of paintings such as 'TKB' 1966 and 'Nico' 1966. In terms of texture, configuration and emphasis on the plane Marden was attempting in screenprint an equivalent for the paintings he included in his first one-man show at Bykert Gallery, New York in the autumn of 1966. Like the paintings, 'Lana 2' and 'Lana 3' have ostensibly calm surfaces which disguise hidden activity.

The opportunity to make screenprints had arisen because Marden was living over the shop. Steve Poleski, its owner, suggested he make use of the facilities during closing hours. The 'Lana' series was the fruit of two weekends' labour.

He had made no prints between 1964 and 1965 because he had no access to equipment and for the same reason another two years elapsed before he embarked on 'Gulf' 1969 (no.16). In 1966 he left Chiron Press

Nico ('s Painting) 1966 Oil and wax on canvas 68 × 100 (26¾ × 39⅜) *Private Collection*

when he was offered his first show at Bykert. 'The Gallery got together some money so I did not have to work and I had several months to finish off the paintings for the show.' The paintings did not sell and after the exhibition he took up a job as Rauschenberg's studio assistant, having been introduced to him by the artist Dorothea Rockburne. He was also teaching at the School of Visual Art in New York City.

Marden's paintings in this period were often named after friends or had titles which suggested landscapes. The paintings did not depict memories but rather evoked them through colour and rhythm: the rhythm of a format (the relationship of height to width), the rhythm of brush strokes or sweeps of the spatula, the resonance, weight and balance of colour. Colour evoked emotions and characteristics associated with the named subject. 'Nebraska' is described by Marden as 'a landscape painting'. 'Nico', he states, 'was based on this idea of blondness, the blondness of a Nordic singer,[17] while '"TKB" was like a mourning painting for a friend of mine that died. There was a whole group of mourning paintings. There was one for Otis,[18] there was a painting called "Passing". There was this Kent State affair[19] and that was my painting. I did that at that time.' Later Marden made the 'Backs' series which were based on the height of his second wife Helen (69 inches) who temporarily had turned her back on him. Each was therefore an equivalent for a human.

Marden has often been grouped with Minimal artists but clearly his purpose was at variance with the aims of Stella, who was interested in literalness and whose blacks within a series rarely varied, or Judd, who created sculptures which asserted their objectness. Marden was dealing with feelings and considered his work to be an extension of the tradition of Abstract Expressionism without the heroic grandiloquence or the hackneyed look of the second generation. Restrained and muted it might have been, but it was nonetheless expressive of reserved emotion. Marden was no more nor less a Minimalist than Carl Andre, whom he befriended early on and whose work he admired for its radicality and its stress on the physical nature of materials. Marden continued to carry in his mind the models of Manet, Zurbarán, Goya and Velázquez, the supreme masters of black painting. The restricted formats and range of colours, the restrained but eloquent surfaces were the 'spartan limitations' within which he worked. 'Within these strict confines ... which I have painted myself into' he wrote, 'I try to give the viewer something to which he will react subjectively. I believe these are highly emotional paintings not to be admired for any technical or intellectual reason but to be felt.'[20] Marden's intentions appear to be similar to Rothko's but, compared to Rothko's optical surfaces, the resulting paintings are more physical. Other painters, such as Robert Ryman, also made paintings of a physical nature, but Ryman's work was concerned with the process of painting and the nature of paint rather than with any associations beyond the canvas. Robert Mangold, on the other hand, painted monochromatic canvases from which all traces of the hand of the artist were expunged by the use of rollers. Like Stella and Judd, his paintings dealt with notions of obviousness and repetition. Stella's often quoted dictum 'what you get is what you see' would describe much of the art of the early sixties but Marden shied away from this credo. The difference between Marden's art and that of his Minimalist contemporaries is that his paintings were actually intended to transcend the fact of their material presence.

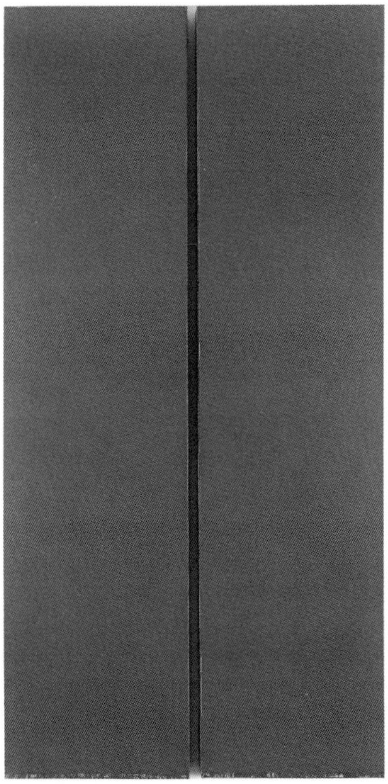

For Helen 1967 Oil and wax on canvas, two panels, overall size 175.2 × 88.9 (69 × 35)
Helen Harrington Marden, New York

Marden did not persist with the monotone canvas, however, for in 1968 he introduced the two-panel, two-toned painting where the panels were joined together. These paintings were a further development of a work of 1967, 'For Helen', in which two vertical canvases were hung a few inches apart, itself a reprise of 'Pair'. He thereby moved from the unitary canvas to the diptych. His principal concern now was how to combine two different colours of equal weight that would create a unified whole. At about this time he also eliminated the border along the bottom edge, since it would have set up a dialogue with the vertical join of the two panels and disturbed the unification of two parts by stressing lateralness. As Linda Shearer pointed out, 'The delicate balance of such reduced elements – color, shape, surface, and a single line – is jeopardized by the juxtaposition of two panels, each containing a line just above the bottom edge.'[21]

By 1969 he had begun to make triptychs which gave him greater scope for exploring different colour combinations. The joined edges were far from perfect surfaces, for Marden retained delicate markings and inconsistencies reminiscent of the lower borders of earlier paintings. Nicks in the surface allowed the viewer to see the layers of underpainting beneath the skin. Their different colours encouraged a deeper understanding of the painting, as though the viewer was penetrating to a new psychological depth.

Marden used the abutted, two-panel configuration in a print titled 'Gulf' which Rosa Esman commissioned from him as part of the 'New York Ten' portfolio. He knew Esman through Chiron Press, which had printed some projects she had published. In its landscape format 'Gulf' differs from most of the diptychs Marden was making at the time but it relates to 'From Bob's House' and 'Urdan' both of which are horizontals. It also retains the bottom border as well as the divide between the panels, which may indicate that it predates the paintings in which the bottom border was eliminated. Finally, the strong contrast of tones in 'Gulf' is a unique characteristic in Marden's oeuvre at this point.

By the time that he came to make 'Gulf' at Chiron Press the workshop had been sold and had expanded its activities to include other kinds of printmaking. In spite of his lack of experience with lithography this medium was assigned to him. As a result of his inexperience and the advice offered to him by the printer,[22] Marden made a lithograph which has the appearance of a silkscreen. Building it up in very much the same way as the 'Lana' prints, he employed tusche over lithographic crayon, which acted like a veil over activity. Marden also drew a line around the whole print and across the middle. This line, which encourages a slight sense of recessive space, is breached in places, thereby reasserting the plane of the paper.

Ten Days: The Return to Etching

'Gulf' brought to an end the early phase of Marden's printmaking but in 1971 he once again became involved in etching. Until the late sixties etching had remained somewhat the domain of full-time printmakers rather than painter-engravers. In the USA lithography and screenprinting had been the preferred media of artists. Screenprinting had made technological advances largely in the service of Pop Art, particularly under the direction of Ken Tyler at Gemini GEL, while a lithographic tradition had become established at Tamarind Press and at Universal Limited Art Editions under the direction of Tatyana Grossman. Although etching workshops were available to artists, as a medium it seemed moribund. In Europe artists such as Hans Hartung, Pierre Soulages, Joan Miró and Max Ernst continued to make etchings as indeed did Picasso whose '347' series, published in 1968, sparked off a more widespread interest in the medium in both Europe and North America. Younger artists, such as David Hockney, had been making etchings since the early sixties. On the other side of the Atlantic Jasper Johns had made his first etchings in 1967, announcing a new restraint and purity in the printed image. This series demonstrated that the intaglio medium could be used in ways other than those of the Hayter tradition. The problem for artists who wanted to make etchings in the USA, however, was to find a printer sympathetic to the new minimal modes of expression, whose standards in the field of etching were as high as those who practised lithography or screenprinting. Etching itself was highly suited to the new, cerebral approach to art.

At the invitation of Robert Feldman, director of Parasol Press, Marden was invited to make etchings in collaboration with Nona Hershey. Feldman states that he had not liked Marden's paintings in the exhibitions he had seen but he was urged by Klaus Kertess, director of Bykert Gallery, and by Chuck Close to look at Marden's drawings. He was impressed by the drawings and immediately asked him to make prints. The three prints which resulted were 'Grid I' (no.17), 'Grid II' (no.18) and 'Untitled' (no.19), all of which turned out to be a disappointment to artist and publisher alike. They released the first two but not the last which they felt was muddy.

That year, however, following a successful print project with Wayne Thiebaud in collaboration with a young printer named Kathan Brown in Oakland, California, Feldman despatched Sol LeWitt to make some etchings with her. These were so impressive that Feldman sent Marden out after him. So began one of the most fruitful printmaking collaborations of the seventies. By the end of his first visit Marden had made eight prints titled 'Ten Days' (no.20), after the number of days which he spent working on the project.

The day before Marden went out to California he spent some time with Paul Walter looking at his considerable collection of Whistler prints. Walter's collection contains a number of prints in different states and the sight of these impressed upon Marden the importance of building up an etching in stages, the value of the delicate touch, the use of blank paper and a delicate wipe to create tone, the variation of depth that could be obtained through the etch and the sheer variety of effects that could be achieved by the intaglio process. Interestingly, Marden recalls that his grandmother had an etching by Whistler and that 'this was the only thing in the family that was like real art'.

When Marden arrived in Oakland he was carrying the plate for 'Untitled' (no.19) and asked Brown to print it up for him. He immediately saw the difference between her approach to inking and Hershey's.[23] Brown uses a hand-wipe method which few, if any, American printers employed at the time, a legacy of her training at the Central School of Art in London.[24]

Marden did not start with any preconceived notion regarding what he would make but, broadly speaking, 'Ten Days' turned out to summarise the themes and configurations of his work to date. It contains the triptych, the diptych, the monochrome and the grid. Grids were employed by many artists, among them Agnes Martin, Sol LeWitt and Jasper Johns. Marden's use of the grid differs from all three artists'. He describes Martin's work as concerning space whereas his work is about denying space, keeping the image right up on the plane. Her paintings, where the grid is superimposed on an exquisitely and delicately painted background colour, are about landscape and atmospherics.[25] By contrast, LeWitt's printed grids were mechanical, precise constructs. Marden's filled grids in 'Ten Days' also suggest more than a passing interest in Johns's 'Alphabets' and 'Numbers' paintings and drawings.[26] However, where Johns employs a graphite wash to unify his drawing, Marden is meticulous in ensuring that most of his cross-hatching is carefully separated from the grid itself, so that the constituent parts of the grid are legible, as in an Andre floor piece. The grid and its contents are of equal weight. Each unit is also of equal value. The image is to that extent non-hierarchical.

The grid had made its first appearance in Marden's printed oeuvre in 'Grid I'. He relates this form to the frottages of tiles he had done in Paris, and subsequent drawings and paintings such as 'Untitled' 1964–5.[27] But Carl Andre was an acknowledged mentor. 'Carl was a very important influence. As mechanical and non-artistic as he tried to make his pieces, one of the great things about them was that none of the shapes was exactly regular. Those mis-shaped things gave much more substance to the image as far as I was concerned.' In Marden's grids, whether open or filled, each rectangle, when examined minutely, contains some kind of mark which distinguishes it from another – whether through foul biting, the imprint of his sweater or deliberate hatching – thus suggesting human intervention rather than the appearance of mechanical repetition and perfection in a LeWitt. Even the grids themselves were imperfectly drawn, the needle sometimes slipping, creating a tail.

The notion of the grid was also concerned with measuring and dividing the rectangle. The large open grid in 'Ten Days' is divided horizontally and vertically down the centre, then each quarter is divided vertically in half again and finally each eighth is divided into thirds. For Marden 'there was an immense difference between dividing a rectangle into halves or into thirds'. 'Grid I' had been divided by multiples of three only. Therefore in Marden's terms the open grid in 'Ten Days' was much more complex.

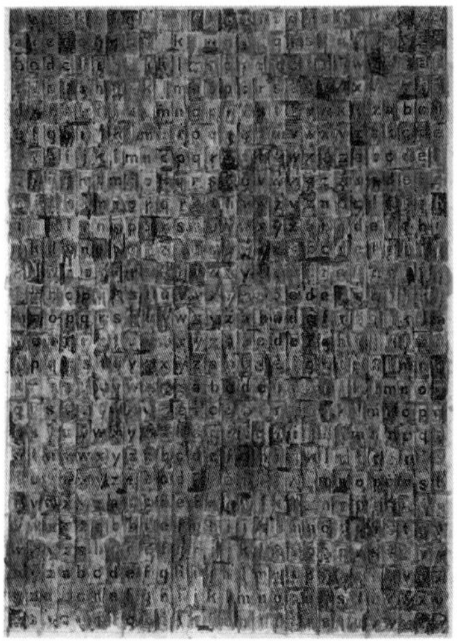

Jasper Johns **Gray Alphabets** 1960 Pencil and graphite wash on paper 97.5 × 70.8 (38⅜ × 27⅞) *Private Collection*

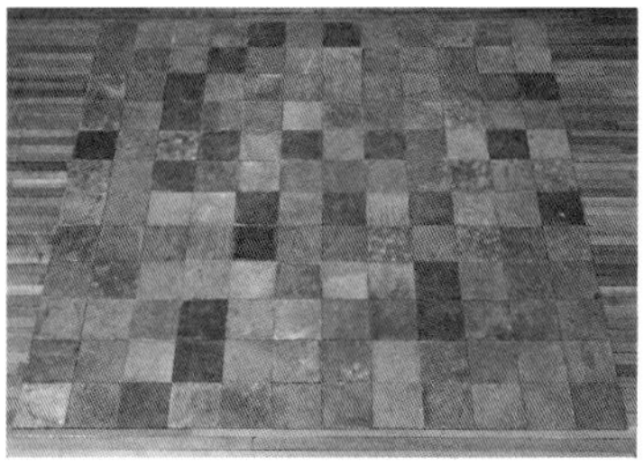

Carl Andre **144 Magnesium Square** 1969 Magnesium sculpture, 1 × 365.8 × 365.8 (⅜ × 143¾ × 143¾) *Tate Gallery. Purchased 1973*

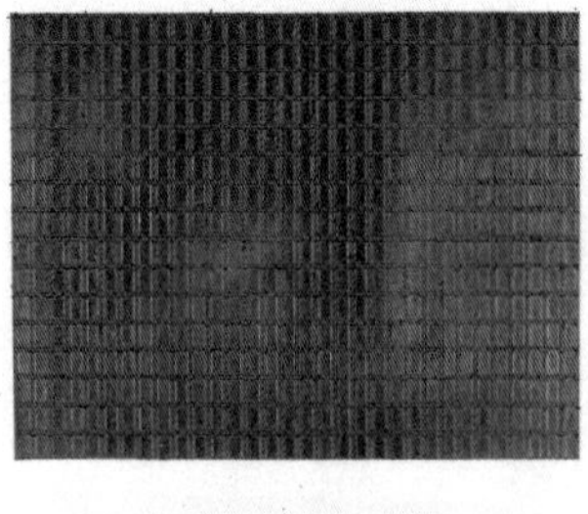

Mosaic Study No.2 1978 Ink and graphite over etching and aquatint on paper 76.2 × 55.8 (30 × 22) *Arnold and Mildred Glimcher*

The grid, according to Marden, 'came out of the shape of the paper or the shape [it] define[s]. There was always some sort of reference, very rarely arbitrary. But with the grids, I always thought drawing on the layers of graphite was the labor of the drawing. It's possessing it, making it yours. You start out with this rectangle and you make it yours by marking it over and over.'[28] Thus even something as supposedly mathematical as a grid takes on a human dimension, as it becomes invested with or taken over by the markings of the artist.

'Ten Days' was the first portfolio of prints that Marden had ever produced and was to set a pattern for his future publications. He did not conceive of it as a series, however, having no idea at the outset how many prints he would make. With no distractions, he simply filled the time available and ended up with eight prints. He took advantage of the professional team to experiment with different approaches, using hard-ground etching, aquatint, burnishing, foul bite, overprinting with a second plate, plates which are handwiped and those where the ink is dragged up (*retroussage*).

The images evolved one from the other, but broadly some of them relate to sketches he made in a notebook for the 'Grove Group' paintings, a series principally executed in 1972 but on which he continued to work until 1976.[29] The 'Grove Group' transmits Marden's impressions of olive groves in Greece, which he first visited in 1971 and to which he has subsequently returned every summer, specifically to the island of Hydra, where he owns a house. The colours of the paintings are variations on grey, green and blue and, in addition to evoking the silvery, green-grey of olive branches, refer to the colours of the sea and the sky. Pages of the 'Grove Group' notebook contain outline sketches of the paintings with indications of their connotations. Thus one image of a rectangle divided into three horizontal panels reads from top to bottom 'leaves-sky | trunk | earth'.[30] The 'Grove Group' paintings were intended as sensuous evocations of the union between man and nature. Marden wrote in the notebook:

> I am seeing my life as part of the struggle between man and nature. I know there is the possibility of some sort of union. This is why I have been forced to take nature as my inspiration.
>
> Any artist who takes the 'art scene ['] or short sighted contemporary history as his inspiration is turning his back on his human self.[31]

Further on in the notebook he comments 'my work comes out of observation and acceptance of nature. Man, part of nature, absorbs and digests and pushes it back out in the form of art.'[32]

The 'Ten Days' portfolio anticipates not only some of the configurations of the 'Grove Group', if not always their actual orientation – 'Grove Group

Grove Group 2 1972–3 Oil and wax on canvas, 2 panels, overall size 182.9 × 274.3 (72 × 108) *Private Collection*

2' is similar to the third print turned through ninety degrees, 'Grove Group 3' corresponds with the first print – but also, in part, the theme of nature. Marden's use of silver grey in two of the prints and cobalt and turquoise in another indicate that he was already thinking of the colours of the 'Grove Group' when he made 'Ten Days'.[33] However the prints should not be seen exclusively as equivalents to landscape, for Marden relates them also to the act of 'looking out onto this Oakland cityscape. What was impressive was that there was lots of sky and it was very open but still it was a city.' 'Ten Days' was as much a response to the environment in which these prints were made as a memory of landscape, indicating that their meaning does not relate precisely to one experience but is multi-faceted.

Although Marden responded to his surroundings, and in spite of his criticism of artists whose work simply feeds off contemporary art, he also acknowledges the importance of artistic precedent in these prints. The murals Rothko painted for Harvard University (1961–2) had really impressed him when he saw them at the Guggenheim Museum[34] and he had visited the Rothko Chapel in Houston, Texas, which was dedicated in 1971. Marden's work was much harder edged than Rothko's compositions, in which soft, blurred forms appear to hover in front of the plane, but the emotional quality with which Rothko invested the rectangle by means of the different densities of paint and by the relationships of colour particularly appealed to him. Interestingly, the Rothko paintings which most closely resemble some of the compositions of the 'Ten Days' prints are the late dark paintings of 1969–70 which became publicly known only in 1971.

Gober 1971 Oil and wax on canvas, two panels, overall size 182.8 × 91.4 (72 × 36) *Jerry and Emily Spiegel, New York*

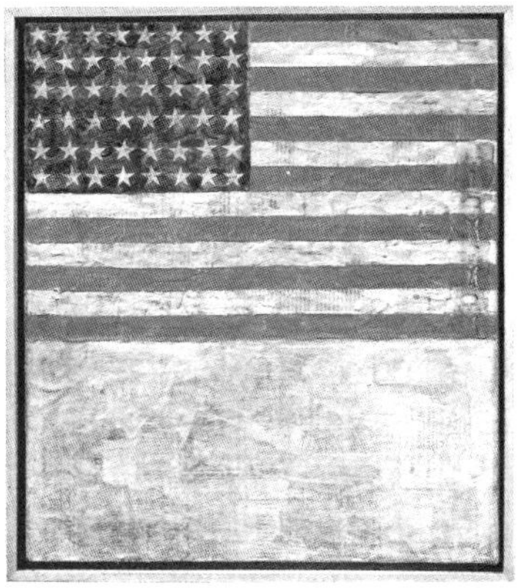

Jasper Johns **Flag above White with Collage** 1955 Encaustic and collage on canvas 57.1 × 48.9 (22½ × 19¼) *Private Collection*

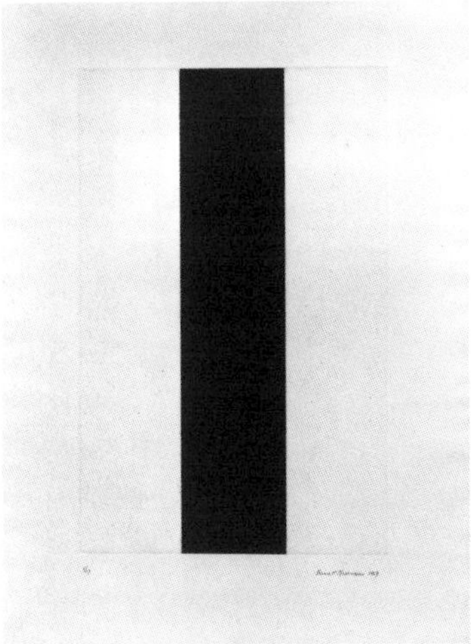

Barnett Newman **Untitled Etching #2** 1969 Etching and aquatint Image size 59.4 × 37.4 (23⅜ × 14¹¹⁄₁₆) *Collection, the Museum of Modern Art, New York Gift of Celeste and Armand Bartos Foundation*

Marden had begun to divide his compositions horizontally, but employed a portrait format in paintings such as 'Urdan' 1970–1 and 'Gober' 1971.[35] Here he invoked a memory not only of Rothko but maybe also of Jasper Johns. In spite of its disturbed surface and evident brushmarks, the muteness of Johns's flag in 'Flag above White with Collage' 1955,[36] and the division of the plane into two differently coloured sections of equal weight, are echoed in Marden's paintings. Johns's depiction of the union flag notwithstanding, his painting is equally impassive. Both this painting and 'Flag above White'[37] were shown in the Jewish Museum retrospective.

Barnett Newman was also of some relevance. Marden recalls that Newman's etchings, especially 'Untitled Etching #1' and 'Untitled Etching #2'[38] published in 1969, had impressed him. Indeed he liked the former so much that he had tried to purchase it in 1971. The superficial affinities between Newman's and Marden's approaches are obvious. Both artists accurately divide up the plane into bands; both make great use of the tone of the paper and both employ a contrast of aquatint and cross-hatching to obtain tonal and textural variation. But Marden's prints have an entirely different feel and a much more subtle understanding of the richness of the etching process. Where Marden activates the whole surface through drawing and touch (such as foul biting, often deliberately created) and insists on the flatness of the plane, Newman's unprinted surface is pristine and the zips represent penetrations of the plane. Marden appreciated Newman's sense of the spiritual more than any formal qualities in his work.

Marden describes 'Ten Days' as like 'an exercise in how much you can keep something the same when you make it look different.' There is a variety in the blacks which he has mixed, and the addition of silver or blue in certain prints increases the range of colour. Furthermore, Kathan Brown's delicate hand wipe[39] provides tone to the areas which ostensibly seem blank, differentiating the colour of the paper in the margins from the tone of the paper where it has been impressed.[40] Marden considers the monotone print to be coloured by virtue of the addition of hardground lines and foul biting. 'There is the plate tone and there is the paper. And it also becomes different because there is a line around it. So I was really reading these as though they were monochromatic, as though I had painted them grey or something'. However, it should be noted that there is a stronger contrast in tones between the blacks and the grey-whites in this series than the contrast of tones that Marden favoured in his paintings in this period. In this sense the prints anticipated the later paintings.

The line around the edge is a common feature of all the prints. Referring to Giacometti's paintings, the memory of which he carried from the early sixties, Marden stated:

> He made the frame and also when he put something in the space you could see it and it was measurable. You could say this was actually one metre from the frame or the plane. I can remember seeing the depiction of some apples on a table and you could say that that apple was 18 inches from the edge of the table. I mean he really depicted things very, very accurately and yet it was full of expression.

At times the bordering line in Marden's prints was eroded by constant rebiting, but the strength of the etch was such that the edge of the plate creates its own line. Most artists would file this away, but Marden preferred not to do so. By retaining a printed edge he differentiated the image from the sheet on which it lay and situated it in space, endowing it with an object quality.

In 'Ten Days' Marden's knowledge of etching had matured considerably. A comparison between 'Untitled' (no.19) printed by Hershey, and the first print of the series indicates not only the superiority of Brown's printing but also of Marden's conception. The composition of the two prints is broadly similar, the difference lying in the disposition of lights and darks. The earlier print is exclusively line while in the example from 'Ten Days' Marden has employed aquatint. Evidently he bit 'Untitled' so deeply because he wanted to create an even tone. The result was a muddy print. He realised, after talking to Kathan Brown, that the effect he desired could have been achieved with greater clarity and transparency by overlaying aquatint and he resorted to this method in a number of the works from this series. Kathan Brown considers that

> the aquatint was a way of smoothing it out, filling it in. The problem with the Hershey print is that it is so crude and spotty.[41] The thing is he wanted to bite these deeply and have a rough appearance but he did not want it to be so crude. So he was using first of all a wax ground. I don't think she used wax. I think she used a varnish which makes it rougher. Wax ground is the traditional ground which is the finest. But it also has to do with the way he drew it – the density, the fineness, the concentratedness of the drawing – but even so you can only build it up so far. I think I must have suggested putting aquatint on it to bind it together.[42]

The resin powder was applied to give an overall tone, biting it for a short time before repeating the application. Care was taken not to bite the plate too deeply, so as not to obliterate the lines drawn beneath the aquatint.

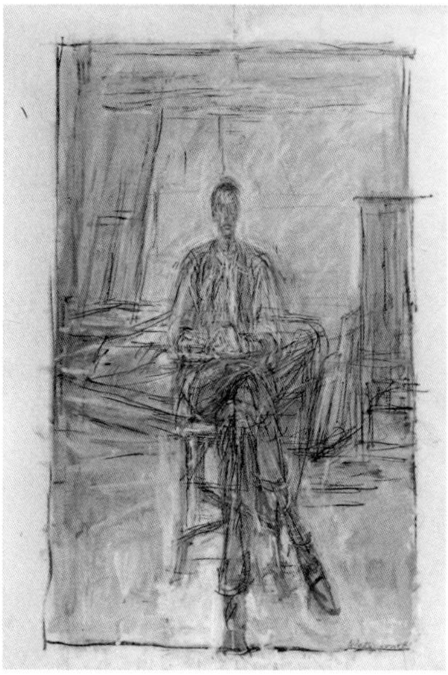

Alberto Giacometti **Seated Man** 1949 Oil on canvas 80 × 54 (31½ × 21¼) *Tate Gallery. Purchased 1949*

Lithography at Captiva Island

'Ten Days' marked the beginning of a decade of intense printing activity for Marden. His next project was commissioned by Rauschenberg along with suites of prints by other artists including Cy Twombly.[43] In February 1972 Marden took up Rauschenberg's invitation to come to his base on Captiva Island, Florida and it was under the latter's imprint, Untitled Press, that he published the works. Marden made six lithographs (no.21), many of which consist of gestural marks over a flat colour, harking back to 'Lana', although revealing more of the ground than in that early print. Working on stone for the first time – 'Gulf' had been drawn on zinc plates – Marden found the materials very seductive. He also felt that his environs had a considerable bearing on his approach.

> Everyday to get to the workshop I had to walk from the house through this jungle. These have much more of a jungle feeling. This is much more vegetal than other [prints]. I worked in a garage and the garage door was up and there were palm trees and things like that, so I am sure that had some sort of effect.

However, the prints also relate closely to Johns's and Rauschenberg's prints in their freedom and their scribbled, almost cancelling lines. Johns's 'Painting with Two Balls I' 1962[44] bears close comparison with the second print in the 'Untitled Press Series', notwithstanding Johns's punning attitude. In terms of Marden's own previous work, however, the lithographs take up the more expressive mode of drawing which he had developed in unique works on paper in 1969[45] and which he had covered up in his paintings; that is to say the brushmarks created on the first application of paint, which he subsequently smoothed over but which were still evidenced in the border of drips. They also look back to the rougher surfaces of the paintings of the early sixties such as 'Three Greys' 1963.[46]

Adriatics: The Subject of the Sea

Marden has not returned to lithography since making the 'Untitled Press Series', largely because he does not enjoy the medium. He finds it self-indulgent and unphysical: 'This is like ice-skating. I'd rather walk through the mud.' A year later he resumed etching, the medium for which he now had a strong preference, when he embarked on the series titled 'Adriatics' (no.22). Returning to Oakland to work with Kathan Brown and Pat Branstead at Crown Point Press, Marden made seven etchings continuing and extending the themes announced in 'Ten Days', but showing a more sophisticated use of aquatint as well as greater control over drawing, especially in the large grids.

Aquatint was alien to the Hayter tradition of printmaking but Marden was one of a number of artists who used it as a primary medium in the early seventies. Johns had utilised it as early as 1967 in the second states of his '1st Etchings' and continued to do so regularly thereafter. Picasso had employed it extensively and inventively in his '347' series. In the seventies, however, the medium itself became a prominent feature in the work of Robert Ryman, Robert Mangold, Gary Stephen and Mel Bochner among others, and Marden himself emphasised it in 'Adriatics'.

In two of the plates which use aquatint Marden returned to the practice of drawing lines through the aquatint, the diagonal lines in the top section of each print continuing downwards in the bottom section, although barely perceptible. The aquatint has been laid heavy enough to create a solid, distinctive tone but not so heavy as to obliterate the line completely. To create the tone in the top section of the first plate the plate was flat-bitten after Marden had deliberately introduced some random markings. He used this process because the light–dark contrast had been too stark. The use of a diagonal line was itself a relatively new development for him, having emerged the previous year in a series of drawings entitled 'Suicide Notes'.[47] It not only divides the plane but establishes its existence as a flat non-void, endowing it with a weight equal to that of the lower, densely inked half. It also allows the viewer to register the size of the upper panel. The combination of two kinds of grid in two of the other prints has the same effect and is roughly equivalent to the depiction of earth and sky or water and sky, in the form of density and lightness.

Marden named these prints after the sea which separates Greece from Italy. 'The first time we went to Greece [in 1971] we sailed from Bari across to Patras. I spent all the time looking out to sea and the 'Sea Paintings' [1973–4][48] were about that. I made all these notes about that. They were about looking at water.' The journey on to Hydra was a further five hours by boat. The larger grids evoke the hypnotic experience of looking out to sea over a long period. While their making requires considerable powers of concentration and great precision, the act of drawing such a repetitive form is meditative and mesmerising. The image is an equivalent for the original experience.

One further plate for 'Adriatics' was made, combining a grid with a solid aquatint which would have rounded off the series. Marden rejected it, possibly because it would have made it too logical – he firmly denies any suggestion that his art is systems based – and because ultimately he was less favourably disposed to the small than to the large grids. The smaller, combined grids 'are too academic, not really felt'. He likes the large grids,

Sea Painting No.1 1973–4 Oil and wax on canvas, 2 panels, overall size 183 × 137.8 (72 × 54¼) *Private Collection*

which of all his prints are among his favourite, for the contrast between regularity and irregularity.

In addition to the 'Sea Paintings' the first three plates of 'Adriatics' relate to the three 'Hydra' paintings of 1972, although the latter do not contain graphic marks comparable to the diagonal lines in the prints. Marden's etchings assert their position halfway between drawing and painting. Like painting, the act of making a print is a physical process. The artist must scratch into the ground; burnishing out an unwanted mark requires considerable effort and application. There is a real involvement with the depth and substance of the materials. The actual printing forces the ink into the paper so that paper and image become one and the pressure of the press creates a difference in levels between image and margins. In a drawing the materials tend to lie on the surface, although Marden's postcard drawings are scraped to such an extent that the inserted image lies in the same plane as the paper. Drawing is relatively resistance-free. The paper accepts the lightest of marks with ease.

At this stage in Marden's career the subjects of his drawings were considerably different from those of his paintings; they were linear, often very free or overtly gridded. The paintings, on the other hand, retained their overwhelming insistence on the primacy of the plane and on the opaque surface. In combining both aspects the prints synthesised Marden's preoccupations.

Another major difference between drawings and prints is that a print can be built up in successive, perceptible layers of ink in much the same way as a painting with paint. This aspect of printmaking was magnificently brought into play in Marden's next suite of etchings, 'Five Plates' (no.23), made towards the end of the 1973.

Five Plates: The Physicality of the Medium

Of all Marden's prints, other than the early 'Lanas', 'Five Plates' is the only suite in which a sense of serial logic is apparent, since it consists of the rectangle divided in two vertically and horizontally, in three vertically and horizontally, and undivided. Four of the prints relate closely to the 'Grove Group' paintings which Marden had executed in 1973[49] while the fourth in the series resembles 'Star (for Patti Smith)' 1972 and 1974.[50]

'Five Plates' is Marden's most painterly portfolio and has an emphasis on surface texture and depth of colour. The depth is built up by applying repeated layers of aquatint. Kathan Brown recalls the plate-making process, with which she closely involved herself:

> We were not as good at making aquatints then as we are now, so we did not get it as even to begin with, which maybe contributes to the beauty of it finally, but it also contributed to the difficulty because, if it was completely even, you could bite [the plate] uniformly and you would not need to rebite it so much. But as it was, you could bite it down so that one part was black and if [the aquatint had not been evenly laid], then another part would not quite be black. By the time you had bitten it down to where the second part was black, the first part had been overdone and a little trough [was created]. So the fact that we did not really have as much control over it then as we do now was a mixed blessing.

The aquatint was repeatedly applied in a very rough form and bitten.

> We would put the powder on and melt it and then bite it as long as we could until we could see that the troughs were starting to occur. Then we would take it out and put more aquatint powder on it and melt it and put it back in again so that it could get [to the point where it would accept] a tremendous quantity of ink. The trouble with that was that when we printed it, it would just kind of splat out. Sometimes we had to throw a number of them away because it went too far, it would come out and make a big glob.

The problem of printing was resolved once Brown and her staff had worked out the right amounts of wiping, of dampness in the paper and of pressure exerted by the press. Varnish was taken around the edge of the plate to protect it from the acid, but sometimes it was nicked, with the result that the acid would bite the edge of the plate causing uneveness and endowing the image with an even greater physical presence. Being a relatively soft material, zinc was receptive to accidents. Marden drew around the edge on most of the plates but, where he did not, the edge appears to have registered anyway. For example Marden did not delineate the bottom edge of the fourth print but according to Brown the printed line 'was caused by us trying to keep this thing from turning into a free form. It was already eroded. We were biting it but it was undercutting because it was bitten so much. So we were trying to put a little bit of varnish on the edge to keep it from underbiting and probably it created a little bit of an edge there, a little line'. Once printed, the sheets were allowed to dry, but shortly before this process was completed Brown and her team took a white rag to buff up the black surfaces.

Marden's idea was to create a very physical print, one which had body, substance and an intensity of colour comparable to his paintings. By referring to the plates on which they were made the title of the series emphasises the objectness of the images. Of all his prints these are the least obviously graphic, although the subtle use of line is crucial to their success. Not only was the depth of aquatint repeatedly built up but the printers also dragged up the ink. Marden added foul bite in many areas to provide tonal contrast, either by drumming on the plate with a needle or by applying a thin ground and letting it break down in the acid. The differences between the unaquatinted areas from print to print are delicately nuanced.

He probably employed this process on the right panel in the first print, the left panel having been coated with asphaltum to stop it out. Marden differentiated between the two whites so that the print would not read 'too conceptually'. When the printers wiped the plates they left a little ink on the blank areas to create a tone to distinguish the image from the margins of the paper, thereby endowing the whole image with a sense of physicality. This was particularly important in the blank plate which, while acting as an equivalent to a monochromatic painting, also evokes a memory of form.

The relationship of prints to paintings had already concerned Marden when earlier in the year he made two screenprints at Simca with Hiroshe Kawanishi. Kawanishi had been printing for Johns – the first time was in 1972 – and Marden had admired his work. Knowing the medium well and having appreciated the standard of work achieved at Crown Point Press when collaborating with professionals, he could see the value of working with a craftsman such as Kawanishi. Marden states that he liked

Winter Painting 1973–5 Oil and wax on canvas, three panels, overall size 183 × 305 (72 × 120) *Stedelijk Museum, Amsterdam*

silkscreen because it was capable of closely resembling painting. As a medium it was easier to understand than etching, which is complicated by image reversal and an almost alchemical process. Silkscreen is comparatively simple.

In the two untitled prints (nos.24 and 25) he introduced strong colour for the first time, namely dark blue and ochre. In their peeling qualities and the intrusion of the lower into the upper surface these prints recall the work of Clyfford Still. They have a close correlation with Marden's paintings of the period, in which he was using long vertical strokes of the spatula to apply the paint, thereby creating a much tighter, less inflected surface. He also painted the screens with long brush strokes.

The difference between these prints and the 'Lana' series, quite apart from the conception, lies in the precision with which they have been registered, the richness of the surface and the colour. The division of the plane into three segments in a ratio of 2:1 in the second of the prints was also a new departure, similarly adopted in 'Winter Painting' 1973–5.[51] The effect is to destabilise the composition and set up a tension between the relative values of the colours and the relative widths of the panels. However, unlike in the paintings, where individual canvases abut one another, the division of the panels in the prints is illusionistic, achieved by a delicate line created by a cut screen.

Five Threes: Moon and Myth

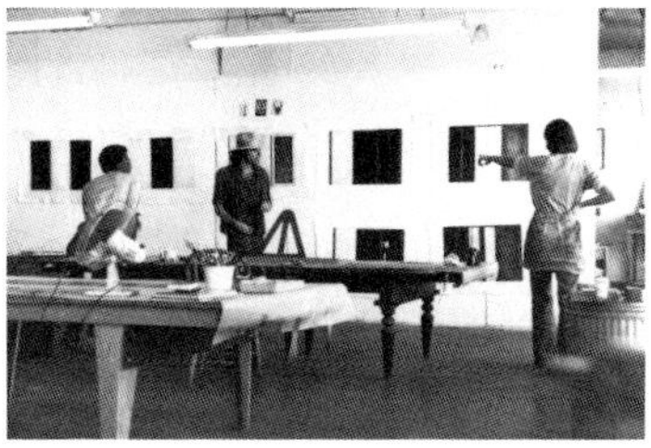

Brice Marden working on 'Five Threes', 1976 at Crown Point Press, then located in Oakland, California

1973 was Marden's most active year to date in terms of printmaking. While he had published some prints independently before the seventies – indeed the 1973 screenprints were also partly self-financed – it was the backing and enthusiasm of Feldman which allowed him to be so prolific. Feldman was responsible for the publication of many important prints by leading American artists, particularly those loosely categorised as Minimalists. Throughout the seventies he published prints by Sol LeWitt, Robert Mangold, Agnes Martin and Robert Ryman, as well as artists of other persuasions such as Richard Artschwager, Chuck Close and Wayne Thiebaud. Feldman created a context in which to promote prints by Minimal artists, although he had a hard time selling any of the work. He was most consistently successful in Europe, American collectors and even museums often ignoring what have turned out to be pre-eminent works.

In spite of the difficulty Feldman encountered in marketing the work, he kept faith with his artists. In 1976 he sent Marden back out to Oakland to make another set of prints. What emerged was 'Five Threes' 1976–7 (no.28). By this time Marden and his family were paying regular visits to Greece and he was stimulated to learn more about Greek culture. Having read Lawrence Durrell's *Alexandria Quartet* while still at Yale, a series of books which gave him a taste for Mediterranean culture, he now steeped himself in Robert Graves's *Greek Myths* and *The White Goddess*, as well as other books relating to ancient art and architecture. In Greece he spent a great deal of time drawing in the landscape and looking at monuments. His paintings and prints begun to be informed by these activities and, just as earlier paintings had referred to specific landscapes and people, so the next works alluded to his new-found interests.

'Five Threes' was made before the three 'Moon' paintings (all dated 1977)[52] to which its formats relate closely. This portfolio also has links with 'For Hera'.[53] In fact Marden conceived of them as studies for the paintings, the first time he had made such a conscious decision. 'The whole configuration of these was a configuration I had worked out before the paintings. This tripartite [format] and the proportion are the same as in the paintings'. For Marden the configuration of the paintings as well as their colours symbolised the three phases of the moon; waxing, full and waning. According to Graves, the Triple Goddess 'was a personification of primitive woman – woman the creatress and destructress. As New Moon or Spring she was girl; as the Full Moon or Summer she was woman; as the Old Moon or Winter she was hag.'[54] The symbolic colours of the moon are white, red and black, white signifying birth and growth, red denoting love and battle and black relating to death and divination. These correspond with the colours of the 'Moon' paintings and in discussing the paintings and the prints Marden alludes to these underlying meanings.

Two of the prints – the fourth and the fifth – anticipated the form of the paintings exactly, while the second bears a strong relation to 'Moon III'. In the paintings, as in these three prints, Marden dealt with the passage of colour or tone from left to right across the image. According to Graves,

> The Moon travels from left to right, the same way as the sun, but as she grows older and weaker rises every night a little farther to the left; then, since the rate of plant growth under a waxing moon is greater than under a waning moon, the right hand has always been associated with growth and strength but the left with weakness and decay.[55]

Thus the fourth print, which corresponds to 'Moon I', is the strongest, having an equally balanced left and right side.[56] In the fifth print, which relates to 'Moon II', the forces are merged in the centre, a still point in the waxing and waning process. However, in the second print all the strength is grouped on the right side, the narrow shaded bands on the left signifying the weaker moon rising. A more complex, though broadly similar, sequence is repeated in the first three prints.

Marden states that he thought of each of the prints as 'Triads, each aspect of the Triad having a definite aspect'. In numerological terms three is a potent number, the first to have a generative middle part and symbolising the highest spiritually creative force by its association with the Trinity. The Pythagoreans called it the perfect number because it has a beginning, a middle and an end. It therefore denotes completeness.

In addition to Greek myth Marden also nurtured an interest in Roman painting which he pursued by reading books and visiting the Metropolitan Museum, where wall paintings from Pompeii are on permanent display.[57] He particularly admired the juxtaposition of colours organised in clearly defined bands and rectangles and the *trompe l'oeil* depiction of panelling and friezes, which he translated into the third in the sequence of 'Five Threes'. The effect was to introduce an illusion of space in a way which previously he had strenuously denied, while at the same time insisting on the flatness of the picture plane. There is therefore a push-pull effect. Different strengths of shading by cross-hatching, scraping and aquatint create different spatial depths, endowing the work with a sense of contrast between inside and outside, facade and interior, brightness and shadow, all of which relate to architecture, a theme which would become integral to Marden's work in the next few years. These themes were also among those on which Edward Hopper elaborated in his celebrated print 'East Side Interior' 1922, where the division of the wall into panels and bands of light and shade, and the depiction of the windows are more than of passing

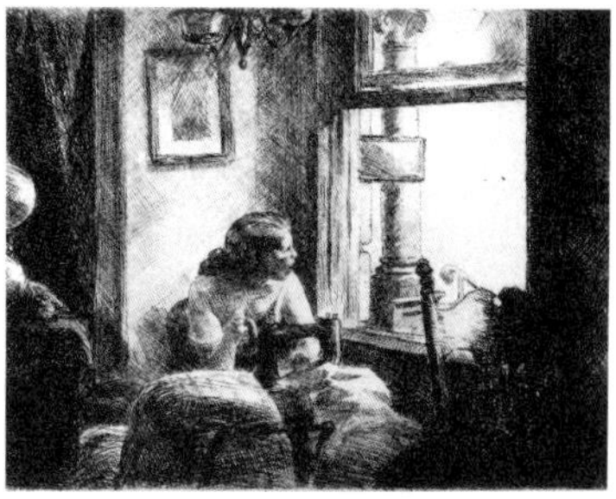

Edward Hopper **East Side Interior** 1922 Etching, image size 19.8 × 25 (7 13/16 × 9 7/8) *Trustees of the British Museum*

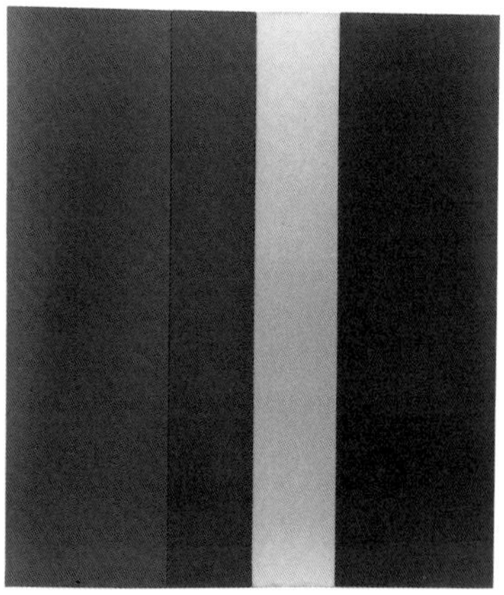

Morada 1976 Oil and wax on canvas, four panels, overall size 213 × 183 (83 7/8 × 72) *Stedelijk Museum, Amsterdam*

Conturbatio (Disquiet) 1978
Oil and wax on canvas, four panels, overall size 213 × 244 (84 × 96)
Private Collection

interest when viewed in relation to 'Five Threes'. While Hopper's execution was broader than Marden's he also obtained delicate effects of light and substance through a variety of cross-hatched marks. Furthermore, in spite of the shallow recession, the image is quite planar with an emphasis on the changes from dark to light and back to dark in a lateral progression across the sheet.

Barnett Newman **Eighth Station** 1964 Oil on canvas 198.4 × 152.4 (78⅛ × 60) *National Gallery of Art, Washington. Robert and Jane Meyerhoff Collection*

The division of the plane into more complex subdivisions was first seen in paintings entitled 'Le Mien' and 'Morada' both of 1976,[58] but 'Five Threes' is considerably more complex. These paintings together with 'Five Threes', foreshadowed the majestic 'Annunciation Series' of 1978, five works individually named 'Conturbatio (Disquiet)', 'Cogitato (Reflection)', 'Interrogatio (Inquiry)', 'Humiliato (Submission)' and 'Meritatio (Merit)'.[59] Each embodies one of 'The Laudable Conditions of the Virgin'. Painted during Helen Marden's pregnancy, this series is a modern-day equivalent to the countless Annunciation paintings of the Renaissance which Marden had been studying, and also invites comparison with Barnett Newman's celebrated 'Stations of the Cross'. While Newman's paintings have been kept together in the National Gallery of Art in Washington DC, Marden's have been split up. Nevertheless they were intended as a narrative cycle of a series of spiritual moments of the same intensity as Newman's. Although

Marden was not specifically thinking of Newman in the making of these paintings or 'Five Threes', he does not deny that Newman's engagement with spiritual themes has had an influence on his art. From a formal point of view, however, 'Five Threes' has an affinity with Newman's etchings, 'Notes' of 1968,[60] which are on a considerably smaller scale. Marden elaborates on the combination of different kinds of cross hatching which Newman employed, often in a single print. But where Newman is content to allow cross-hatching alone to create different spatial depths, Marden applies an aquatint to suffuse the whole print in gentle nuances of blue light, creating a far more delicate and complex set of spatial relationships. In the two black and white prints he disrupted the perfection of the aquatint surface with fine lines which create a barely perceptible silvery, flickering light. The subtlety of the surface, and the stealth with which it reveals itself bring to mind the strategies of Ad Reinhardt in his late black paintings where the inner image is only revealed after prolonged observation.

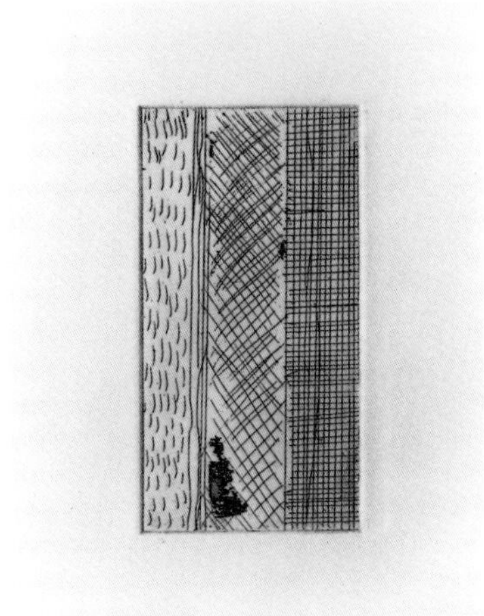

Barnett Newman **Note 1** 1968
Etching, image size 150 × 75 ($5\frac{15}{16} \times 2\frac{15}{16}$) *Private Collection*

Marden worked on 'Five Threes' principally in the summer of 1976, returning to Oakland to complete the project on one day in January 1977. In the spring of 1975 he had had a one-man exhibition at the Guggenheim Museum which was the culmination of a series of exhibitions devoted to his Minimal peers. Earlier that year he showed etchings at Knoedler Gallery in the company of his former teacher William Bailey. That 1976 was a relatively quiet year in terms of exhibitions was not, therefore, unexpected but in 1977 he held his second solo show in Rome, the first having taken place the previous year. He took the opportunity of his stay in Rome to travel to Pompeii, to look at Roman painting *in situ*, noting the interaction between columns and lintels. The division of the plane by the columns and the employment of bright colours struck a resonant chord which was soon translated into Marden's art. In addition he had been reading *Earth, the Temple and the Gods* by Vincent Scully,[61] a book about sacred Greek architecture which he describes as having been very important to him. Scully presents an analysis of the relationship of the temple to the land, sacred building to sacred location, stressing that they form an architectural whole.

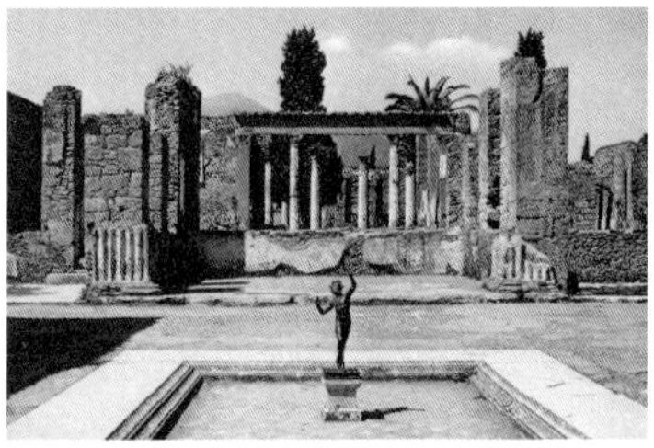

Atrium, the Faunas's House, Pompeii

> All Greek sacred architecture explores and praises the character of a god or group of gods in a specific place. The place itself is holy and, before the temple was built upon it, embodied the whole of the deity as a recognised natural force. With the coming of the temple, housing its image within it and itself developed as a sculptural embodiment of god's presence and character, the meaning becomes double, both of the deity as in nature and the god as imagined by men. Therefore the formal

elements of any Greek sanctuary are, first, the specifically sacred landscape in which it is set and, second, the buildings that are placed within it.[62]

While landscape had always made an impact on Marden he was now beginning to assimilate his experience of ancient Greek and Roman architecture with their rectilinear compositions of post and lintel. From now on his paintings would refer to land and structure in both form and colour.

'12 Views': The Impact of Greece and Rome

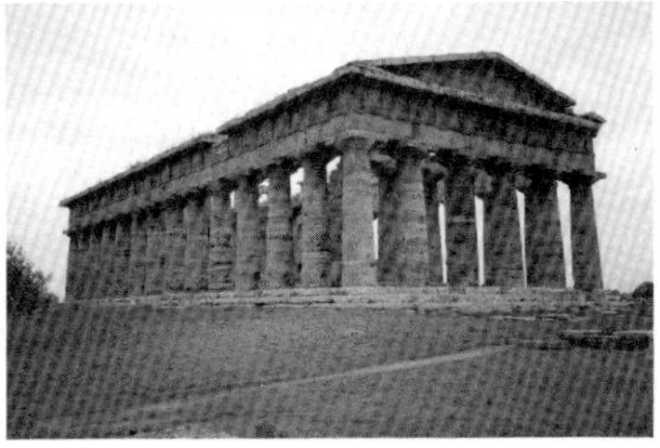

Temple of Neptune dedicated to Hera, Paestum. Photograph: Krzysztof Cieszkowski

Among the first instances of the impact of Greek and Roman architecture on Marden are in the prints entitled '12 Views for Caroline Tatyana' (no.29) which he began in 1977 and completed in 1979. In comparison with the paintings of this period they are radical in their division of the plane and in their suggestion of doorways and windows. Once again Marden plays on the contrast between notions of inside and outside in a manner related to the appearance of the facade of a Greek temple. Looking at a temple, the individual columns of a facade appear to make up a single plane of light and shade. Describing the second temple of Hera at Paestum Scully writes:

> The first impression the eye retains is of an absolute unity and balance. It then sees, without ever losing that first impression, that the unity is made up of totally separate parts and that the balance is between completely dissimilar units. The columns of the front and rear are six; one may count them if one wishes, but the eye takes them in at a glance forming a single shape. Accepting this as one, the eye then feels the whole shape to be taking on direction as the side columns recede into space. The temple is both open and closed. In the optimum angle the eye can slip between the columns of the front and the flank, but, moving, it may be prevented, for example, from entering between the columns of the side, which thus form one plastically rhythmical wall. As the observer changes position these relationships change; the eye will penetrate at the side and will slowly slide out along the columns of the front until they in turn become an impenetrable facade ... The temple is both open and closed, solid and void, interlocking inside and outside in a splendidly measured rhythm of column and wall.[63]

This description of the perception of Greek temple architecture might easily be applied to Marden's '12 Views'. He contrasts burning, brilliant light with engulfing shade, density with lightness, substance with ether and depth with flatness. Each image has its complement and both are brought together in the doubles. Marden's original intention was to employ delicate shades of contrasting red and green as well as blue and brown in the double images. He was looking for 'a push-pull' action. These were also among the colours which the Greeks used to decorate the temple friezes and statuary, creating bright, optical effects. Furthermore, Marden's initial choice of paper was one with a green cast which affected the whole tone of the image and linked it to notions of landscape, green being derived from the earth. By printing the image on a paper with a green tone Marden would integrate image and ground in a way analogous to the integration of landscape and temple. However, the colours which Marden employed were so subtle that they were barely perceptible.

Although Greek architecture and Roman painting had a considerable impact on Marden he was equally receptive to other ancient cultures. He also visited Egypt, 'looking at some tombs that had false doors'. The sense of blocking up an opening is implicit in a number of these images.

The composition of each single plate consists of seven vertical columns topped by a horizontal lintel. On one occasion some columns are divided in two by shading in opposite directions. According to Scully

> Recent psychological studies have shown that there is a limitation in the human capacity to comprehend numbers of objects in a rapid glance. It has been demonstrated that human beings can assimilate up to seven objects without reference to the tedious counting process, but eight is on the very limit of that capacity and beyond it for many.[64]

Seven is the most mysterious of numbers. It cannot be produced by multiplication. It recurs with frequency in the Bible, particularly in the Book of Revelations which Marden read while working on the Basle window project (see below).[65] It is also connected to the moon, which traditionally has four phases, lasting seven days each, which together make a calendar month. In terms of the occult the number seven governs the cycles and rhythms of life and for the same reason it is regarded as a number of completeness. There are seven colours in the spectrum, seven notes in the musical scale, Seven Deadly Sins and seven orifices of the male body. Finally, according to biblical tradition God created the world in six days and on the seventh he rested. Seven is therefore a potent number. While Marden's choice of seven as the base number for these prints may have been intuitive, he was not without a knowledge of numerology, through his reading of alchemical texts and books by Aleister Crowley concerning magic and alchemy.[66]

Besides the notion of doorways and windows these prints evoke images of the Old Testament cross, particularly the first print with its undivided

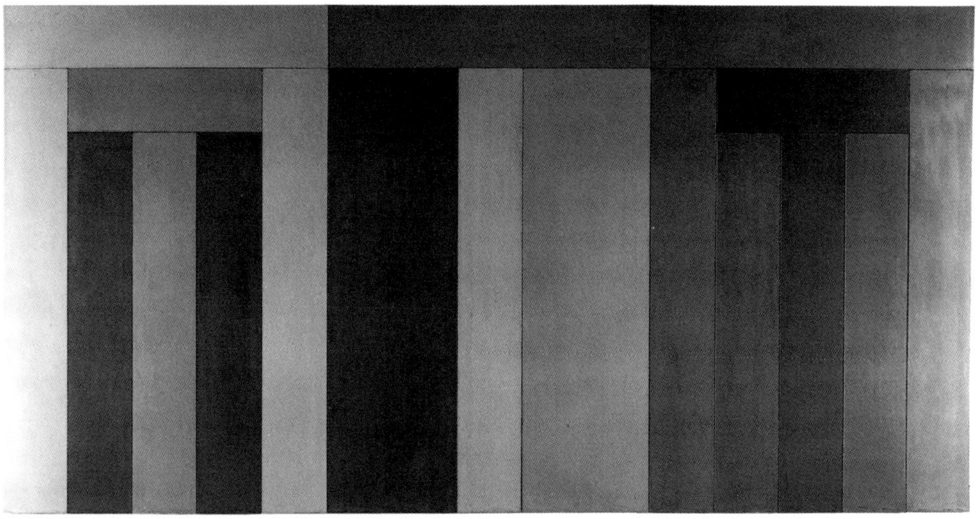

Thira 1979–80 Oil and wax on canvas, 16 panels, overall size 244 × 457 (96 × 180) *Museé national d'art moderne, Centre Georges Pompidou, Paris*

central vertical column. The ambiguity of the reading was deliberate. This theme was given its fullest treatment in 'Thira' 1979–80,[67] which can be interpreted as a Golgotha. Here the forms are articulated by the use of colour opposites derived from the colour circle of Johannes Itten.[68] Marden is drawing with colour in a manner not too dissimilar from Matisse in his paper cut-outs, butting one discrete panel of colour up against another.

It was not without coincidence that during this period Marden had begun work on a commission to make stained glass windows for the cathedral of Basle. He was first approached in 1977 and presumably this stimulated him to pay closer attention to earlier forms of Christian expression. The studies he made for some of the windows – the project was never completed – indicate that he was thinking in terms of vertical columns of coloured glass, each column consisting of a single colour related to the four elements. Red and green were juxtaposed to signify fire and earth, blue and yellow were placed beside each other to denote water and air. These combinations broadly followed Itten's arrangements which demonstrate that when adjacent, complementary colours intensify their luminosity to their maximum. They are also fundamental to alchemy.

A basic tenet of alchemy is that all substances are composed of four elements: air, earth, fire and water. Aristotle emphasised that these four elements are bearers of fundamental properties, dryness and heat being associated with fire, heat and moisture with air, moisture and cold with water and cold and dryness with earth, thus creating a continuum. All other substances were supposed to be combinations of the four elements and the properties of substances were thought to reflect their elemental composition. Thus Greek thought encompassed the idea that all matter could be understood in terms of elemental qualities but that the elements themselves were non-material.

Marden describes his experience of working on stained glass as being equivalent to alchemy. 'You put silver into the glass to get yellow. You did all these things which alchemists worked on. I figured that if I had mixed the colours absolutely right I could make an actual transformation. To me that is an actual possibility'. '12 Views for Caroline Tatyana' were made alongside Marden's earliest stained glass studies and therefore his introduction of colours should not be considered unrelated to the alchemical issue. A notebook, dated '1979–82/84',[69] indicates that Marden was thinking exactly along these lines.

The portfolio was not published until 1985. Editioning had begun at Crown Point Press in 1979 but halfway through Feldman asked Brown not to proceed because he was having such trouble marketing 'Five Threes'. He considered the two sets of prints to be too closely related to be able to sell them simultaneously. The plates were retained and when they were finally printed in Santa Monica by Doris Simmelink, Marden dispensed with the colours, other than the use of a blue in the doubles, and chose a larger, brilliant white paper in place of the handmade one with the green cast. The fact that he finally printed green with black in 'Focus I–V' (no.32) may have persuaded him not to repeat the experiment when editioning '12 Views'; he has demonstrated both before and since that he is most comfortable in etching when using varying tones of black.

Grids and Tiles

If Feldman felt nervous at releasing the '12 Views' portfolio he nevertheless agreed to publish a subsidiary project entitled 'Tiles' (no.31), which Marden made while waiting for proofs of the principal series to be pulled. 'Tiles' relates closely to the grid drawings which he had been making since 1973. These were a development of 'Suicide Notes', where the plane of the rectangle was fractured, and which further evolved in the Basle cathedral drawings, where Marden divided vertical panels of colour horizontally by thin black bars.

'Tiles' was conceived alongside 'Tile I' (no.30) and derives from an idea Marden had of making ceramic tiles. Inspired by a set of fake Delft tiles in his kitchen, he wanted to have a group of ceramic ones glazed with a grid pattern, over which he might apply paint. He intended to put them together in various combinations to form a mural composition. He obtained a close approximation of the intended effect when he asked Kathan Brown to print four plates on one sheet in a square of adjoining images. She produced a series of these proofs over which Marden drew more elaborate grids. In describing this project Marden draws an analogy with 'an apartment building in New York [which is like] a grid [where] completely different things are happening in one aspect of the grid which is the exact same measure as the next apartment.' Marden asked Pace Editions to manage the project but it never materialised, largely through a lack of organisation. However, Marden extended the idea when he drew and painted on off-cuts of marble in Greece in 1983.

'Tiles' are remarkable for Marden's method of drawing on the plate. Since 1972, besides pencils, he had been drawing with ailanthus twigs cut from a tree near his home. Dipping one end into ink, he found that he was able to draw with the whole forearm, rather than from the wrist, and could extend the length of the stick by attaching it to a pole. The twig would respond to the slightest movement. It was therefore an instrument of greater sensitivity than the pencil and although it imposed a greater distance between hand and support, paradoxically the relationship between the two was more intimate. Analogies may be made not only with Pollock's practice of painting with sticks – although Pollock dripped his paint rather than allowing the applicator to touch the surface – but also with Matisse's method of making drawings for the ceramic tiles for the chapel in Vence.

Marden began 'Tiles' by sketching on the plate with a twig dipped in a sugar solution, adding the hardground etched lines and some aquatint afterwards. The sugarlift method allows the artist to draw on the plate as if on a piece of paper. There is no ground to break through and no resistance. The plates were repeatedly bitten allowing the foul biting to get progressively deeper. With the sugarlift Marden achieved remarkable variation in the density of the ink, using bubbles to introduce areas of light within otherwise dark areas of aquatint. He evidently enjoyed the freedom of sugarlift and its proximity to his methods of drawing and henceforth it would become his principal method of etching.

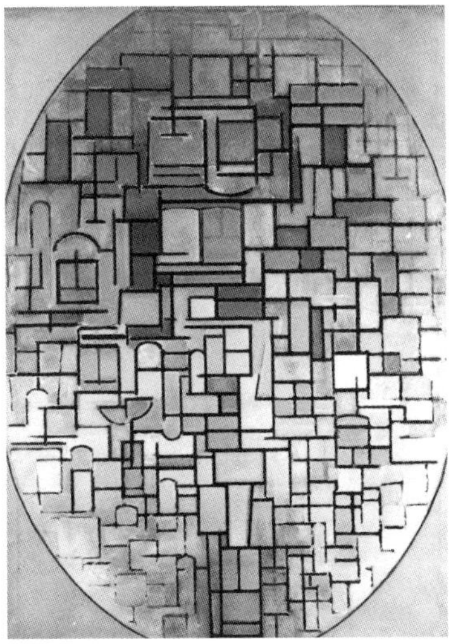

Piet Mondrian **Oval Composition (Tableau III)** 1914 Oil on canvas 140.5 × 102 (55 5/16 × 40 1/8) *Stedelijk Museum, Amsterdam*

'Tiles' marks the end of Marden's collaboration with Kathan Brown, since she no longer printed for independent publishers and discontinued her relationship with Parasol Press. In any event, with the arrival of two further children by his second marriage, Marden concluded that he could no longer afford to take time away from his family. Only one further print was editioned, a work which Marden considers incomplete, namely 'Untitled' 1979 (no.35). He refers to it as the 'boogie woogie' print because it recalls Mondrian's 'Broadway Boogie-Woogie' 1942-3 in terms of its complexity, although it is also reminiscent of the latter's paintings of 1914. He also stated that he had intended 'to make a big, beautiful etching, like one of the great Cubist Braque etchings.'

A Change in Direction

At the beginning of the eighties Marden suffered a mid-life crisis and temporarily removed himself from his family to live in his studio on Bond Street. His personal problems were compounded by a sense of aimlessness, a feeling that he had pushed his painting as far as it could go in the particular direction he had taken it. He had reached a point where a fundamental decision had to be taken. While he liked the paintings he had been making 'it just got really boring making them. I figured you either change or you die before your time'.[70] As well as a heavy drinker, Marden had been a regular user of narcotics, all of which helped him to achieve the meditative state which gazing at his paintings was meant to induce. 'I used to smoke marijuana all the time ... It was built into the philosophy of the paintings. Then you hit middle age, and your metabolism is different. It just makes you tired, and you can't get your work done.'[71] Marden basically had a choice to wean himself off drugs and alcohol or lose his family and blow his career. Relations were repaired with the family but he was feeling increasingly at odds with his representatives at Pace Gallery.

> Here I was at Pace Gallery, which was really making me very nervous, because I am in no way relating to these people. They are not getting my art and I am not terribly enthusiastic about what they are doing commercially. And I don't see the situation as getting any better and I'm in debt to them. I think, well, what are you going to do, how are you going to get this straightened out, are you stuck here doing this for the rest of your life?

At around this time Marden was producing work for and based on the window project which he took on as 'a way to expand my ideas'. The window project allowed him to think in terms not only of breaking up the rectangle – one of the windows he was commissioned to make was a rose, another was an arched window – but also to see the plane as translucent, no longer an opaque, built up surface. He was dealing with an immaterial flatness rather than a sense of physicality, and this sense of translucence and corresponding spatial depth invaded his paintings, as it had already done in his drawings and prints such as 'Tiles'. His paintings were now approaching the freedom of his graphics as he applied paint in a more liquid state, without wax, to encourage bleeding and drips. While he had retained such accidents in the lower border of the early paintings, they were now featured in the main body of the image.

The impetus to change his art came not only from the crisis in which he found himself but from his growing appreciation of oriental calligraphy,

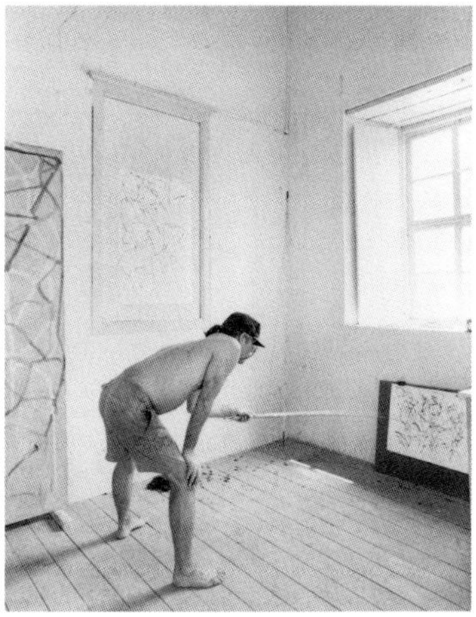

Marden in his studio in Greece.
Photograph by Bill Jacobson

and Eastern mysticism and religion. At the end of 1984 he was impressed by an exhibition held jointly at the Japan House Gallery and the Asia Society Galleries entitled *Masters of Japanese Calligraphy 8th–19th Century.* He had previously rejected oriental culture as being irrelevant to his vision but now it acted as a catalyst. He visited the exhibition on repeated occasions and when his wife Helen encouraged him to join her and the children in Thailand at Christmas there was no question but of his going.

In calligraphy Marden found a way not of complicating what he was already doing but of actually breaking away from it. He had conceived a plan that he would train to be a calligrapher while he was in Thailand, but heard that it was necessary to be right-handed. This proved subsequently to be untrue, but he believed it sufficiently to be discouraged from enacting his fantasy.

The marks he had been making in drawings from 'Suicide Notes' onwards had often had a calligraphic quality, but now Marden took the opportunity to study first Japanese calligraphy and then Chinese, which he admired considerably more. Using sticks, he made hundreds of drawings in Asia, and subsequently in Hydra, and then made a conscious decision to allow his paintings and drawings to coalesce. Whereas before they had been separate activities, the drawings being more overtly expressive and nervous, the paintings impassive and authoritative, now Marden began to make serpentine strokes with brushes attached to long sticks, the paint thinned with turpineol and erased in places by rubbing and scraping, so that overlapping strokes would not build up a surface density. The images he produced were webs, glyphs and motifs resembling crystal structures. They were painted over coloured grounds and arranged in vertical columns like Chinese characters, although they bore no narrative. The grid had not disappeared but had gone underground, as lines crisscrossed between vertical columns to disguise the orderliness of the composition. The paintings had become graphic. While there was a certain automatism to Marden's mark-making, it was disciplined by much fore and after thought.

Etchings to Rexroth and the Art of the East

It was during this transitional phase that Marden began to make 'Etchings to Rexroth' (no.40). He had not made any etchings for a long time but, through the publisher Peter Blum, he had been commissioned to make an etching for an issue of *Parkett* (no.39) to be devoted to his work. Blum also invited him to publish some prints and made arrangements for him to work with Jennifer Melby in New York. The *Parkett* etching relates closely to the window drawings. Marden worked on it twice a week during October 1985 and returned to Melby in January 1986 to start work on the second project, which would last until June.

According to Melby, Marden was having difficulty in deciding what to do. Originally he attempted variations on the *Parkett* theme in a larger size but he arrived one day

> with some notebooks with a lot of drawings he had done in Greece. Pen and ink drawings. And we were talking and I said 'You can do the same sort of thing you have done in these sketchbooks on copper plates, just drawing with sugarlift'.[72]

Marden was delighted with the idea. Marking a grid lightly onto the edge of the plate he started to produce independent glyphs but, as he warmed to the task and the series progressed, so he began to join them up. He remembers the fifth print as being one 'that really clicked' and by the time he had reached the ninth he had drawn a configuration with a tightness which excited him. 'This is the one where it started. I figured this is what I want to get in the drawings and in the paintings', which were still posing him problems. What particularly pleased him was the spiralling effect, which communicated the energy and the layers of meaning contained in the drawings which he had done in the Far East.

> One day I would draw a tree, the next day we would go to the same place and I would draw a sea shell on top of it, and then the next day we would go somewhere else and I would draw rocks, and I would layer it all on top on the same drawings … You are observing nature and yet you are just trying to respond to it. You are not trying to draw a picture of it … It deals with a certain kind of abstraction. You can accept that as energy coming through and going back out into [drawing and] painting.

Marden enjoys the variety and complexity of nature. 'If you look at a curve in nature it does more naturally than your own hands [could do] and it's a way of educating your hands and eyes and it's also about the energy. When you draw a tree you get a certain kind of energy and just by drawing the way it grows it's about the energy of that organism.' Back in the studio, however, he would rework the drawings with the result that they became less recognisably studies after nature. 'You do lots of botanical studies but then three years later you are working on the same drawings in another town. I'm not trying to make them look less like vegetation but they are just not there, they are not in that place, but that basic energy is usually there.'

While in Thailand Marden had visited a seashell museum. He was attracted to their markings and has since then been a collector. He is particularly interested in volutes which bear spiralling, skeletal markings on their exteriors. 'The great thing about seashells [is that] they [are] portable, natural objects and they never repeat themselves.' Many of the drawings he made in Thailand were based on them and markings of that type were incorporated into the Rexroth project. Other images for the portfolio came from drawing the landscape in Greece, 'the shape of mountains and the sea beyond. I drew these spaces between mountains and then just started bringing them together.'[73] Yet another source may have been the triangular symbols he drew in the 1979–82/84 notebook derived from the table of correspondences.[74] The problem for Marden was how to transmit his feelings in front of nature, the energy he tapped into, without depicting the literal object. According to John Hay

> If there is any single, fundamental characterisation of [Chinese] calligraphy, it is that of a line of energy, materialising through the brush into the ink-trace. Hence many terms such as 'brush strength' (pi-li), are essentially aspects of energy. The characterization is so natural and effective that it is taken for granted. But in fact, it should count as one of the most original and effective achievements in all of art theory.[75]

Marden recognised that Chinese calligraphy could provide a model. Chinese is a conceptual language in which certain signs are carriers of meaning and their grammatical status is determined by their position in a sentence. Meaning is extended by associative ideas triggered by a particular character or group of characters. The language is therefore a system of layering, literally one ideograph on top of and beside another, and extends to over fifty thousand characters. Despite the freedom accorded to personal style, the creation of a character follows very strict rules and its disposition is governed by a grid. The discipline, the interconnectedness and the interlinking all appealed to Marden who had begun to evolve a limited vocabulary of signs and glyphs.

The configurations have no specific meanings but after repeated use become as archetypal as the images encountered in Marden's earlier work. Being left-handed he starts in the top right corner and works downwards in columns. His images can be read either vertically or horizontally and resonate accordingly. Beginning with separate glyphs, as though learning new words, he disposed them on the plate in a disconnected manner. However as his confidence grew in the use of this new vocabulary, so he started to link the glyphs as though forming sentences, so that the original forms became almost indecipherable as discrete units but could be conjugated by the viewer in many different ways.

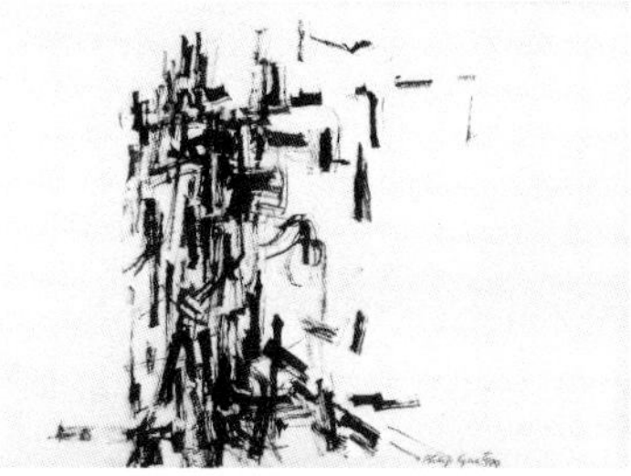

Philip Guston **Untitled** 1954
Pen and ink on paper 45.6 × 61 (18 × 24) *Tate Gallery. Purchased 1991*

Marden was the not the first American artist to be interested in oriental calligraphy. Franz Kline denied its influence but he was certainly aware of

Far Eastern art. Philip Guston's quill pen drawings of the fifties, with their accumulated strokes, also have an oriental feel while Mark Tobey studied in a Zen monastery in Japan in 1934. Among European artists Marden was interested in Henri Michaux by whom he owns a work. However the artist of the mid-century whose graphic work bears the closest resemblance to Marden's new-found style is David Smith, some of whose drawings recall ideographs while others consist of interlacing webs of lines.[76] Smith's drawings mostly relate to his own sculptural forms but the calligraphic gesture came from his admiration of oriental art. Marden's work differs from his, however, not only in terms of the scale of the mark and the deliberateness of the gesture – Smith's work is very fluid and gives the impression of having been executed at speed – but it is clearly based on a grid. The diagonal lines have their origins in the divided rectangle as much as in the forms of nature. In this respect an interesting parallel can be drawn again with Mondrian whose tree paintings, whether naturalistic or Cubistic, have a strong affinity with Marden's recent work. Like Mondrian's Cubistic paintings, however anarchic Marden's configurations may appear to be, they are always held in check.

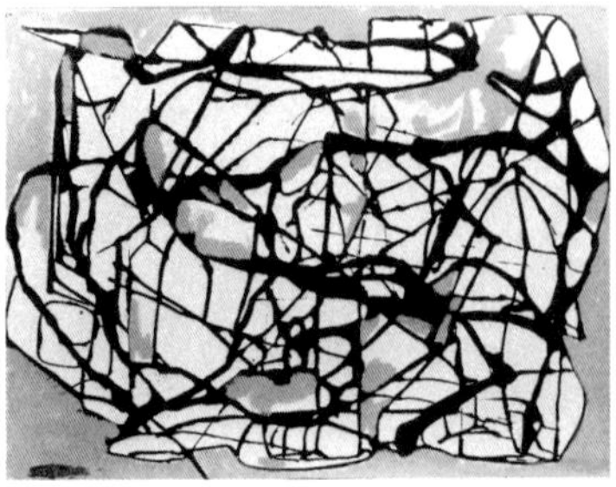

David Smith **Untitled** 1955
Egg, ink and tempera on paper
66 × 50.8 (26 × 20)
Private Collection

If Smith's images are derived from a common interest in oriental art the range of mark Marden makes within one image is far greater. He combines broad slashing bands with filigree threads, stuttering lines with full-blooded puddles, flicks of the wrist with carefully controlled drags, deeply bitten sugarlift with delicate, transparent washes of flat-biting all of which communicate different levels of energy like the three primary modes of Chinese script – cursive, semicursive and standard.

'Etchings to Rexroth' was something of an experiment and for some time Marden did not know how to use the plates he had drawn. He tried printing three plates on one sheet, then two plates separated by another plate of pure colour as though thinking in terms of his earlier triptychs. He also tried printing some coloured proofs and at one point resorted to *chine collé* to try to resolve the colour issue.

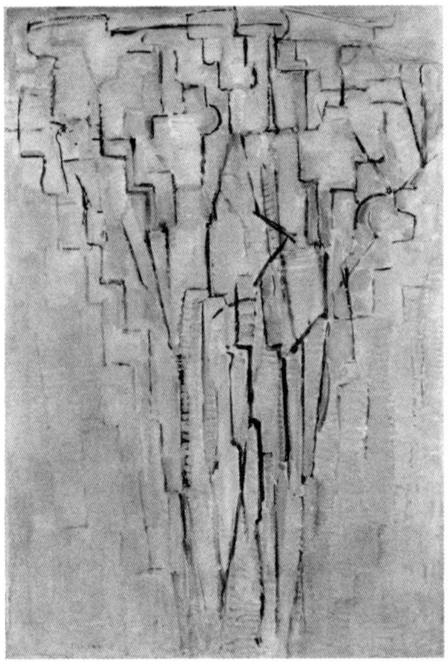

Piet Mondrian **Tree** *c.*1913 Oil on canvas 100.3 × 67.3 (39½ × 26½)
Tate Gallery. Purchased 1977

Cold Mountain: The Rhythms of Nature

Marden's achievement in the 'Rexroth' etchings was not only to develop a new vocabulary but to create a suite of plates in which his manipulation of the media was as inventive and expressive as his new vocabulary of forms. In the 'Tu Fu' print (no.41), made in 1987 to accompany the book of 'Etchings to Rexroth', Marden draws upon all his experience of the previous year to make an image of exquisite tonal contrasts suggestive of delicate botanical forms or waterfalls, or perhaps even figures. In this etching, like some of the Rexroth works, he creates a dynamic by contrasting straight, vertical, horizontal and diagonal strokes with gently bleeding and fluttering shapes. Triangular structures are still the dominant motifs as they were in early prints such as 'Untitled' (no.2).

Marden's most recent prints, 'Cold Mountain Series. Zen Studies 1 – 6' (no.43), are more linear and have an affinity with Pollock, whose looping, rhythmic gestures, creating serpentine skeins of paint, have been such an inspiration to Marden in the last few years. Although he had looked at Pollock's work throughout his career it is only comparatively recently that he has come to admire him above all other artists. He has a special affection for Pollock's mature paintings, where

> it seems to me he has gone from being some sort of highly sophisticated western painter into some other realm. Paintings like 'Scent'[77] ... [are] about forces of nature. Somehow he can make that image but it's not necessarily an image. 'Scent' is very peculiar to me, like a real mother earth kind of image. It's very strange. I mean he is kind of lost. Pollock is an incredibly sophisticated and intelligent artist but he sort of loses all that and it just becomes very direct, human expression.

Marden believes that above all other artists, Pollock had the ability to subordinate himself to nature, to receive its energy and to transmit that directly through his painting. In the light of this Pollock's claim 'I am nature' becomes immediately comprehensible. This view of Pollock is coloured by Marden's own aspirations which are informed by his interest in Zen.

Helmut Brinker writes:

> Characteristic of Zen – and, in a sense, characteristic indeed of the oriental mind in general – is the attempt to understand and experience the things of this world, whether animate or inanimate, from *within:* to let oneself be seized and taken by them instead of trying to comprehend them, as we in the West do, from a point of view external to them. Thus to a degree unparalleled in any other form of art, Zen art requires of the beholder tranquil and patient absorption, a pure and composed hearkening to that inaudible utterance, which yet subsumes in itself all things, and which points to the absolute *Nothingness* lying beyond all form and colour.[78]

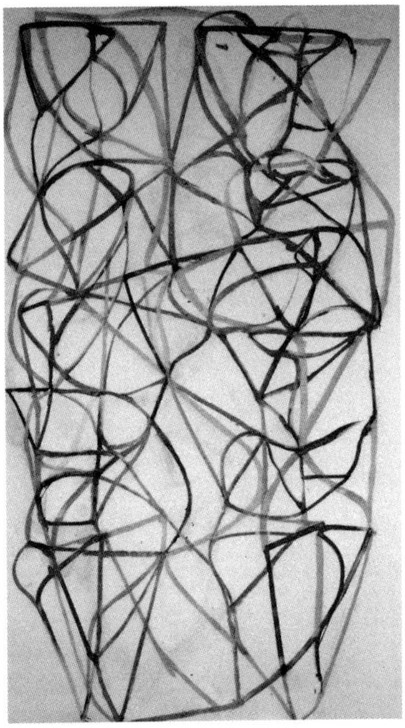

Couplet III 1988–9 Oil on canvas
274 × 152 (107⅞ × 59⅞)
Tate Gallery. Purchased will assistance from an anonymous donor 1990

This definition of Zen almost defines Marden's desire to receive and transmit the energy of nature and its elemental dynamics through the meditative act of painting and drawing.

Between the 'Rexroth' etchings and the 'Cold Mountain' works Marden began paring down his paintings, reducing the amount of colour and thinning the surfaces. They had an altogether leaner, sparer look. As in Cubist paintings, and indeed in many of Pollock's, lines would be drawn to a point just inside the edge. Thus a form would extend outwards only to loop back in on itself, thereby creating a sense of compressed tension and an endless, spiralling rhythm invoking the notion of the double helix. The paintings were less dominated by triangular motifs and scaffolding and became looser and more free-flowing.

Simultaneously Marden immersed himself in oriental literature. He discovered an edition of *The Collected Songs of Cold Mountain* translated from the Chinese by Red Pine[79] in which the English and the Chinese are printed in parallel. He had already come across the poet Cold Mountain in Kenneth Rexroth's translations but the combination of the Chinese with the English allowed Marden to begin to think about the meaning of individual ideographs. Marden does not understand the Chinese language, but he has established relationships between signifier and signified.

Cold Mountain was one of the great poets of the Tang dynasty whose output amounted to about three hundred poems. They can be playful, touching or bitter or a combination of all three. They frequently describe the landscape of the mountains where Cold Mountain sought refuge from the Imperial court, with its burbling streams, lush vegetation, carpets of wild flowers, roaring waterfalls, echoing gorges and singing birds; a landscape of solitude in nature. While retaining occasional hankerings for the worldly life he had left behind, Cold Mountain wrote about his lifelong pursuit of the Tao, 'a state of intuitive understanding in which the unity of "I" and "other" is experienced as vividly as the heat of fire or the coldness of ice. Once this has taken place, [the Taoist] can thenceforward respond with total spontaneity to every situation, just as plants bend spontaneously towards sunlight'.[80] In his desire to lose control in making art, to act simply as a receiver and transmitter of the energy of nature, Marden aspires to a Taoist attitude.

The way in which he makes the work to some degree depends on automatism. 'I think the closest I get to any sort of meditative state is when I'm drawing' he stated in an interview with his fellow painter Pat Steir.[81] 'It's about joining things up, making relationships, but at the same time letting the drawing itself do the work ... Ideally, the drawing is working and I'm working with it'. The proximity to Zen and Tao thought is apparent, although Marden never completely loses control. 'You take something out of control and bring it into control'.[82]

If Marden comes near to losing control in the drawings, he never does in the paintings. 'I keep wanting to lose control but I can't quite do it. I make a mark, and at that moment I can lose myself but then I come back and look at it and scrape it off. My paintings are not gestural although they

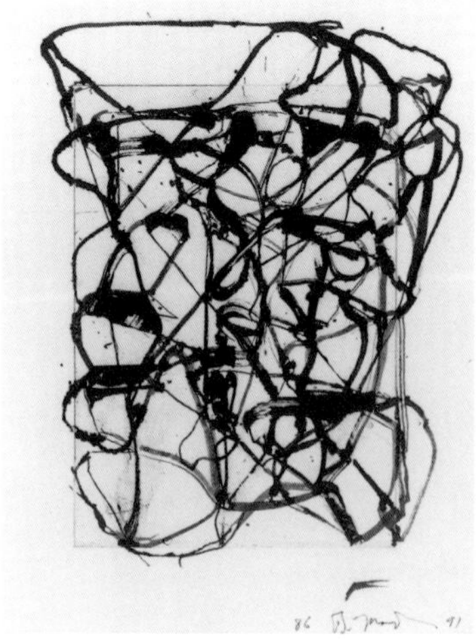

Tu Fu Dog 1 1986–91 Ink over etching and aquatint on paper
24.1 × 17.7 (9½ × 7)
Richard Brown Baker, New York

Cold Mountain 3 (Open) 1988–91
Oil on linen 274.3 × 365.8
(108 × 144) *Collection of the Artist*

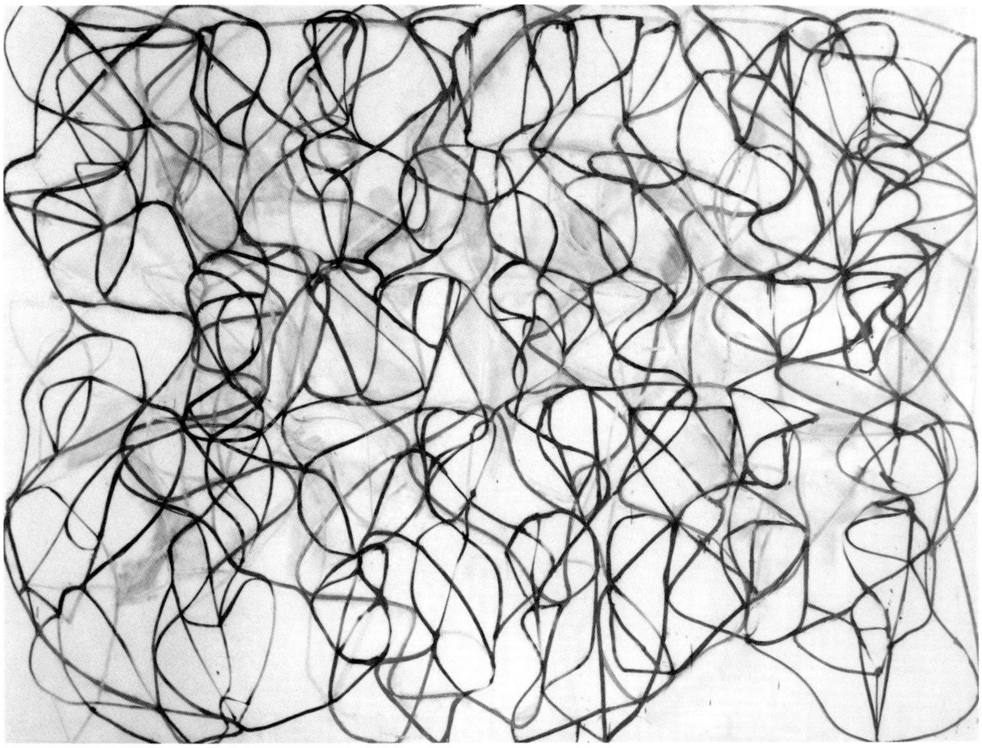

may look like it. De Kooning's might appear gestural. I looked at them that way but they weren't. They were controlled too.'

The 'Cold Mountain' paintings consist of six large canvases. With the exception of the first in the series which was made in 1988–9, the others were made side by side in 1990–1. Each canvas consists of four couplets, five characters deep, arranged vertically across the canvas in a grid and painted over a ground of relatively neutral colour. This organisation parallels the structure of Cold Mountain's poems. In the first canvas, which corresponds to the sixth print, Marden retains the clear identity of the grid but in the subsequent paintings he links the two individual columns of the couplet and then the couplets themselves, disguising, although not completely losing, the original structure. He thereby creates an all-over unity, a nexus of figures which communicate with each other in a multiplicity of ways. Compared to his earlier chords of subtly varing colours within a resticted range, these paintings, in all their cyclical complexity, are fugues.

The paintings were preceded by and made alongside hundreds of drawings. Whereas the paint surface is rubbed down to avoid a build up of paint, the drawings are quite densely worked, especially when Marden applies gouache to paint out unwanted lines. The ink seems to sit on top of the paper, whereas the constant rubbing of the surface of the canvas creates the illusion that paint and canvas are in one plane. This is further enhanced by the fact that the paintings are painted right to the edge, whereas many of the smaller drawings are bordered by wide margins. The prints parallel the paintings in both these respects, for not only are they worked to the edges of the plate but the press forces the ink into the paper.

The drawings do, however, vary in character. Some consist of lines densely woven together, while others depict more isolated marks descending in trickling columns, as though gravity has determined their fall. Marden occasionally applied white gouache to obliterate earlier marks, to thicken up the surface and endow it with spatial depth or to provide highlights. The images are drawn over either a coloured ground or one left bare. Some images evoke dancing figures, while others remain indecipherable. They frequently tail off towards the bottom leaving a border, which brings to mind Marden's earlier practice.

In terms of mark-making the prints lie somewhere between the drawings and the paintings. In general they are less densely worked than the drawings and, as in the paintings, there is a greater sense of space and depth. In a print the artist can build up an image in stages and alter anything he does not like by burnishing it out, leaving no indication of its previous existence. However, the strength of the mark is not determined by the application of pressure from the hand but by the length of time the plate remains in the acid. Thus while Marden may aspire to lose control in applying the sugar solution, he is fully in control when determining the length of the bite. When the plate is printed the resulting line is crisp and slightly raised, whereas in a drawing the ink often bleeds and sinks.

Marden began each print by drawing individual shapes onto the plate using sticks dipped in sugar solution – he tried spitbite at first, but did not like it. The compositional structure of each print follows that of the paintings: four couplets, five characters deep, arranged vertically in a grid. As he continued to work them he began to join up the characters within each couplet and then linked the couplets themselves, except in the sixth print where they remain separate. Again, this echoes the paintings which were worked alongside. Marden equates the junction of characters and couplets with the way that he reads the poems: 'You read the characters against each other a little bit. The first phrase joins up to the next phrase. It's a much more open kind of translating than that which is done in Western poetry.'

Compared with the 'Rexroth' prints the 'Cold Mountain Series, Zen Studies 1–6' are looser, more cursive and relaxed. The surface does not seem hard-won and remains pure even where aquatint has been scraped out. Indeed they seem effortless. The line is more confident, controlled and fluid as befits the increased scale of the plates, but varied in its width, rhythm and speed.

In the thirty years Marden has been making prints his imagery and concerns have developed considerably, but however different the 'Cold Mountain' prints appear to be from the etchings of his student days, they share a number of similarities. Marden has always been receptive to accident, has always drawn with a combination of nervous and assured line and has respected the flatness of the picture plane while searching for depth either through line or layering. The composition has always been governed by an organising grid and has remained resolutely abstract while assuming wider connotations beyond art itself. Finally, however restrained or impassive Marden's work has appeared to be it has never been unyielding and has always been expressive of emotions. As he states:

> Rothko was talking about painting, about death and I was much more interested in that than in Judd's Minimalist aesthetic. Emotions? I wanted to keep that open. Subject matter was no longer valid but I felt my work was much more of a continuation of Abstract Expressionism than a rejection of it.

Of all the print media he has encountered, etching remains his favourite because it involves a physical engagement with materials. 'It's about touch and it's about feeling and it's very direct.' But it is also disciplined and slow. These are the fundamental characteristics of Marden's oeuvre.

Notes

1 This and all subsequent quotations attributed to Marden are taken from a series of interviews conducted between the author and Marden in 1991, unless otherwise stated.
2 Repr. Lanier Graham, *The Prints of Willem de Kooning. A catalogue raisonné 1957–71*, 1, Paris 1991, p.39.
3 Repr. Paul Cummings et al., *Willem de Kooning Drawings Paintings Sculpture*, exh. cat., Whitney Museum of American Art, New York 1984, pp.190 and 194 respectively.
4 Repr. *Parkett*, no.7, 1986, p.29 (col.).
5 Marden had married Pauline Baez while still a student and together they had a son, Nicholas.
6 Repr. *Manet 1832–1883*, exh. cat., Galeries nationales du Grand Palais, Paris 1983, p.274 (col.). This painting was recently included in the exhibition *Connections*, which Marden selected and hung at the Museum of Fine Arts Boston (Mar. – July 1991). This exhibition combined works from many different departments of the museum's permanent collection with paintings and drawings by Marden himself.
7 Marden's interest in Zurbarán was encouraged by Vicente.
8 Feb.–Apr. 1964.
9 Repr. Alan R. Solomon, *Jasper Johns*, exh. cat., The Jewish Museum, New York 1964, no.1.
10 Dec. 1963 – Feb. 1964.
11 Repr. Linda Shearer, *Brice Marden*, exh. cat., Solomon R. Guggenheim Museum, New York 1975, p.31.
12 'When you get intimidated you start working small.'
13 Quoted in 'Brice Marden Interviewed by Saul Ostrow', *Bomb*, Winter 1988, p.31.
14 Ibid.
15 Repr. Shearer 1975, p.29.
16 Repr. Peter Schjeldahl, *Art of Our Time: The Saatchi Collection*, 1, 1984, no.64 (col.).
17 Ibid., no.65 (col.). Nico was a singer for Velvet Underground.
18 'For Otis Redding' 1968 repr. *Art Minimal II*, exh. cat., C.A.P.C. Musée d'art contemporain, Bordeaux, Dec. 1986 – Feb. 1987, p.69 (col.).
19 In May 1970 student demonstrators at Kent State University, Ohio were shot dead by the National Guard. This event was also memorialised by Richard Hamilton in a screenprint entitled 'Kent State' 1970 (see *The Tate Gallery 1984–86: Illustrated Catalogue of Acquisitions*, 1988, pp.371–5 repr.).
20 Quoted in *Brice Marden: Paintings Drawings and Prints 1975–80*, exh. cat., Whitechapel Art Gallery, 1981, p.54.
21 Shearer 1975, p.19.
22 The name of the printer has not been traced.
23 Kathan Brown still retains the proof she printed but has never seen Hershey's edition.
24 See n.39 below.
25 See for example 'Night Sea' 1963, repr. Schjeldahl 1983, no.75 (col.).
26 Repr. Nan Rosethal and Ruth E. Fine, *The Drawings of Jasper Johns*, exh. cat., National Gallery of Art, Washington 1990, pp.139 and 135 (col.).

27 Repr. *Parkett*, no.7, 1986, p.39 (col.).
28 Quoted in Ostrow 1988, p.34.
29 The 'Grove Group' was the subject of an exhibition at Gagosian Gallery, New York in 1991. The notebook and the paintings are reproduced in Robert Pincus-Witten, *Brice Marden: The Grove Group*, exh. cat., Gagosian Gallery, New York 1991.
30 Repr. ibid., p.14.
31 Ibid., p.26.
32 Ibid., p.27.
33 Since the notebook contains the names, addresses and telephone numbers of both Robert Feldman and Nona Hershey he probably began to use the notebook before embarking on 'Ten Days' since he did not return to Nona Hershey after making 'Grid I', 'Grid II' and 'Untitled'.
34 Apr. – June 1963.
35 Repr. Shearer 1975, p.41.
36 Repr. Michael Crichton, *Jasper Johns*, New York 1977, no.2.
37 Repr. ibid, p.31.
38 Repr. Hugh M. Davies, *The Prints of Barnett Newman*, New York 1983, pp.91 and 93.
39 Most printers use a cloth to wipe the plate but Kathan Brown had been taught, in England, the French method of wiping the plate with her hand, having previously taken off only the excess with a tarlatan. Brown studied printmaking at Central School of Art, London under Merlyn Evans, Tony Harrison and Jack Coutu, and painting and drawing with Roger Hilton and William Turnbull.
40 Although Patricia Branstead is credited with having printed 'Ten Days' Kathan Brown was principally responsible. Brown had only recently taken on Branstead as an apprentice and although she had played the leading role in the printing, nevertheless generously agreed to attribute it to Branstead.
41 These remarks were made in front of the version which Brown printed.
42 This and further quotations attributed to Kathan Brown are taken from an interview held with the author on 19 and 20 July 1991.
43 See Jack Cowart and James Elliott, *Prints from Untitled Press, Captiva, Florida*, exh. cat., Wadsworth Atheneum, Hartford, Connecticut 1973.
44 Repr. Riva Castleman, *Jasper Johns: A Print Retrospective*, Museum of Modern Art, New York 1986, p.62.
45 Repr. Herrman Kern and Klaus Kertess, *Brice Marden: Drawings*, exh. cat., Kunstraum München, Munich 1979, nos.4 and 5.
46 Repr. *Parkett*, no.7, 1986, p.28 (col.).
47 See Brice Marden, *Suicide Notes*, Lausanne 1974.
48 Repr. Schjeldahl 1984, nos.70 and 72 (col.).
49 Marden went out to Oakland to work on 'Five Plates' at the beginning of November 1973 and completed the project in eight days. The 'Grove Group' paintings had largely been completed by then.
50 This painting is reproduced in its early state in Shearer 1975, p.44 but has since been painted so that the two outer bands are of a similar tone, therefore closely resembling the print. The dimensions of this painting are taken from the height and shoulder width of the poet Patti Smith, so that it becomes an equivalent to a portrait.
51 Repr. *Brice Marden: Paintings Drawings and Prints 1975–80*, exh. cat., Whitechapel Art Gallery, 1981, p.17 (col.).
52 'Moon I' and 'Moon III' repr. ibid., pp.23–4 (col.).
53 Repr. ibid., p.25 (col.).
54 Robert Graves, *The White Goddess*, 1948, American paperback version New York 1966, p.386.
55 Ibid., p.445.
56 This configuration was also employed by Johns in 'Study for Painting with Two Balls' 1957, repr. Solomon 1964, p.12.
57 Repr. Maxwell L. Anderson, 'Pompeiian Fresoes in the Metropolitan Museum of Art', *The Metropolitan Museum of Art Bulletin*, vol.16, Winter 1987–8.
58 Repr. Whitechapel Art Gallery 1981, pp.20–1.
59 All repr. Whitechapel Art Gallery 1981, pp.27–31.
60 Repr. Hugh M. Davies 1983, pp.71–89. 'Notes', a portfolio of eighteen etchings, was made in 1968 but released posthumously in 1978. Thomas B. Hess devoted an article to it in *PCN*, vol.2, Jan.–Feb. 1972, pp.121–2 in which he reproduced four of them. Marden may have been aware of the prints before he made 'Five Threes', although it is unlikely.
61 Yale University 1962, revised eds. 1969 and 1979.
62 Ibid., pp.2–3.
63 Ibid., pp.60–1.
64 Ibid., p.235, n.14.
65 In the interview with Saul Ostrow, Marden stated that the window project for the cathedral in Basle included a 'program of images based on The Revelations.'
66 Marden remembers in particular *Vel Prolegomena Symbolica Ad Systemam Sceptico-Mysticae Viae Explicandae, Fundamentum Hieroglyphicum Sanctissimorum Scientiae Summae*, published in London in 1909, of which he had a facsimile edition, published in Berkeley in 1980. This text comprised a table of correspondences between religions, numbers, alphabets, symbols, colours, etc.
67 Repr. Whitechapel Art Gallery 1981, p.32 (col.). The Greek word 'thira' means door.
68 See Johannes Itten, *Design and Form*, 1963, revised ed. 1975, reprinted 1983, p.33.
69 Repr. *Brice Marden: Recent Work*, exh. cat., Pace Gallery, New York 1984 pp.[5–16].
70 Marden quoted in Kay Larson, 'Different Strokes', *New York*, vol.24, 21 Oct. 1991, p.79.
71 Ibid.
72 This and all subsequent statements attributed to Melby are taken from an interview conducted with her on 17 July 1991.
73 See 'Thirteen Drawings' 1983 repr. Pace Gallery 1984, pp.[35–7].
74 See nn.69 and 66 above.
75 Quoted in Yoshiaki Shimizu and John M. Rosenfield, *Masters of Japanese Calligraphy 8th–19th Century*, exh. cat., Japan House Gallery and Asia Society Galleries, New York 1984, p.33.
76 See for example nos.76 and 87 in Paul Cummings, *David Smith: The Drawings*, exh. cat., Whitney Museum of American Art, New York 1979, repr.
77 Repr. Ellen G. Landau, *Jackson Pollock*, 1989, p.235 (col.).
78 Helmut Brinker, *Zen in the Art of Painting*, trans. George Campbell, 1987, p.1.
79 Port Townsend, Washington 1983.
80 John Blofeld, *Introduction* in Pine 1983, [n.p.].
81 Published in *Brice Marden: Recent Drawings and Etchings*, exh. cat., Matthew Marks, New York 1991.
82 Quoted in Ostrow 1988.

12 Four 1966
Image size: 28 × 40 (11 × 15¾)

14 Lana 2 1966
Image size: 28 × 40 (11 × 15¾)

15 Lana 3 1966
Image size: 28 × 40.1 (11 × 15⅞)

16 **Gulf** 1969
Image size: 34.3 × 50.7 (13½ × 19 15/16)

20 Ten Days 1971, pub. 1972 Print (b)
Image size: 55 × 27 (21⅝ × 10⅝)

20 Ten Days 1971, pub. 1972 Print (c)
Image size: 38 × 30 ($14\frac{15}{16}$ × $11\frac{3}{4}$)

20 Ten Days 1971, pub. 1972 Print (e)
Image size: 30.5 × 38.5 (12 × 15⅛)

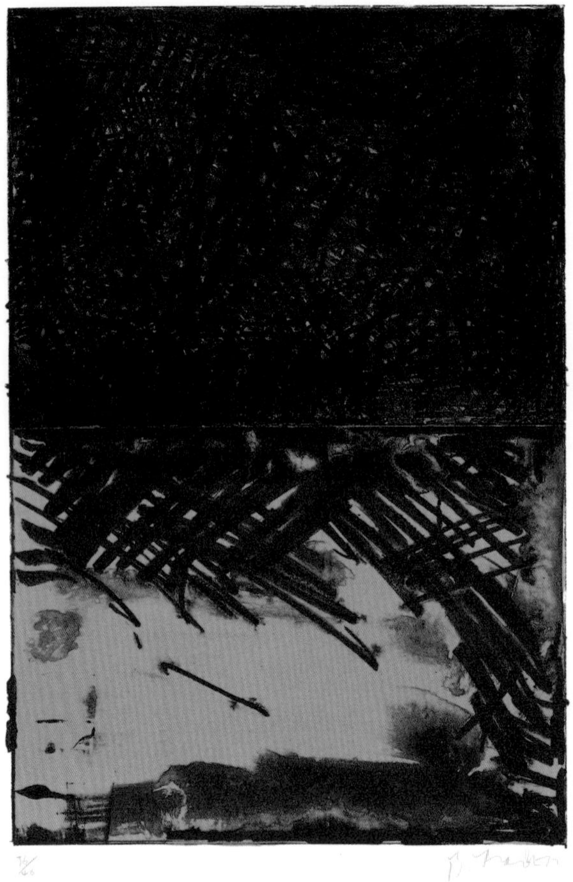

21 **Untitled Press Series** 1972 #3
Image size: 40.7 × 26.7 (16 × 10½)

24 Untitled 1973
Image size: 49.2 × 39.3 (19⅜ × 15½)

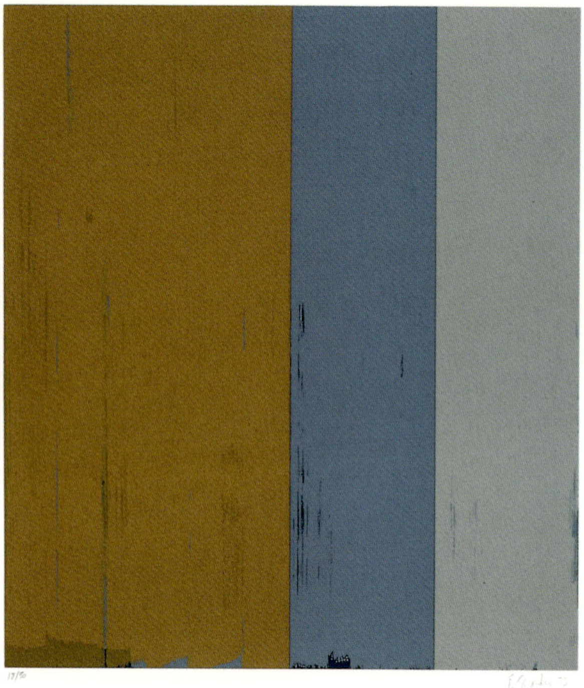

25 Untitled 1973
Image size: 45.8 × 39.5 (18 1/16 × 15 1/16)

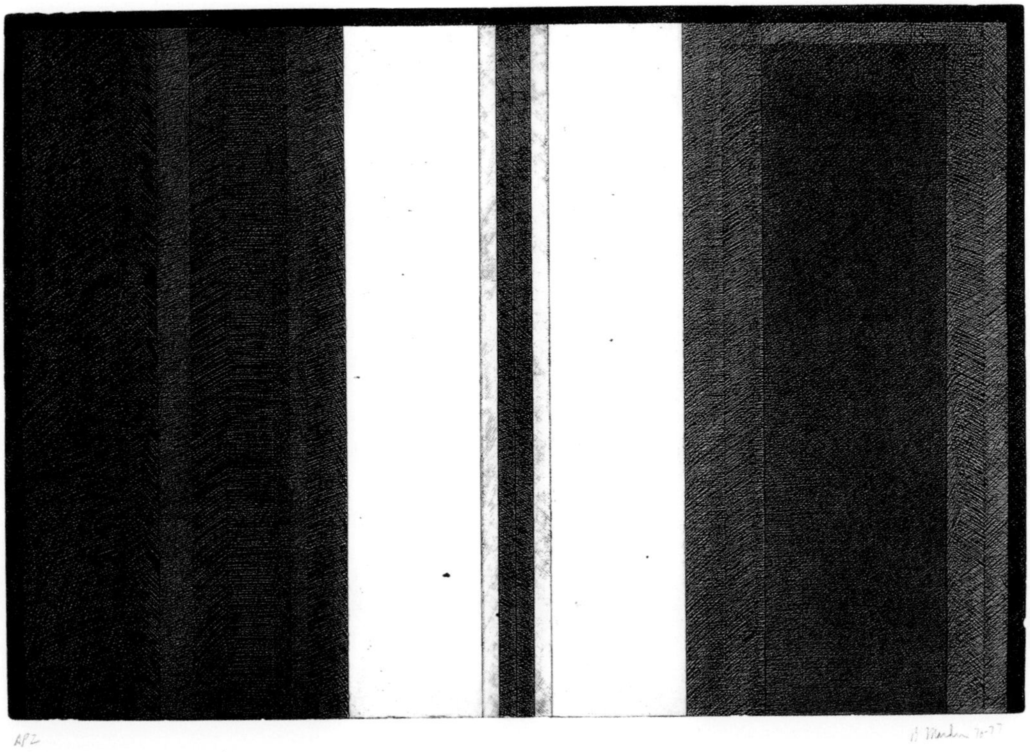

28 Five Threes 1976–7 Print (a)
Image size: 53.3 × 75.8 (21 × 29⅞)

28 Five Threes 1976–7 Print (b)
Image size: 53.2 × 75.6 (21 × 29¾)

28 Five Threes 1976–7 Print (c)
Image size: 53.3 × 75.5 (21 × 29¾)

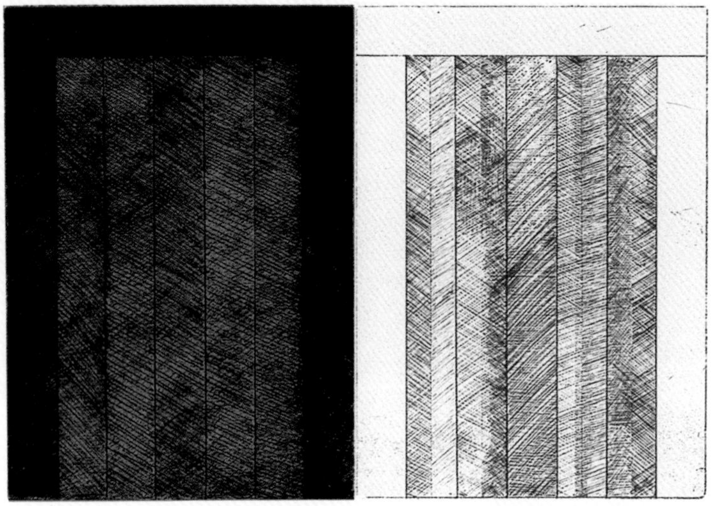

29 12 Views for Caroline Tatyana 1977–9
pub. 1989 Print (k)
Image size: 25 × 35.2 (9⅞ × 14)

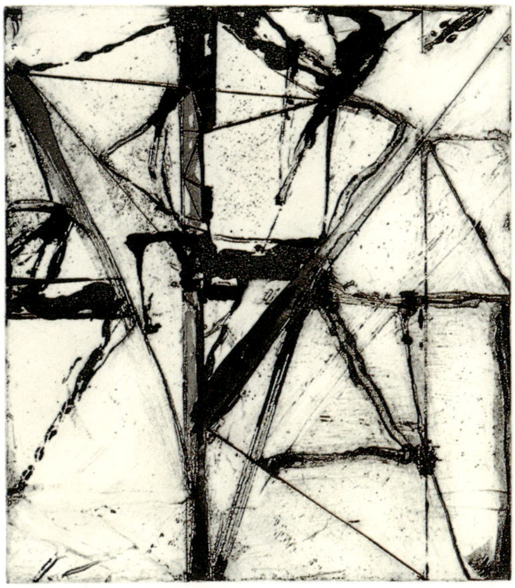

40 **Etchings to Rexroth** 1986 Print **18**
Image size: 20.3 × 17.8 (8 × 7)

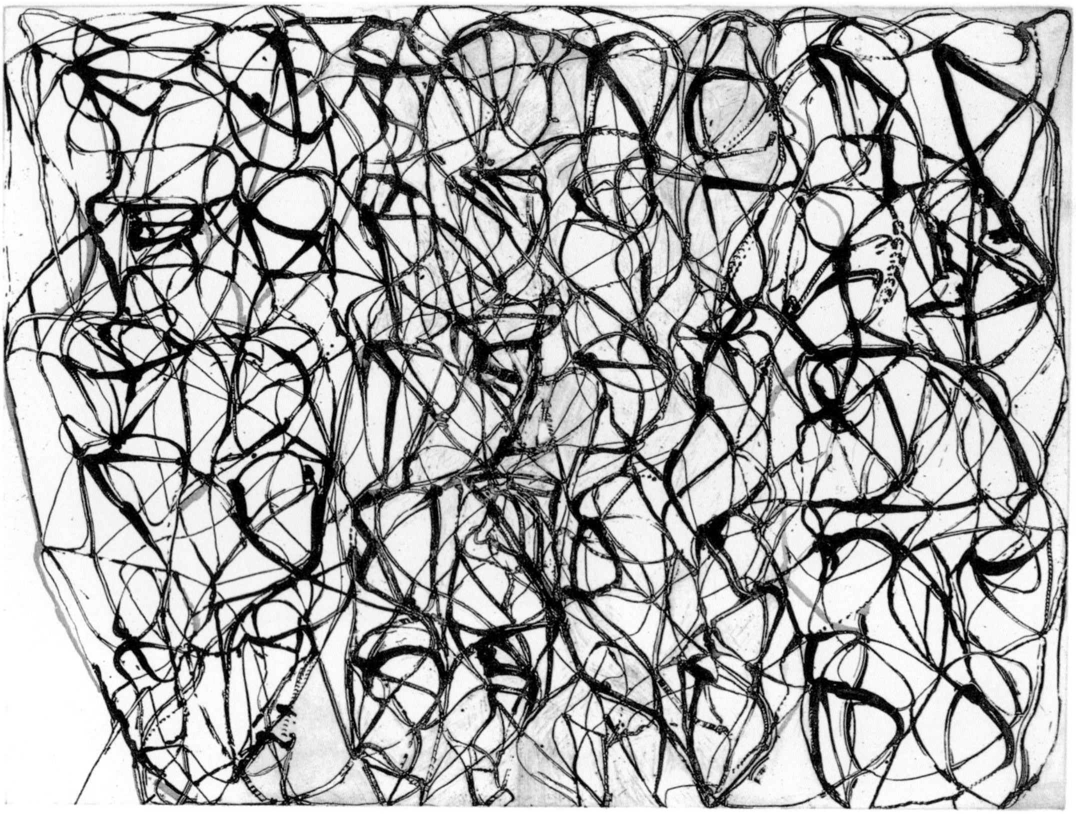

43 **Cold Mountain Series, Zen Study 4** 1991
Image size: 52.5 × 68.6 (20⅝ × 27)

Catalogue Note

Measurements are given in centimetres followed by inches in brackets; height before width. The colour of the paper is white unless otherwise indicated. Most etchings are printed on paper with a deckle-edge. Paper sizes may therefore vary between editions. For the purpose of reproduction in most cases the edges of the paper have been trimmed. 'Inscribed' means inscribed by the artist; all prints are inscribed in pencil. Works marked with an asterisk are included in the exhibition.

The following prints by Brice Marden are in the collection of the Tate Gallery:

No.23 'Five Plates' 1973 (P01739–01743) Presented by the Contemporary Art Society 1975
No.31 'Tiles' 1979 (P07849–07852) Purchased 1983
No.29 '12 Views for Caroline Tatyana' 1979, pub. 1989 (P77336–77347) Purchased 1989
No.40 'Etchings to Rexroth' 1986 (P77208–77232) Purchased 1987

Abbreviations: General

AP	artist's proof
BAT	Bon à tirer, also know as right to print (RTP)
cm	centimetres
col.	colour
ed.	edition
etching	hardground etching
exh.	exhibition
exh. cat.	exhibition catalogue
in	inches
lit	literature
p.	page
[n.p.]	not paginated
p.[ ]	unpaginated
PP	printer's proof
pub.	published
repr.	reproduced in
t.l.	top left
t.r.	top right

Abbreviations: Literature

All books cited are published in London unless otherwise stated.

Kunstraum München *Brice Marden Drawings 1964–1978*, exh. cat., Kunstraum München, Munich 1979

Parkett *Parkett*, no.7, Jan. 1986

PCN *Print Collector's Newsletter*

Schjeldahl Peter Schjeldahl, *Art of our Time: The Saatchi Collection 1*, 1984

Shearer Linda Shearer, *Brice Marden*, exh. cat., The Solomon R. Guggenheim Museum, New York 1975

Stedelijk *Brice Marden: Paintings, Drawings Etchings 1975–1980*, exh. cat., Stedelijk Museum, Amsterdam 1981

Whitechapel *Brice Marden: Paintings, Drawings and Prints 1975–1980*, exh. cat., Whitechapel Art Gallery, 1981

1 **Untitled** 1961
Etching on ivory wove paper
Image size: 7.6 × 12.6 (3 × 5)
Paper size: 12.6 × 18.1 (5 × 7⅛)
1 plate
Colour: black
Printed by the artist at
Boston University
Not editioned. Proofs only
Inscribed 'B. Marden 61' below
image b.r. and 'artist's proof' below
image b.l.

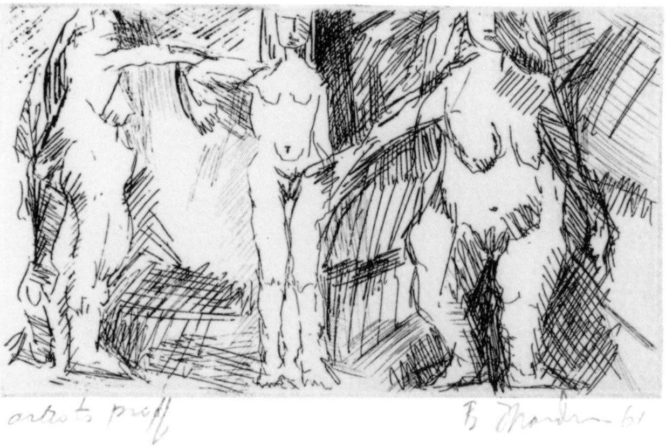

This is one of Marden's earliest known prints, although he remembers having made woodcuts at Boston University. The image depicts three nude figures, probably in a landscape, in a manner related to Cézanne and to Picasso.

For further discussion of this print see p.12.

*2 **Untitled** *c.*1961
Etching and drypoint on ivory wove paper
Image size: 7.5 × 12.5 (3 × 5)
Paper size: 13.3 × 17.5 (5$\frac{3}{16}$ × 6$\frac{7}{8}$)
1 plate
Colour: black
Printed by the artist at Boston University
Not editioned. Proofs only (at least 5)
Inscribed 'B. Marden' below image b.r.

The image depicts the head and upper part of the torso of a female nude. At Boston, Marden was painting and drawing from poses set up in the life class. In this and the previous etching Marden states that he 'was being freer' than in the life class. He has divided the plane with diagonal lines which not only indicates an interest in Cubist faceting but also anticipates his strategy, in later works, of breaking up the flatness of the plane. The surface is more densely hatched than the previous print and is more deeply bitten. The markings are cruder and more forceful.

For further discussion of this print see p.12.

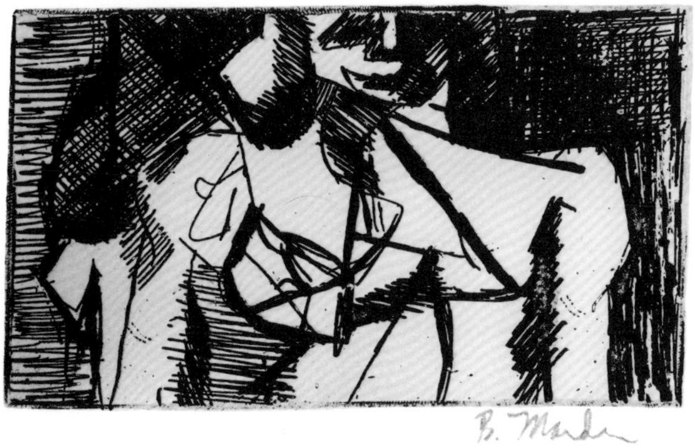

3 **Untitled** 1961
Etching on ivory wove paper
Image size: 7.6 × 12.6 (3 × 5)
Paper size: 11.5 × 18.3
(4½ × 7¼)
1 plate
Colour: black
Printed by the artist at
Boston University
Edition: 5 plus at least 1 AP
Inscribed 'B. Marden 61' below
image b.r. and numbered below
image b.l.

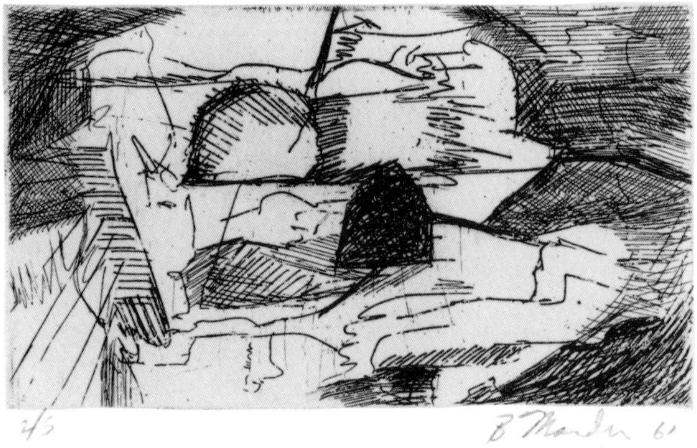

The image depicts an abstract landscape with a building structure at centre. At this time Marden did many drawings out of the car window when travelling down to New York to visit exhibitions.

For further discussion of this print see p.12.

4 **Things** 1961
Etching on ivory wove paper
Image size: 14.4 × 22.2
(5¾ × 8¾)
Paper size: 36.1 × 44.4
(14¼ × 17½)
1 plate
Colour: black
Printed by the artist at Yale Summer School of Music and Art, Norfolk, Connecticut
Not editioned. Proofs only
Inscribed 'B. Marden' below image b.l. and 'Things' below image at centre

One impression of this print has been found. Marden has retained the plate and a further proof was printed for record purposes in 1991 by Jennifer Melby in New York.

The image depicts a still life of a glass, a mug and possibly a jug on a table. The objects have been distorted, suggesting Marden's interest in Cézanne.

For further discussion of this print see p.12.

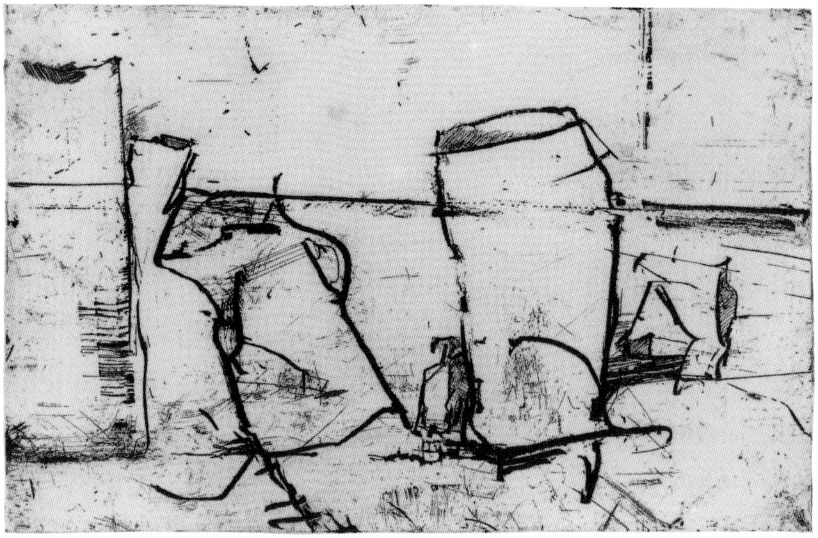

*5 **Untitled** 1961
Etching, sugarlift aquatint and aquatint on Rives paper
Image size: 39.9 × 30 (15¾ × 11 13/16)
Paper size: 50.8 × 38.5 (20 × 15 3/16)
1 plate
Colour: black
Printed by the artist at Yale University
Not editioned. Proofs only.
Inscribed 'B. Marden' below image b.r. and 'artist's proof' below image b.l.

Only one proof of the final state of this print has been found, although it exists in two other states which are also signed and inscribed 'artist's proof'. The earliest proof consists of gestural lines applied with a brush using sugarlift. These marks are reminiscent of the work of Franz Kline. In the first state Marden has employed a landscape format, the composition running diagonally downwards towards the bottom right corner. In the second state he has retained the landscape format and added areas of aquatint, particularly to the left side and the far right. The effect is to reduce the emphasis on the calligraphic quality of the early state. In the third and, as far as is known, final state the image has been turned through ninety degrees to become a portrait format. Some of the sugarlift has been burnished out and partially scraped out towards top left and bottom right. All three states are inscribed identically, with the exception of the third which is not dated. The image recalls works by de Kooning of the late fifties as well as Kline.

For further discussion of this print see p.14.

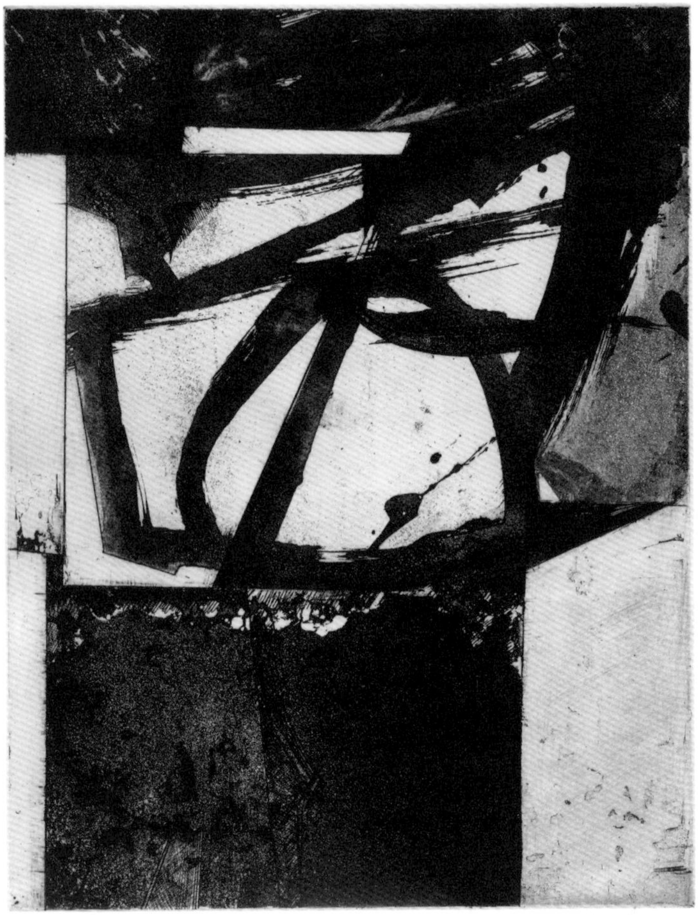

5

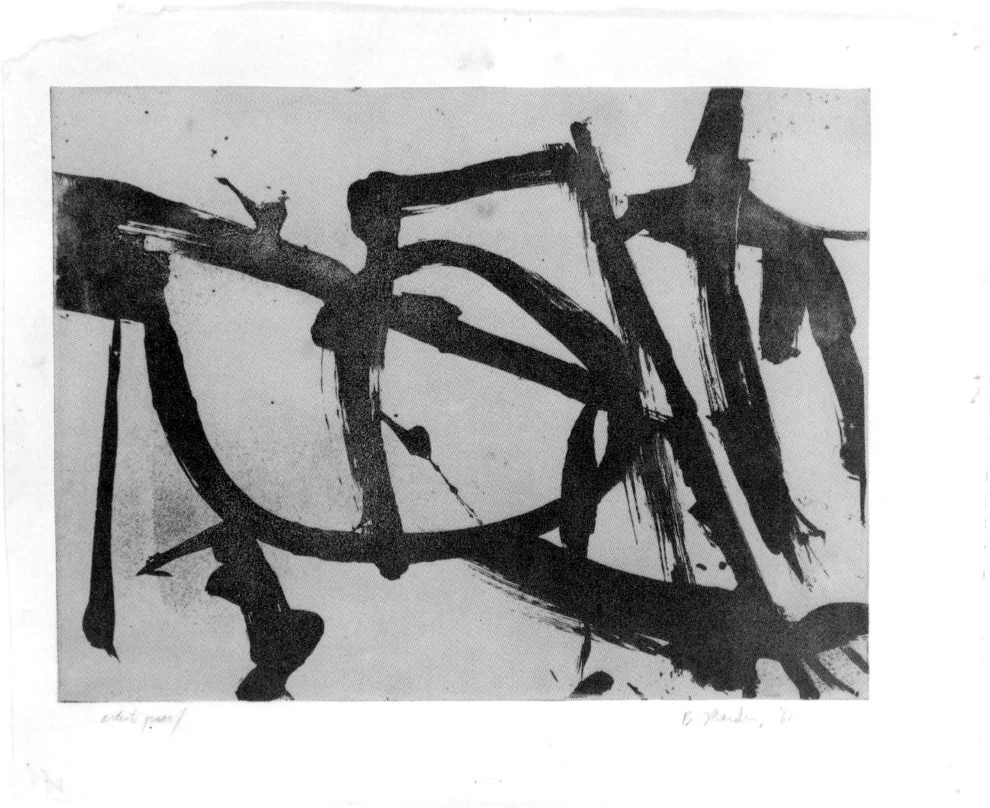

5 1st state

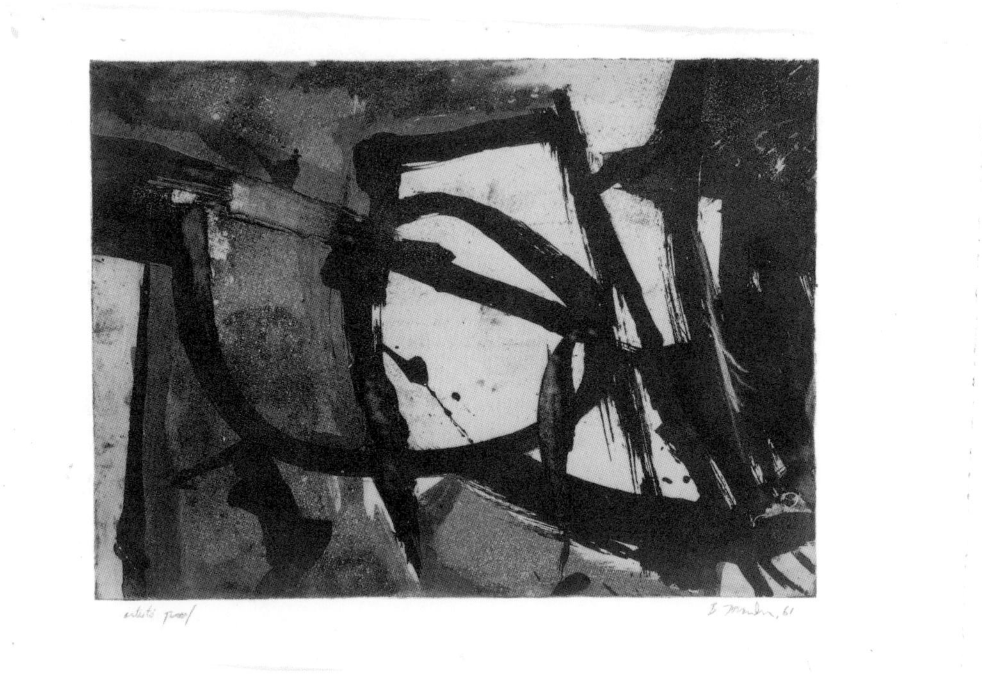

5 2nd state

6 **Untitled** 1961
Etching with sugarlift aquatint and aquatint on ivory wove paper
Image size: 29.8 × 24.7 (11¾ × 9¾)
Paper size: 35.2 × 29.8 (14⅛ × 11¾)
1 plate
Colour: black
Printed by the artist at Yale University
Not editioned. Proofs only
Inscribed 'B. Marden' below image b.r and 'artists proof I' below image b.l.

Two states of this print are known. In the second state Marden has scraped out the motifs in the bottom two-thirds of the first state, creating an area of tone enlivened by ghost images from the earlier state. The configuration of dark above light anticipates some of the images in later works, particularly 'Ten Days' (no.20). The first state is inscribed 'B. Marden, 61' below image b.r. and 'artist's proof' below image b.l.

For further discussion of this print see p.15.

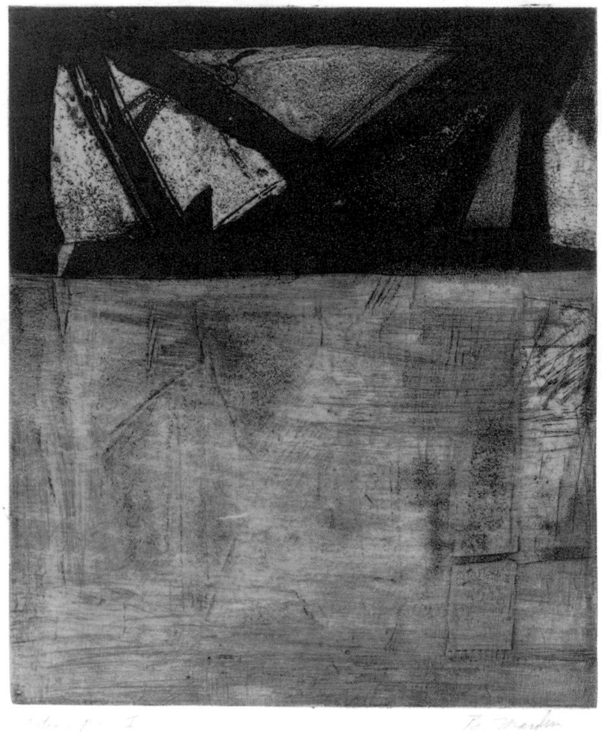

6

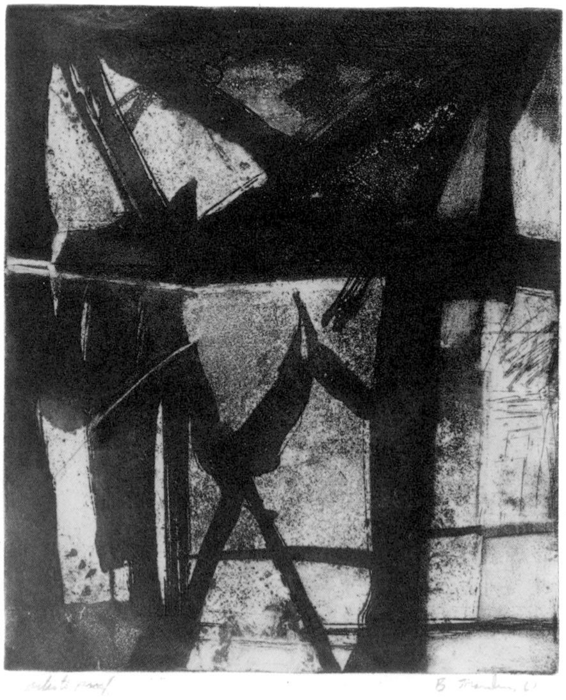

6 1st state

7 **Untitled** 1961
Etching, sugarlift aquatint and aquatint on ivory wove paper
Image size: 24.7 × 29.8 (9¾ × 11¾)
Paper size: 31.1 × 40 (12¼ × 15¾)
1 plate
Colour: black
Printed by the artist at Yale University
Not editioned. Proofs only
Inscribed 'B. Marden, 61' below image b.r. and 'artist's proof' below image b.l.

A print in a similar style to the previous two entries. Marden's interest in textural invention is evident here. The copy illustrated is dedicated to Chuck Close, Marden's fellow student at Yale.

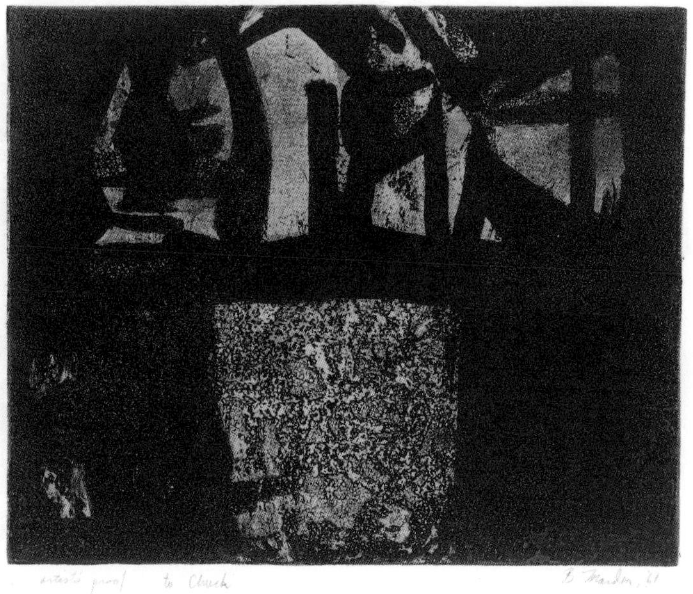

8 Untitled 1961
Etching and aquatint on ivory, wove paper
Image size: 19.6 × 29.8 (7⅞ × 11¾)
Paper size: 31.4 × 41.2 (12⅜ × 16¼)
1 plate
Colour: black
Printed by the artist at Yale University
Not editioned. Proofs only
Inscribed 'B. Marden, 61' below image b.r. and 'artist's proof' below image b.l.

Only one proof of this image has been found. It is not known in any other state. Marden's interest in de Kooning's paintings and drawings of the late forties is evident here. The tonal contrasts are achieved principally through line and scraping, rather than aquatint.

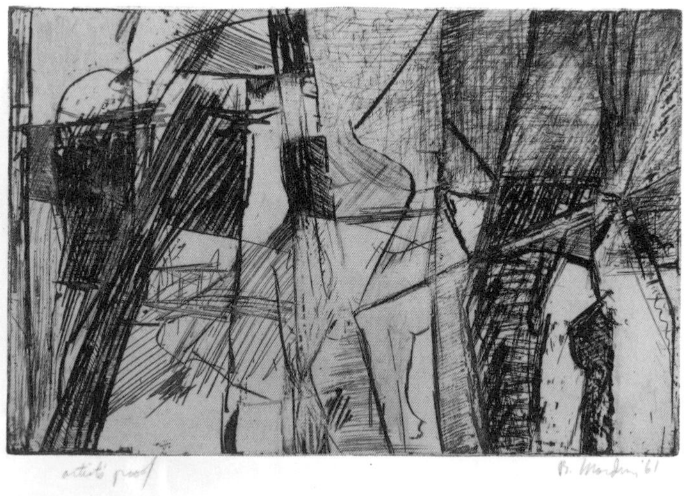

***9 Untitled** *c.*1963
Etching on ivory wove paper
Image size: 14.7 × 15 (5 13/16 × 5 7/8)
Paper size: 19.5 × 19.7 (7 5/8 × 7 3/4)
Colour: black
Printed by the artist at
Yale University
Not editioned. Proofs only
Inscribed '#1' below image b.r.

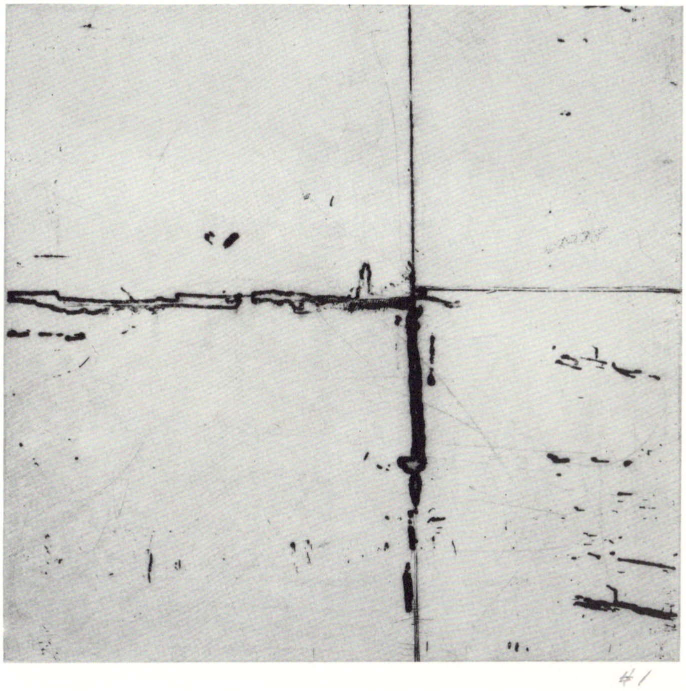

The image is divided into four rectangles. One line runs in varying thicknesses from top to bottom and is met by two separate lines at different heights, one coming from the left edge and the other from the right. Each line is located off-centre and each rectangle is of a different size. The image and the paper are not quite square. The perfection of the square is thus subverted. The surface has been enlivened by the use of foul biting, while the marks have been strengthened by prolonged immersion of the plate in the acid.

The almost square format of this print is rare in Marden's oeuvre and indicates an interest in the work of Mondrian which Marden relates to 'a definite attempt to get away from the compositional excess of Abstract Expressionism'. He has generally avoided the square because of its spiritual connotations within the history of twentieth century art.

The image looks forward to the grid drawings and prints such as 'Tiles' (no.31) and is one of a number of works executed in this period where the plane is divided into four (see 'Untitled' 1962–3, repr. *Parkett*, p.29 in col.)

For further discussion of this print see p.15.

*10 **Untitled** *c.*1963
Etching on ivory wove paper
Image size: 10.8 × 15 (4¼ × 6)
Paper size: 31.3 × 39.1
(12¼ × 15½)
1 plate
Colour: black
Printed by the artist at
Yale University
Not editioned. Proofs only

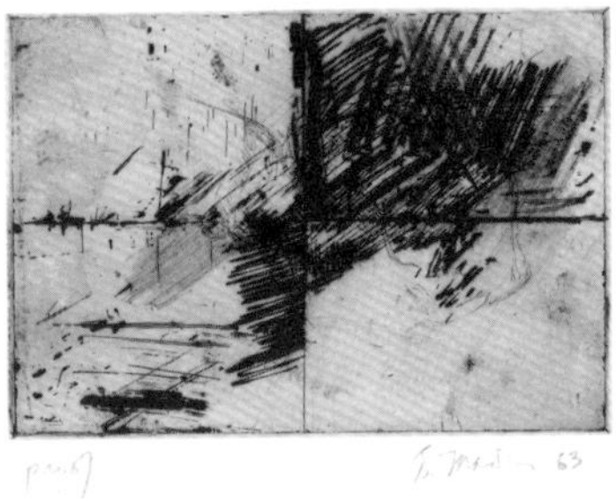

No original proofs of this work have been found, but Marden retained the plate from which one proof was pulled for record purposes by Jennifer Melby in 1991 in New York. It is inscribed 'B. Marden 63' below image b.r. and 'proof' below image b.l. This image and the previous one relate to 'Untitled' 1962–3 (repr. *Parkett*, p.29 in col.) and to many drawings of the period.

Parts of the image have been deeply bitten to produce a very high relief.

*11 **Watsonville** 1963
Etching on ivory wove paper
Image size: 14.3 × 11 (5¾ × 4$\frac{5}{16}$)
Paper size: 20 × 16 (7⅞ × 6¼)
1 plate
Colour: black
Printed and published by the artist at Yale University
Edition: 25 plus at least 1 AP
Inscribed 'B. Marden "Watsonville"' and numbered below image

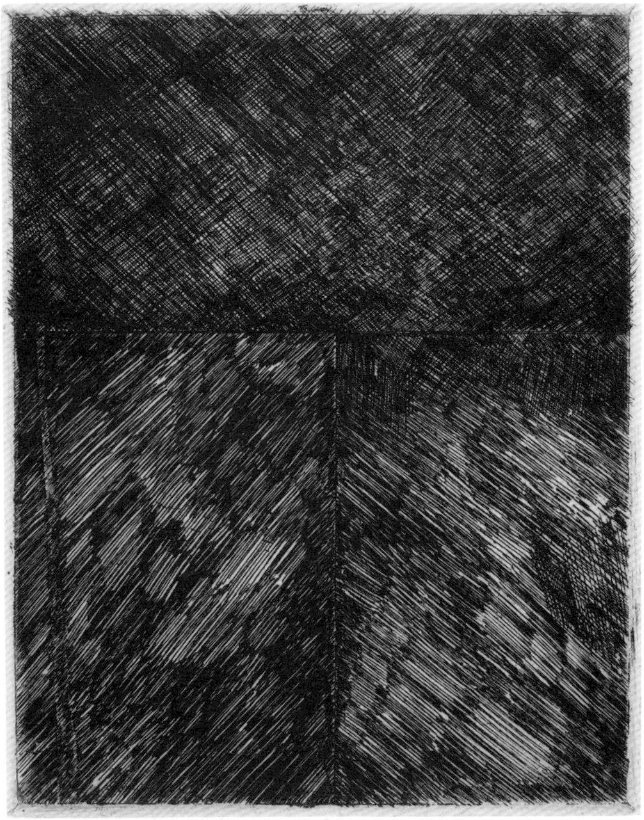

The image is divided into three rectangular sections by two lines, one spanning the width of the image, the other rising vertically from the bottom edge, just to the right of centre, to meet the first line. The rectangles are of three different sizes although the two vertical ones look similar. The top rectangle is cross-hatched, whereas the two upright rectangles are predominantly diagonally shaded. The diagonal lines draw attention to the near-central division and suggest the notion of perspective without creating an illusion of it. Thus the image remains emphatically planar. In its reliance on line for tonal gradation 'Watsonville' anticipates some of the 'Ten Days' prints (see no.20), although the mark-making is coarser and admits more light.

A number of Marden's paintings in this period contained vertical and horizontal divisions. The introduction of the horizontal element anticipates the post and lintel motif (see no.29).

For further discussion of this print see pp.15–16.

*12 **Four** 1966
Screenprint on paper
Image size: 28 × 40 (11 × 15¾)
Paper size: 50.8 × 60.3
(20 × 23¾)
3 screens
Colour: first screen dark grey, second screen intermediate grey, third screen light grey
Printed by the artist at Chiron Press, New York and published by him
Edition: 5 plus at least 1 AP
Inscribed 'B. Marden' below image b.r., 'Four' below image at centre and numbered below image b.l.
Reproduced in colour on p.57

The image consists of four upright, separated panels of similar dimensions in light grey with a predominantly dark grey lower border. The print is built up in three layers of three different tones of grey. The imperfections along the edges of each panel are the result of poor registration and were not intended by the artist. The first two greys were drawn onto the screen with a crayon. The light grey is flat-printed on top.

A graphite drawing of the same configuration in the artist's collection is one of a number that he was making at the time. He explained that 'they were ideas of paintings which were never executed'. Marden has made at least three drawings using 'Four' as a base (one repr. Kunstraum, Munich, no.2). In the one cited he has transformed the configuration into a diptych. In another, 'Painting Study 1' 1980 (repr. p.19), he has superimposed a grid.

The single, narrow, vertical format was first used in 'Decorative Painting' 1964–5 (repr. p.20 and Shearer, p.29). Marden employed two separated, vertical panels in 'For Helen' 1967 (repr. p.23 and Shearer, p.33). The surface of 'Four' is fairly smooth and is equivalent to the surface of Marden's wax paintings, the first of which, 'Wax I', was made in 1966.

For further discussion of this print see p.20.

*13 **Lana** 1966
Screenprint on paper
Image size: 28 × 40 (11 × 15¾)
Paper size: 49.9 × 60.3
($19\frac{11}{16}$ × 23¾)
Two screens
Colour: first screen black, second screen grey-blue
Printed by the artist at Chiron Press, New York and published by him
Edition: 11 plus at least 2 APs
Inscribed 'B. Marden' below image b.r., 'Lana' below image at centre and numbered below image b.l.

See entry for no.15 below.

*14 **Lana 2** 1966
Screenprint on paper
Image size: 28 × 40 (11 × 15¾)
Paper size: 50.8 × 60.8 (20 × 23 15/16)
3 screens
Colour: first screen black, second screen grey-blue, third screen warm grey
Printed by the artist at Chiron Press, New York and published by him
Edition: 11 plus at least 1 AP
Inscribed 'B. Marden' below image b.r., 'Lana 2' below image at centre and numbered below image b.l.
Reproduced in colour on p.58

See entry for no.15 below.

*15 **Lana 3** 1966
Screenprint on paper
Image size: 28 × 40.1 (11 × 15⅞)
Paper size: 50.8 × 61 (20 × 24)
3 screens
Colour: first screen black, second screen grey-blue, third screen grey-pink
Printed by the artist at Chiron Press, New York and published by him
Edition: 11 plus at least 1 AP
Inscribed 'B. Marden' below image b.r., 'Lana #3' below image at centre and numbered below image b.l.
Reproduced in colour on p.59

Each of the 'Lana' prints consists of a rectangle of colour, with a border along the bottom containing marks which spilled over beyond the confines of the rectangle during the process of drawing on the screens. 'Lana' and 'Lana 2', although editioned as independent prints, are equivalent to stage proofs for 'Lana 3'. According to Marden each succeeding 'Lana' print employs the screens of the previous image in the same order of printing, before a new screen is added. However, close examination of 'Lana 3' suggests that the screens for the previous two prints only have been used, the pink in 'Lana 3' turning to grey where it covers black and grey-blue. Marks which appear in the border of this print and which do

not appear in 'Lana 2' may either have occurred as a result of cleaning the screen after use for 'Lana 2' or have been added.

The first screen was drawn with a crayon. The second screen was a solid colour. The texture of 'Lana' is broken and in this respect is an equivalent to the paintings entitled 'Last Dylan Study' 1964–6 and 'Plumb II' 1964–5. It is close to a number of drawings Marden made at the time where he emphasised gesture and texture. In 'Lana 2' he superimposed a further solid colour which finds its equivalent in the paintings Marden began to make using wax, the broken marks from the previous screen showing through like the brush marks of a painting. 'Nico' 1966 (repr. p.22 and Schjeldahl, no.65 in col.) is close in feel and format to 'Lana 2' and 'Lana 3' in this respect. The same screen in a different colour is employed for the final printing of 'Lana 3'. The process by which a screenprint can be built up in layers of colour was considered by Marden to be a graphic equivalent for his painting technique.

The border along the bottom is intended not only to provide a sense of scale to the solid rectangle but to demonstrate the build up of colours as 'an index of the painting'. Marden stated that he 'used to be very conscious of the way these things dripped at the bottom so these were really drawn at the bottom'. He deliberately transgressed the edge of the rectangle he had delineated. The 'drips' did not occur by accident.

Marden had not actually intended to make three prints but, as he explained, 'I think the reason I did not work it all into one was because I liked what I was getting on the way.'

Very few, if any, of these prints were sold and they were mostly given to friends as presents. Marden has drawn over a number of proofs, two as late as 1980 (one repr. Whitechapel, p.44 and detail on front cover in col.). The prints were named after a friend of the artist.

For further discussion of these prints see p.21.

*16 **Gulf** 1969
From 'New York Ten' portfolio
Lithograph on Rives paper
Image size: 34.3 × 50.7
($13\frac{1}{2} \times 19\frac{15}{16}$)
Paper size: 51 × 66 ($20\frac{1}{16} \times 26$)
2 zinc plates
Colour: black and warm grey
Printed by Chiron Press, New York and published by Tanglewood Editions, New York
Edition: 100 plus 10 APs numbered in roman and 1 BAT
Inscribed 'B. Marden 69' below image b.r. and numbered below image b.l.; printer's stamp b.r. and publisher's stamp b.l.
Reproduced in colour on p.60

'Gulf' has a landscape format and consists of a dark rectangle above a lighter one. The two rectangles have ragged edges which permit the paper to show through. A line has been drawn around the edge of the print and across the centre to define the image and to emphasise the irregularity of the colour areas. The gap between the two colours emphasises their separateness. The horizontal division was unusual in Marden's work at this time but was used in 'From Bob's House' and 'Urdan'.

The title of the work refers to the Gulf of Mexico. Rauschenberg's home on Captiva Island is in the Gulf of Mexico. Marden considers the image to be an equivalent to the view from Rauschenberg's house. He was commissioned to make the print by Rosa Esman for a portfolio by ten young artists working or exhibiting in New York. The artists were Alan Cote, David Diao, Ronald Landfield, Lee Lozano, Brice Marden, William Pettet, Alan Shields, Kenneth Showell, Lawrence Stafford and Peter Young. Marden had met Esman when he worked at Chiron Press.

For further discussion of this print see p.24.

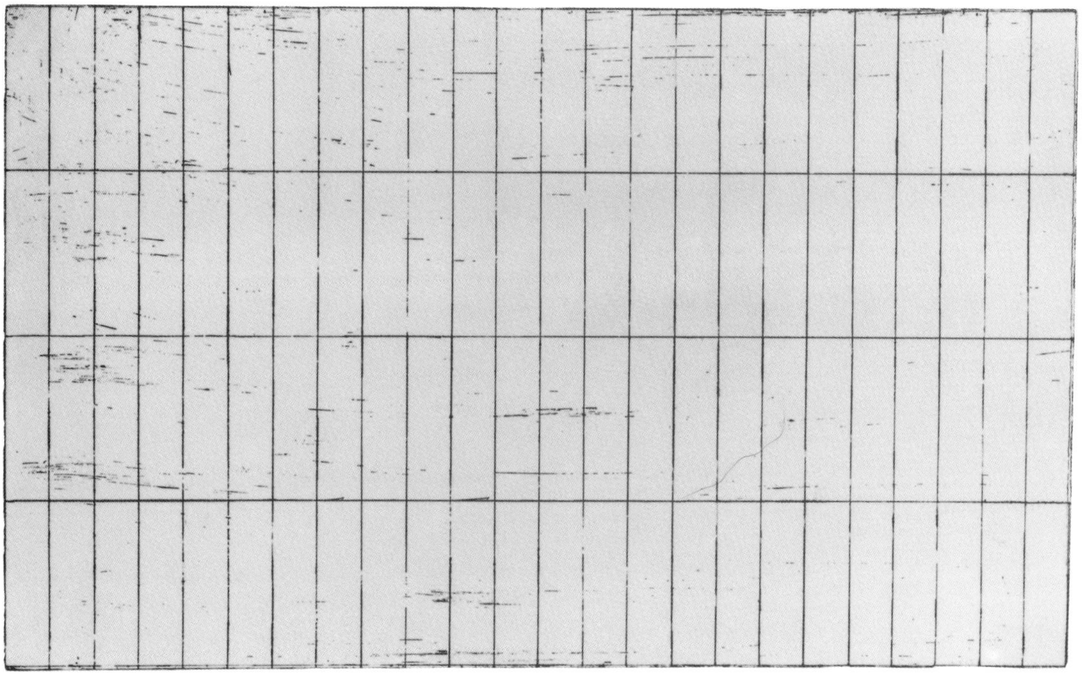

17 Grid I 1971
Etching on Arches paper
Image size: 37.5 × 60.5 (14¾ × 23⅞)
Paper size: 56.5 × 76 (22¼ × 30)
1 plate
Colour: black
Printed by Nona Hershey, New York and published by Parasol Press, New York
Edition: 50 plus at least 1 AP
Inscribed 'B. Marden 71' below image b.l., 'Grid I' below image at centre and numbered below image b.l.

The image consists of a grid of ninety-six rectangles. Three lines run horizontally across the plane while twenty-three are drawn vertically. Marden began by dividing the plate into three panels and then divided each of those in half. He halved the six resulting panels and then the consequent twelve, making a total of twenty-four. He then divided them horizontally by three lines to form four vertical bands. The grid, therefore, employs a system based on the numbers two and three.

The lines are drawn imperfectly and the plate contains a lot of foul biting. The imperfection of the grid is deliberate and invests it with a sense of human intervention. It also permits a more complex reading of space. The double line at the bottom of the print was not desired. It has occurred because the edge of the plate itself has printed.

Marden states that in his drawings he had been using grids 'to keep the tension even across the surface of the plane. It also became a measuring thing.'

This and nos.18 and 19 were the first prints Parasol Press commissioned from Marden.

For further discussion of this print see p.25 and pp.26–7.

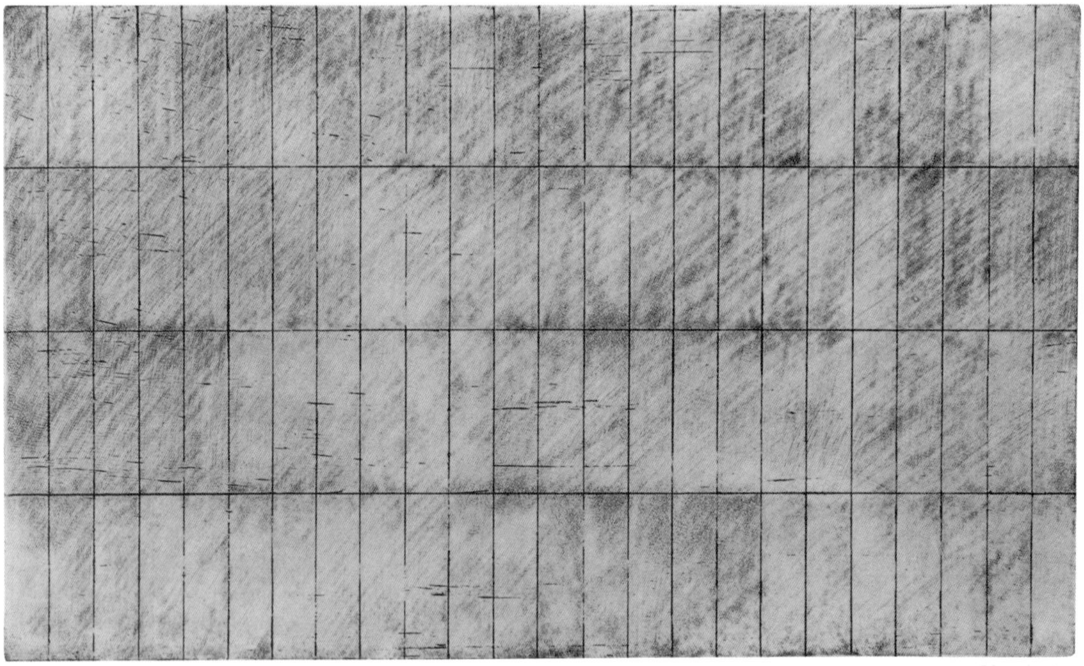

18 **Grid II** 1971
Etching and aquatint on Rives BFK paper
Image size: 37.1 × 60.3 (14⅝ × 23¾)
Paper size: 55.8 × 75.9 (22 × 29⅞)
1 plate
Colour: black
Printed by Nona Hershey, New York and published by Parasol Press, New York
Edition: 31 plus some APs
Inscribed 'B. Marden 71' below image b.r. and numbered below image b.r.

Marden applied aquatint to the plate he used for 'Grid I' (no.17) and scraped it back to create the uneven surface.

Robert Feldman states that he gave half of the remaining prints in the edition to Marden and half to Bykert Gallery when it closed.

19 Untitled 1971, pub. 1982
Etching on Arches paper
Image size: 37.5 × 59.6 (14¾ × 23½)
Paper size: 58.4 × 74.7 (23⅛ × 29⅜)
1 plate
Colour: black
Printed by Nona Hershey, New York and published by Parasol Press, New York
Edition: 50 plus some APs
Inscribed 'B. Marden 71' below image b.r. and numbered below image b.l.
Repr: *Order and Experience*, exh. cat., Arts Council of Great Britain 1975, p.[8] (as 'From Five Plates')

Made alongside 'Grid I' (no.17) and 'Grid II' (no.18), this print consists of three adjoining panels moving from light to dark to intermediate, reading from left to right. In addition to the edition of fifty, seven stage proofs are known to exist, plus a further proof printed by Kathan Brown (see p.25).

Tone is created by hatching rather than by aquatint. Its strength is determined by both the density of marks and the length of time the plate has been exposed to the acid.

The stage proofs indicate that the right-hand panel of the print began as a series of 'combed' horizontal marks together with an incomplete elliptical mark above the centre of the left panel. The combed marks were created by a threaded rod. There were also some vertical sweeps. Marden continued by drawing lines, making the horizontal marks less evident, possibly because they subverted the uniformity of the plane. The central panel also became progressively denser although the changes between states were less marked than in the right panel. He drew a line around the edge of the plate and between each panel for definition. The panels are distinguished from one another not only by tone but by the rhythms and directions of the marks.

'Untitled' relates very closely to a drawing, 'Untitled' 1969 (repr. Sotheby's, New York, *Contemporary Art Part II*, 14 Nov. 1991, lot 147 in col.) which is slightly larger but has the same sequence of tones. In its tripartite division the print also compares with a number of paintings, among them 'Grand Street' 1969 (repr. Schjeldahl, no.68 in col.) and 'Point' 1969 (repr. ibid., no.69 in col.).

For further discussion of this print see pp.25–6, 30 and 94.

*20 **Ten Days** 1971, pub. 1972
Portfolio of 8 etchings with other media on Arches paper
Image size: variable
Paper size: variable
Zinc plates
Colour: variable
Printed by Patricia Branstead and Kathan Brown at Kathan Brown Workshop, Oakland, California and published by Parasol Press, New York
Edition: 30 plus 20 APs lettered A–T
Each inscribed 'B. Marden 71' below image b.r. and numbered below image b.l.; printer's stamp b.r.
Lit: 'Prints and Photographs Published', *PCN*, vol.3, Sept.–Oct. 1972, p.85; Philip Larson, 'Aquatints Again', *PCN*, vol.8, July–Aug. 1977, pp.62–3 (print d repr.); *No Title: The Sol LeWitt Collection*, exh. cat., Weslyan University, Middletown, Connecticut 1981, p.75 (print f repr. transposed as 'detail from *Five Plates*')
Also repr: 'Prints and Multiples', *Arts Magazine*, vol.46, Mar. 1972, p.27 (print d repr.); *Eighteenth National Print Exhibition*, exh. cat., Brooklyn Museum, New York 1972 [n.p.] (print e repr.); *Bulletin of Rhode Island School of Design*, vol.59, April 1973, pp.[62–3] (print d repr.); Diane Kelder, 'The Graphics Revival', *Art in America*, vol.61, July–Aug. 1973, p.112 (print d repr.); Fenella Crichton, 'Brice Marden at Hester Royen', *Art International*, vol.29, 20 Apr. 1975, pp.39–40 (print c repr.); Frances Carey and Antony Griffiths, *American Prints 1879–1979*, exh. cat., British Museum 1980, no.132 (print f repr.)

(a) Etching and aquatint
Image size: 39.6 × 52.5 (15 9/16 × 20 5/8)
Paper size: 56 × 76 (22 × 30)
1 plate
Colour: black

(b) Etching and aquatint
Image size: 55 × 27 (21 5/8 × 10 5/8)
Paper size: 76 × 56.3 (30 × 22 1/8)
1 plate
Colour: 50% black, 25% cobalt and 25% turquoise blue mixed
Reproduced in colour on p.61

(c) Etching and aquatint
Image size: 38 × 30 (14 15/16 × 11 3/4)
Paper size: 76.1 × 56.3 (30 × 22 3/16)
2 plates
Colour: 90% black, 10% silver mixed
Reproduced in colour on p.62

(d) Etching
Image size: 30.4 × 38.3 (12 × 15 1/16)
Paper size: 56.3 × 76 (22 1/8 × 30)
1 plate
Colour: black

(e) Etching and aquatint
Image size: 30.5 × 38.5 (12 × 15 1/8)
Paper size: 56.7 × 76 (22 5/16 × 30)
2 plates
Colour: black and silver grey
Reproduced in colour on p.63

(f) Etching and aquatint
Image size: 59.8 × 37 (23 1/2 × 14 1/2)
Paper size: 76 × 56.3 (30 × 22 1/8)
1 plate
Colour: black

(g) Etching and aquatint
Image size: 36.7 × 60 (14 7/16 × 23 5/8)
Paper size: 56.3 × 76.7 (22 1/8 × 29 3/4)
1 plate
Colour: 70% black, 30% burnt umber mixed

(h) Etching
Image size: 37.2 × 60 (14 5/8 × 23 5/8)
Paper size: 56.4 × 76 (22 3/16 × 30)
1 plate
Colour: 70% black, 30% burnt umber mixed

'Ten Days' is the first portfolio that Marden made. When he arrived in Oakland he had no preconceived plans for the project. He handed the plate for 'Untitled' (no.19) to Brown and asked her to print it up. As Brown recalls: 'he was trying to explain to us that he wanted it to be very rich and deep, he wanted to bite it and he wanted a line that was somewhat rough, not a fine line. And he wanted it heavily bitten but he did not want it muddy.' The first plate of 'Ten Days' repeats this composition but, instead of relying on a deep bite for darker tone, which had muddied the earlier print, Brown suggested he used aquatint. The marks are also finer with none of the sweeping lines of 'Untitled'.

Initially Marden asked Brown to put on a ground to encourage foul biting. A similar approach was taken with all the prints. In print (a) in addition to familiar imperfections in the plate, there is also an impression from Marden's sweater where he must have leaned on the plate while drawing. A similar impression is found in other plates, as well as finger marks. Although these were not put on deliberately, had he so wished, he could either have eliminated them or taken care to avoid making them. From Marden's point of view, however, they activate the surface and ensure that 'blank' panels read as surfaces and not as voids.

The ground was put on with a roller and in some of the prints the roller mark is still visible; for example, the smudging in the top right corner of the last image. Marden drew a line around the edge of many of the plates, for example in the first, second and third prints, while in the two filled grids he omitted to do so. On occasions the line was eroded by repeated biting as in the second print. This also occurred in the third print where a line was drawn to distinguish between the two areas of tone. In order to preserve a line around the edge, even if it had eroded in the acid, Marden specifically asked Brown not to file the edges of the plate too much, so that they would print. A comparison between 'Untitled' (no.19) and the first print of 'Ten Days' reveals the difference between a plate which has been filed and one which has been left virtually unfiled. The edge of the latter is considerably sharper.

In addition to drawing the line around the edge Marden also began by dividing the plates into the intended panels or sections by scratching ruled lines through the ground.

Although most of the prints have the appearance of being black, many of them are mixtures of tones. The third print combines black and silver grey to print an equivalent of graphite, while the second print is a mixture of blue, turquoise and black. The second of the filled grids combines a black aquatint, on a separate plate, with the grid drawn on the plate of the previous print printed silver grey. Marden had initially printed the silver ink on its own but felt it was insufficiently strong. The transparency of the silver ink – it probably had a fair amount of extender – allows the black to show through. Even where an image is printed in one colour, this could either be black or a mixture of black with burnt umber. The choice of tone was important to Marden, for whom black is as much a colour as any other.

All the plates were hand-wiped. In the 'blank' areas Marden wanted a light, general tone and these were the most difficult to ink. In print (f) Brown dragged up the ink (*retroussage*) using a cheesecloth after the plate was wiped. As she explains the method: 'You just very lightly tickle [the plate] and it pulls the ink up to the surface and covers over anything.' This produces a more solid layer of ink.

Brown describes the way in which Marden obtained variations in the blacks. Each time a proof was taken 'you [had] to put the wax [ground] back on again. When you put the wax back on again it's a little difficult to get it down into all the grooves that are already etched in there.' Where the wax covering was imperfect, the lines that were re-exposed to the acid were bitten even more. Although Marden may not have precisely anticipated it he accepted it as part of the etching process. These lines have a rougher appearance than lines drawn late in the making of the print. There is a distinction to be made, however, between the action of the acid and the effect of drawing many lines side by side, which can sometimes have the same appearance of density.

When aquatint was applied care was taken not to obliterate the lines beneath (see the first print for example). As Brown explains, 'he put those lines in on purpose, so we could not go down so deeply. The deeper the plate bites the more the spot expands, so if you bite it enough you can cover your sins. But you could not do that if you didn't want to obscure the line. So the best thing to do is put in a fine [aquatint] and bite it only a little.' Aquatinting was done step by step in a collaborative process between artist and printer until the right density was achieved. Print (f) however is the only print where there is no hatching beneath the aquatint, which is printed solid.

Marden has indicated that there is no specific order to the prints and that the order adopted here is acceptable. The prints just evolved as he was working and he worked on several plates together.

Four stage proofs exist for the second print, showing progressive stages of hatching and aquatinting as well as different colour trials. The second plate in the third print has been deliberately slightly misregistered, creating a line just inside the plate mark.

Paintings may be compared to prints as follows: print (a) relates to 'Blue Painting' 1972 (repr. Shearer, p.42) in the sequence of tones from light to dark, and is a variation on 'Three Deliberate Greys for Jasper Johns' 1970. It also anticipates 'Shunt' 1972. Print (b) is similar to 'Smith' 1971 in format and in its juxtaposition of dark above light. Print (c) has a format similar to 'Rodeo' 1971 but the light–dark relationship is reversed. Prints (d) and (e) look back to 'Untitled' 1964–5 (repr. *Parkett*, p.39 in col.) and forward to the prints entitled 'Painting Study' 1974 (nos.26 and 27). They also relate to many grid drawings of the period. Print (f) is reminiscent in format to 'Fave' 1968–9 (repr. Shearer, p.36) and adumbrates 'Five Plates' 1973 (no.23). Print (g) returns to the horizontal format of 'Gulf' 1969 (no.16) but in its division into two areas of similar tone relates to 'For Helen' 1967 (repr. p.23 and Shearer, p.33). The final print looks back to 'Grid I' (no.17) of the same year, to 'Untitled' 1964–5 (see above) and to Marden's preoccupation with grids in 'Adriatics' 1973 (no.22).

A number of proofs were taken by Marden and overdrawn. These include 'Mosaic Study no.2' 1978 (repr. p.26 and Whitechapel, p.36). Here Marden took a proof on which had been printed an aquatint ground followed by the outline grid of plate (d) prior to the addition of shading. He then added further lines in graphite and blocked in the grid with ink heightened with graphite.

Crown Point Press have retained the plate for print (b).

Although the colophon and printer's stamp indicate that Patricia Branstead was the printer, Kathan Brown recalls that Branstead had only just joined her workshop and that Brown herself did most of the work, with Branstead acting as her assistant. Marden confirms this. Because Brown does not like to list more than one printer, she included her own name by referring to Kathan Brown's workshop rather than Crown Point Press. In addition she was unsure at this early stage whether she wanted the name of Crown Point Press, hitherto associated with printing and publishing artists' books (for example by Wayne Thieband and Richard Diebenkorn), to be linked to jobbing work.

For further discussion of 'Ten Days' see pp.25-30.

20 (a)

20 (b)

20 (c)

20 (d)

20 (e)

20 (f)

20 (g)

20 (h)

*21 **Untitled Press Series** 1972
Series of 6 lithographs, 1 with screenprint
Image size: various
Paper size: various
Colour: various
Printed by Richard Wilke, assisted by Steven Hartman at Untitled Press Inc., Captiva Island, Florida and published by Untitled Press Inc.
Edition: various
Each inscribed 'B. Marden 72' below image b.r and numbered below image b.l.; publisher's stamp b.r. and publisher's copyright stamp on back b.l.
Lit: Jack Cowart and James Elliott, *Prints from Untitled Press, Captiva, Florida*, exh. cat., Wadsworth Atheneum, Hartford, Connecticut 1973, pp.5–6 and 20–5; 'Prints and Photographs Published', *PCN*, vol.4, May–June 1973, p.37 (#2 repr.); Ronny H. Cohen, 'Minimal Prints', *PCN*, vol.21, May–June 1990, p.44 (#5 repr.)

* #1
Lithograph on Italia paper
Image size: 45.5 × 23 (17⅞ × 9)
Paper size: 66.2 × 48.7 (26 1/16 × 19)
1 stone
Colour: light grey and warm grey
Edition: 42 plus 5 APs, 5 colour trials, 1 progressive proof, 1 BAT, 1 Change Inc. and 1 Captiva Con.

* #2
Lithograph and screenprint on Italia paper
Image size: 38.2 × 40.8 (15 × 16)
Paper size: 49 × 66.5 (26⅛ × 19⅛)
3 stones
Colour: first stone flat-printed white-grey, second stone blue-grey and third stone green-grey
Screenprint in black added at Styria Studio, New York
Edition: 48 plus 5 APs, 1 progressive proof, 1 BAT, 1 Change Inc., and 1 Captiva Con.

* #3
Lithograph on Rives paper
Image size: 40.7 × 26.7 (16 × 10½)
Paper size: 65 × 48.7 (26 3/16 × 19 3/16)
3 stones
Colour: first stone grey flat, second stone warm brown-black, third stone grey-blue and same colour as in #6
Edition: 40 plus 3 APs, 1 progressive proof, 1 BAT, 1 Change Inc., and 1 Captiva Con.
Reproduced in colour on p.64

* #4
Lithograph on Italia paper
Image size: 49.1 × 34.6 (19⅓ × 16½)
Paper size: 66.5 × 48.9 (26¼ × 19¼)
3 stones
Colour: first stone cool green, second stone green-black, third stone black
Edition: 46 plus 7 APs, 1 progressive proof, 2 colour trials, 1 BAT, 1 Change Inc.

#5
Lithograph on Italia paper
Image size: 28 × 28.4 (11 × 11 3/16)
Paper size: 66.4 × 48.8 (26 3/16 × 19¼)
1 stone
Colour: brown-black
Edition: 44 plus 6 APs, 1 progressive proof, 1 BAT, 1 Change Inc., 1 Captiva Con. and 1 Untitled Press

#6
Lithograph on Italia paper
Image size: 20.5 × 26.8 (8 1/16 × 10½)
Paper size: 66.9 × 48.8 (26⅛ × 19⅛)
1 stone
Colour: mixture of brown-black, monstral green and flame red
Edition: 46 plus 5 APs, 1 progressive proof, 1 BAT, 1 Change Inc. and 1 Captiva Con.

These lithographs were published by Robert Rauschenberg's Untitled Press. Marden executed them between 13 February and 4 April 1972 at Rauschenberg's base on Captiva Island, Florida. The series comprises four diptychs, one triptych and a singular format in which areas of flat colour are contrasted with gestural strokes of lithographic crayon.

The press was located on a property adjoining Rauschenberg's and according to Cowart and Elliott was 'made accessible by cutting a road through the subtropical vegetation with the help of resident friends.' Rauschenberg's idea was to create an atmosphere which was relaxed and away from commercial pressures.

Marden states that the gestural nature of his prints partly derived from the impact of the surroundings. He explained, 'Every day to get to the workshop I had to walk from the house through this jungle. These have much more of a jungle feeling. This is much more vegetal than other prints.' However, although these images are much freer than anything Marden had previously produced, such a gestural approach was not confined to prints. It is also found, to a lesser degree, in drawings such as 'Untitled' 1969 (repr. Kunstraum, Munich, no.5) and 'Suicide Notes' (repr. Brice Marden, *Suicide Notes*, Lausanne 1974) which Marden began that year. Furthermore, it relates to the underpainting on Marden's canvases where paint was applied with strokes of the brush before being smoothed over with a spatula. However, unlike in the paintings where actual depth is created by the layering of paint, in the lithographs Marden creates an illusion of space by the juxtaposition of colours and marks. Of all Marden's prints these have the greatest sense of depth.

In their gestural quality they have an affinity with the prints of Jasper Johns (see p.31) and Rauschenberg, whose screenprints and lithographs were often enlivened by such marks.

Unlike Marden's only other lithograph, 'Gulf' (no.16), this series has the look of lithography. Marden states that he was seduced by the medium, with its lack of resistance, but ultimately he disliked it.

All the prints are uniquely lithographs with the exception of the second, to which Marden added screenprint on his return to New York. This was done at Styria Studio (see Cowart and Elliott, p.6). He used each stone once only with the exception of the stone used for '#6', which he had previously employed in the top panel of '#3'. According to Marden the variation in the size of the editions resulted either from a lack of paper or from an inability to obtain more good impressions from the stones. The description of the proofs and colours above is that given by Cowart and Elliott.

Other artists who published prints with Untitled Press were Cy Twombly, David Bradshaw, Robert Petersen, Hisachika Taka Hashi and Robert Whitman.

For further discussion of these prints see p.31.

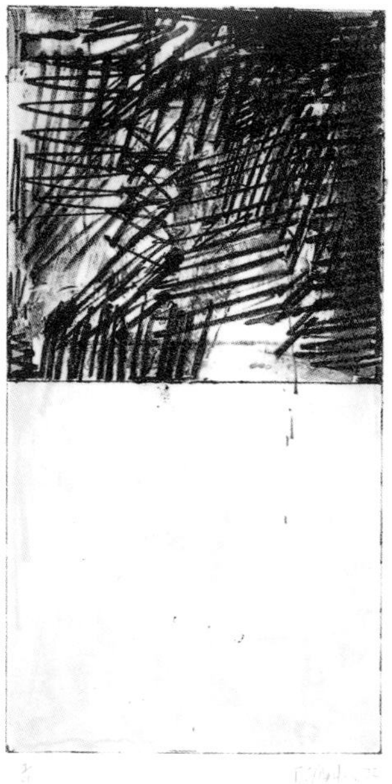

21 #1

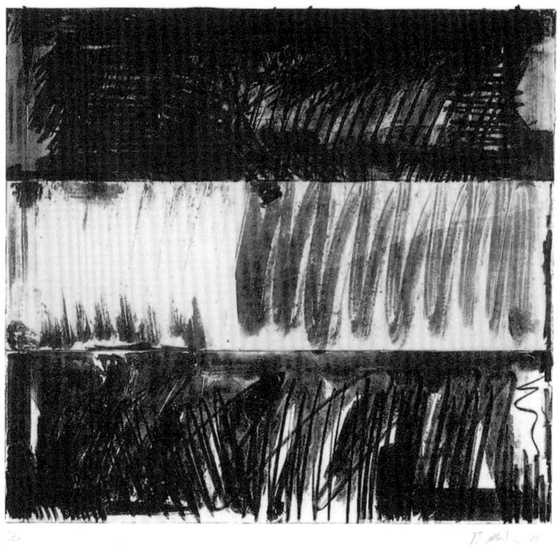

21 #2

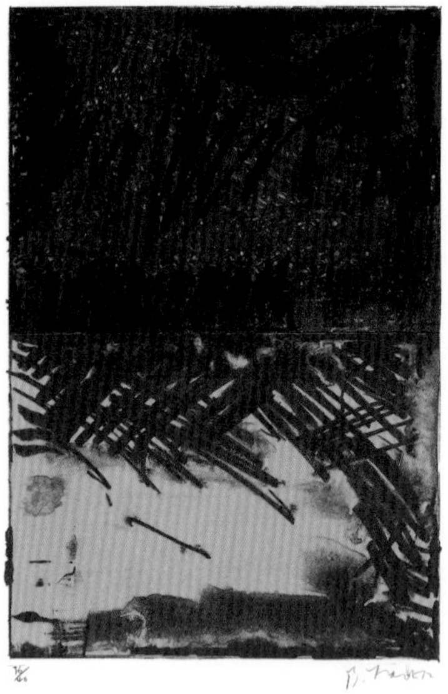

21 #3

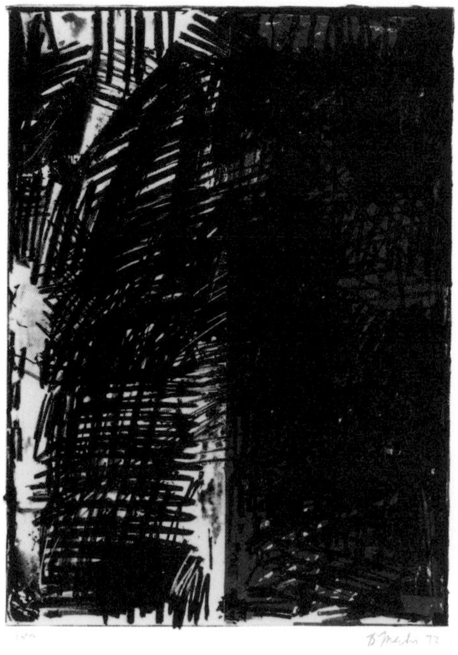

21 #4

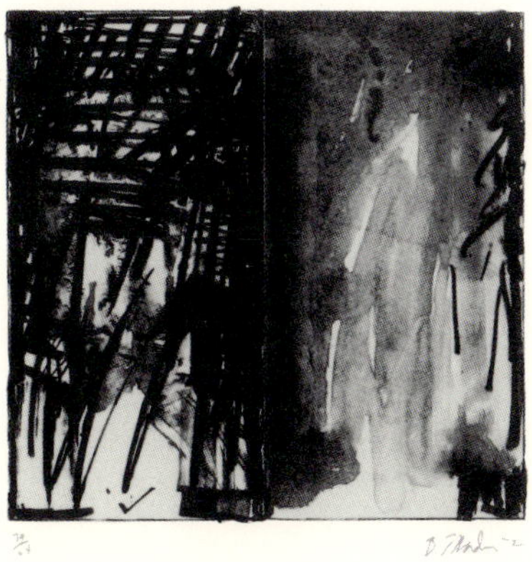

21 #5

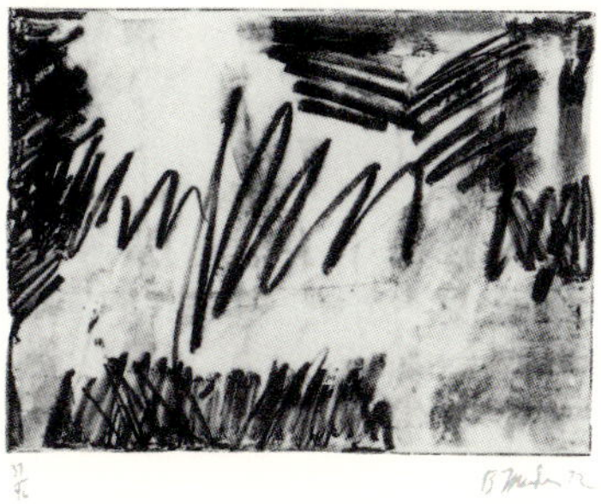

21 #6

***22 Adriatics** 1973
Portfolio of 7 etchings with other media on Rives BFK paper
Image size: various
Paper size: various
1 copper plate each
Colour: black
Printed by Patricia Branstead and Kathan Brown at Crown Point Press, Oakland, California and published by Parasol Press, New York
Edition: 40 with the exception of prints (f) and (g) of which only 35 were printed, plus 12 APs
Each inscribed 'B. Marden' below image b.r. and numbered below image b.l.; printer's stamp b.r.
Lit: 'Prints and Photographs Published', *PCN*, vol.5, May–June 1974, p.41; Fenella Crichton, 'Brice Marden at Hester Royen', *Art International*, vol.29, 20 April 1975, pp.40–1; Stephen Bann, 'Adriatics – à propos of Brice Marden', *Twentieth Century Studies*, nos.15–16, Dec. 1976, p.128; Ronny H. Cohen, 'Minimal Prints', *PCN*, vol.21, May–June 1990, p.44
Repr: *Prints: Bochner, LeWitt, Mangold, Marden et al.*, exh. cat., Art Gallery of Ontario, Toronto 1975, p.32 (print g); *Minimal Druckgraphik*, exh. cat., Kestner Gesellschaft, Hanover 1976, pp.41–3 (prints d, e and f)

*(a) Etching and aquatint
Image size: 60 × 35.7
(23⅝ × 14 1/16)
Paper size: 82.8 × 56.5
(32 9/16 × 22¼)

*(b) Etching and aquatint
Image size: 60.5 × 35.8
(23¾ × 14 1/16)
Paper size: 83 × 56.5
(32⅝ × 22¼)

*(c) Etching and aquatint
Image size: 60 × 35.8
(23⅝ × 14 1/16)
Paper size: 82.5 × 56.4
(32½ × 22 3/16)

(d) Etching
Image size: 59.3 × 35.2
(23 5/16 × 13⅞)
Paper size: 87.2 × 60.5
(34⅜ × 23⅞)

(e) Etching
Image size: 59.3 × 35.2
(23 5/16 × 13⅞)
Paper size: 87.2 × 60.5
(34⅜ × 23⅞)

*(f) Etching
Image size: 60.5 × 71.5
(23¾ × 28 3/16)
Paper size: 82.8 × 92.4
(32 9/16 × 36⅜)

(g) Etching
Image size: 60 × 70.5
(23¾ × 27¾)
Paper size: 82.8 × 91.4
(32⅝ × 36)

Marden worked on 'Adriatics' between 12 and 21 March and 2 and 10 November 1973. The formats of the images are diptychs and grids. The title of the prints refers to the sea between Italy and Greece. Marden journeyed across this sea on the way to his house on the Greek island of Hydra. He states that 'Adriatics' is about the difference in weight and density between sea and sky. It also suggests the monotony and meditative state induced by gazing at the sea. The series relates to 'Sea Painting 1' (repr. p.33) and 'Sea Painting 2' both dated 1973–4 (both repr. Schjeldahl, nos.70 and 72) and also to 'Hydra I', 'Hydra II' and 'Hydra III' all dated 1972. In particular the first three prints in the portfolio repeat the same light-above-dark configuration of 'Sea Painting 1' and the 'Hydra' paintings.

Each of the first three plates is divided in half and has a line drawn around the edge and horizontally through the centre. In (a) Marden covered the bottom half in aquatint and drew five lines diagonally in the top half before continuing them vertically downwards to the bottom edge. The lines in the top section are sometimes reinforced by a parallel line. The top half of the plate has also been flat-bitten, probably because Marden found the light–dark contrast too strong. In plate (b) he has hatched over the aquatint, whereas in (c) the aquatint is preserved unaltered. In both plates the top half is cleaner than in (a), any tone coming from gentle hand wiping and foul biting.

Marden recalls that he did one of the large grids first 'and it really knocked me out'. Print (f) is one of his favourites and he reused the plate for 'Untitled' (no.35). The combination of grids of different sized rectangles in two of the prints is a variation on the dark–light contrast. Indeed, Marden perceives the grids as equivalents to colours. Each grid has a different value. When combined they create an ambiguous sense of space and depth, and appear to hover in front of the plane of the paper. This is encouraged by the fact that, as in all etchings, the ink is printed slightly in relief.

While the grids are plotted accurately, Marden made and retained a number of random marks. As in earlier grids he liked the way in which apparently mechanical production could be subverted by the human touch, whether through foul biting or the impression of his sweater. Similarly a roller mark is retained in print (d). This directly contrasts with the etchings of Sol LeWitt which were printed to perfection by Kathan Brown. The foul biting was carefully controlled by Marden. In the top left corner of the first print Marden has semi-scraped out some marks which he may have found on the plate or which he may have added and subsequently disliked.

As with many of Marden's earlier works, the bottom of three of the four grids is left open while in the fourth he has drawn a line to close it in.

'Adriatics' was printed from copper plates which is a harder material than zinc. As a result the lines of the grids are crisper than in the grids of 'Ten Days'.

Marden made a plate for an eighth print which was portrait format. He divided it in half horizontally and juxtaposed a solid aquatint with a grid overprinted with aquatint. Beneath the solid aquatint were two horizontal lines. The grid was enlivened by diagonal, vertical and cursive, freehand lines. The plate was abandoned and cancelled but has been retained by Crown Point Press.

The last two prints were published in an edition of thirty-five because the plates broke down in the printing. Therefore only thirty-five complete portfolios were released. However both prints were numbered out of forty. The prints are stamped with a printer's stamp consisting of the letter 'K'. This stands for Kathan Brown. Brown states that she worked on the prints with Patricia Branstead but officially credited the printing to her. She is unsure why her stamp as opposed to Branstead's was used.

During the course of making 'Adriatics' Marden also worked on a series of very small plates which he intended to publish as 'Suicide Notes'. He has never published them because he felt that he did not have thirty which were good enough. He may yet do so at a later date. The images of these prints are in the spirit of the drawings of the same name.

The colophon states that there were ten APs but Parasol Press have confirmed that there were in fact twelve.

For further discussion of 'Adriatics' see pp.31–4.

22 (a)

22 (b)

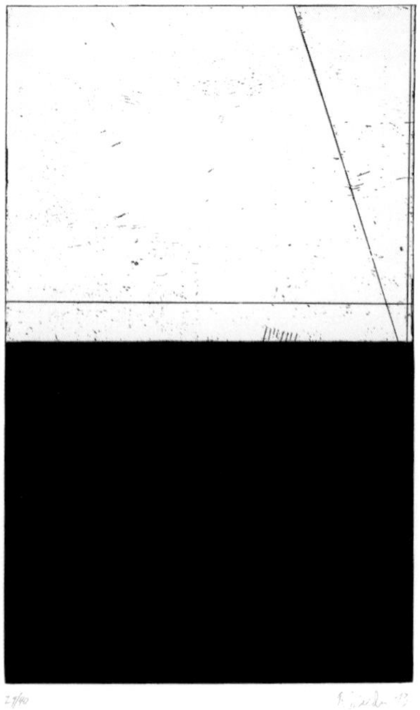

22 (c)

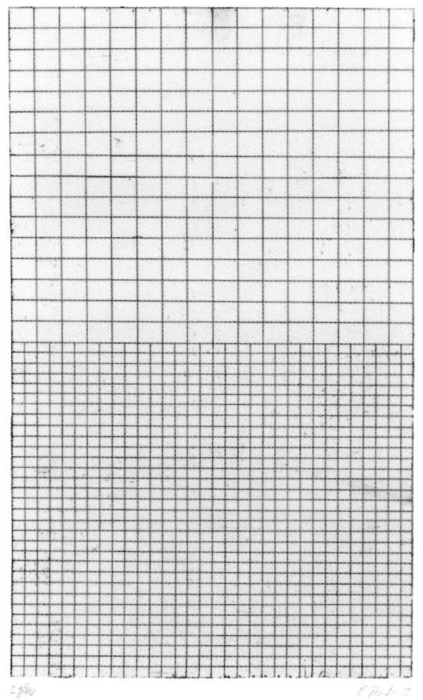

22 (d)

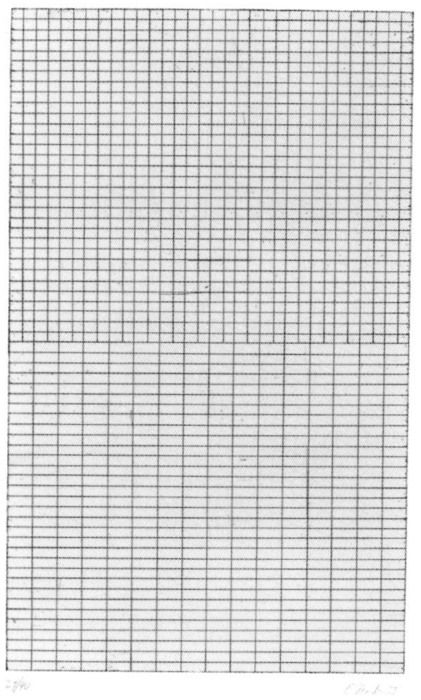

22 (e)

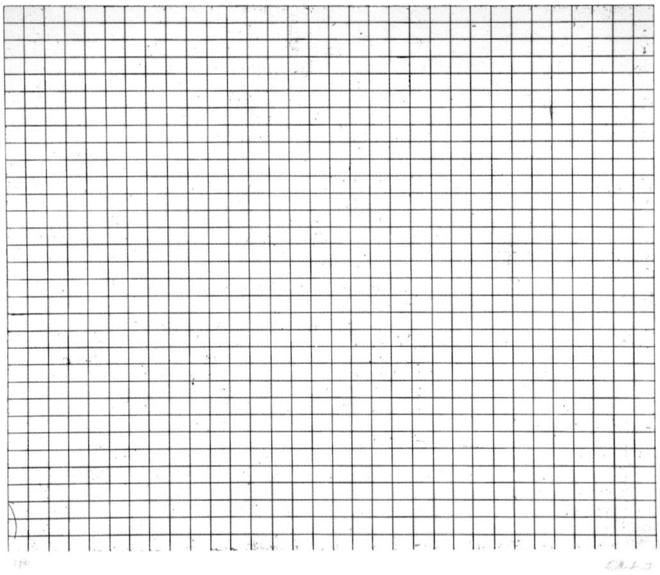

22 (f)

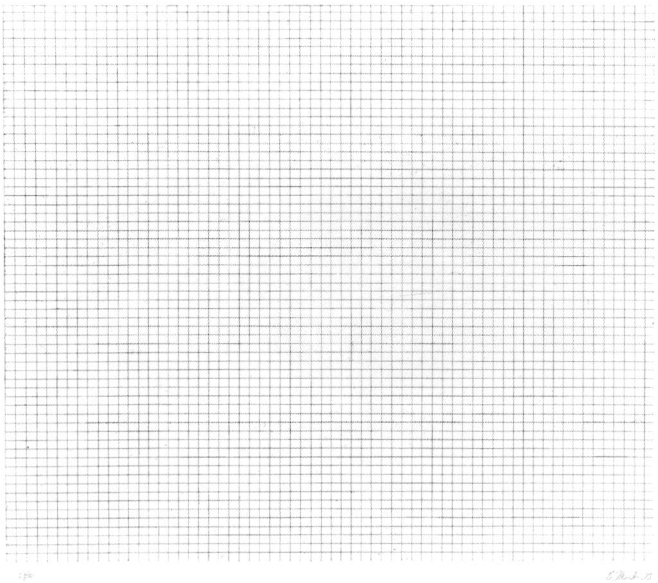

22 (g)

***23 Five Plates** 1973
Portfolio of 5 etchings with other media on Rives BFK paper
Image size: various
Paper size: various
1 zinc plate each
Colour: black
Printed by Patricia Branstead and Kathan Brown at Crown Point Press, Oakland, California and published by Parasol Press, New York
Edition: 50 plus 15 APs lettered A–O
Each inscribed 'B. Marden 73' below image b.r and numbered below image b.l.; printer's stamp b.r.
Lit: 'Prints and Photographs Published', *PCN*, vol.5, Jan.–Feb. 1975, p.151; Fenella Crichton, 'Brice Marden at Hester Royen', *Art International*, vol.29, 20 Apr. 1975, p.41; Richard S. Field, *Recent American Etching*, exh. cat., Davison Art Center, Weslyan University, Middletown, Connecticut 1975, [n.p.], nos.28–30 (print a repr.); Jeremy Lewison, *American Art: Minimal Expression*, exh. broadsheet, Tate Gallery, 1984, p.[4] (print b repr.); Ronny H. Cohen, 'Minimal Prints', *PCN*, vol.21, May–June 1990, p.44.
Also repr: *Prints: Bochner, LeWitt, Mangold, Marden et al.*, exh. cat., Art Gallery of Ontario, Toronto 1975, p.34 (print a); *Minimal Art: Druckgraphik*, exh. cat., Kestner Gesellschaft, Hanover 1976, pp.44–5 (prints d and a)

(a) Etching and aquatint
Image size: 69.6 × 48.8 (27⅜ × 19¼)
Paper size: 101.2 × 73.4 (39⅞ × 28⅞)

(b) Etching and aquatint
Image size: 69.7 × 49.8 (27 7/16 × 19¾)
Paper size: 101.7 × 73.2 (39⅞ × 28 13/16)

(c) Etching and aquatint
Image size: 69.7 × 49.8 (27 7/16 × 19 7/16)
Paper size: 101.3 × 72.9 (39⅞ × 28¾)

(d) Etching and aquatint
Image size: 69.5 × 50.8 (27⅜ × 20)
Paper size: 101.7 × 73.8 (40 × 29⅛)

(e) Etching
Image size: 69.8 × 49.8 (27½ × 19⅝)
Paper size: 101.3 × 73.7 (39⅞ × 29)

Marden worked on 'Five Plates' between 2 and 10 November 1973 during the session in which he completed work on 'Adriatics' (see no.22).

The plates were made by Patricia Branstead and Kathan Brown but the prints were editioned by Branstead alone. The images are a further elaboration on those in 'Ten Days' (no.20) and 'Adriatics' and consist of one monochrome, two two-panel and two three-panel compositions. That Marden was able to complete these at the same time as 'Adriatics' suggests that either he had little to do on that set or that, because little drawing was involved in 'Five Plates', the principal work was proofing and printing them.

Marden drew a line around the edge of most of the plates and, where intended, subdivided them, although in the fourth print the bottom was left open and the edge of the plate has printed. Both Marden and Kathan Brown recall that he worked on the monochrome plate first. The plate marks are uneven because the prints were subjected to the acid so many times and for such a long duration that they eroded.

The successful results Marden was achieving on the aquatint plates of 'Adriatics' must have encouraged him to work on a set of etchings in which the principal medium was straight aquatint. His idea was to make a set of prints which had a real sense of physicality by building up layers of aquatint as he would build up layers of paint in a painting. The aquatint has been applied and the plates have been bitten unevenly, largely owing to a lack of technical sophistication. In order to increase the density of the ink the printers dragged it up to the surface (*retroussage*). As Brown recalls 'We were just trying to get this physical thing. We were just creating this physicality that is different from the other prints.' The density of aquatint and ink on 'Five Plates' is immediately apparent when compared with 'Adriatics'. For a description of the aquatint process involved in making these plates see p.34.

In addition to delineating the edge of the plate, Marden deliberately marked the monochrome plate so that foul biting would show in the printing and give the image substance. It was then delicately hand-wiped.

Marden recalls that he knew in advance that he was going to make a group of five prints, because they were to relate to the five paintings of the 'Grove Group' which were already in progress. The compositions of 'Five Plates' mimic exactly those of the 'Grove Group' except that they have been rotated ninety degrees to become portrait format. Marden stated that by concentrating on similar themes in the prints which were solely black and white, he could be 'involved with the more romantic subject matter of the "Grove Group". Since the formal aspect of the composition was worked out I could concentrate in the "Grove Group" on the light and colour and the idea about place.' In this sense 'Five Plates' can be regarded as not only a variation on the 'Grove Group' but as a study for it. In addition to the 'Grove Group', the fourth print in the series relates to 'Star (for Patti Smith)' 1972 and 1974. In its first state this painting had two outside panels of differing tones, one light and one dark. When it was repainted in 1974 the two outer panels were of equal tone and value and were black, echoing the format of the print.

For further discussion of these prints see pp.34–5.

23 (a)

23 (b)

23 (c)

23 (d)

23 (e)

*24 **Untitled** 1973
Screenprint on Rives BFK paper
Image size: 49.2 × 39.3
($19\frac{3}{8} \times 15\frac{1}{2}$)
Paper size: 105.5 × 75.7
($41\frac{1}{2} \times 29\frac{3}{16}$)
3 screens
Colour: blue (hand-cut screen), blue-grey (tusche), blue (hand-cut screen)
Printed by Hiroshe Kawanishi at Simca Print Artists, New York and published by them and the artist
Edition: 50 plus 6 APs
Inscribed 'B. Marden 73' and numbered to the right of bottom centre; printer's stamp b.r.
Reproduced in colour on p.65

See entry for 'Untitled' 1973 (no.25).

***25 Untitled** 1973
Screenprint on Rives BFK paper
Image size: 45.8 × 39.5
(18 1/16 × 15 9/16)
Paper size: 105.5 × 76
(41 5/8 × 29 7/8)
5 screens
Colour: blue (hand-cut screen), blue-grey (tusche), grey (tusche), ochre (tusche) and blue (hand-cut)
Printed by Hiroshe Kawanishi at Simca Print Artists, New York and published by them and the artist
Edition: 50 plus 6 APs
Inscribed 'B. Marden 73' below image b.r. and numbered below image b.l.; printer's stamp b.r.
Reproduced in colour on p.66

Marden had been impressed by the screenprints that Jasper Johns had made with Hiroshe Kawanishi, 'Flags I' (repr. Riva Castleman, *Jasper Johns: A Print Retrospective*, exh. cat., Museum of Modern Art, New York 1986, p.105 in col.) and 'Flags II' both of 1973, especially by the way in which Kawanishi had managed to create a very painterly surface. Marden wanted to make some colour prints which, in his experience, were easier to do in screenprint than in etching.

Marden re-employed the three screens of the first print in the second print with the edges of the tusche taped up at the top to make a straight edge. He then added two further screens. The screens which were used to print lines were hand-cut. Marden painted directly onto the others using long vertical strokes. This was the way he was now applying paint to canvas to create a more even, tighter surface. Marden thinks that he may have employed a ruler to ensure the rectitude of the stroke.

The composition of no.25 resembles that of a number of paintings of this period where Marden would divide the plane vertically into two halves, and further divide one of them into half again (see for example 'Winter Painting' 1973–5, repr. p.36 and Whitechapel, p.17 in col. and 'Join' repr. ibid., p.59 t.l.). This format anticipates the greater complexity of the 'Annunciation Series' 1978 (repr. Whitechapel, pp.27–31 in col.).

The location of the signature at the bottom of the sheet in no.24 is unusual for Marden, who tends to favour a signature just below the image. He explained that he signed it in this novel position for compositional reasons. Because the image had a ragged edge 'the whole sheet read in a different way.'

26 Painting Study 1 1974
Screenprint with wax on ivory Dutch Etching paper
Image size: 24.3 × 17 (9¾ × 6⅝)
Paper size: 76 × 55.5 (29⅞ × 22¼)
2 screens
Colour: black and white
Printed by Styria Studio, New York and published by them and Multiples Inc., New York
Edition: 50 plus 12 APs
Inscribed 'B. Marden 74' and numbered bottom centre; printer's stamp b.r.; artist's and Multiples Inc. copyright stamp on back

See entry for 'Painting Study 2' (no.27) below.

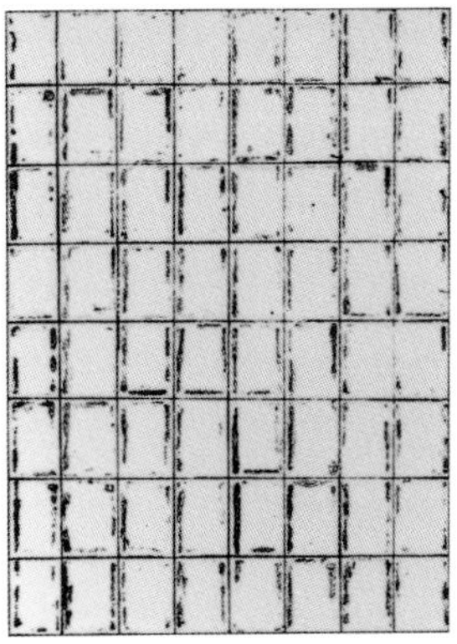

27 **Painting Study 2** 1974
Screenprint with wax and graphite on ivory Dutch Etching paper
Image size: 24 × 17 (9½ × 6⅝)
Paper size: 75.9 × 55.4 (29⅞ × 22⅞)
2 screens
Colour: grey and black
Printed by Styria Studio, New York and published by them and Multiples Inc., New York
Edition: 50 plus 12 APs
Inscribed 'B. Marden 74' and numbered bottom centre; printer's stamp b.r.; artist's and Multiples Inc. copyright stamp on back
Lit: Gene Baro, *30 Years of American Printmaking Including the 20th National Print Exhibition*, exh. cat., Brooklyn Museum, New York 1976, no.186 (repr.)

Marden was approached to make both this print and the previous one by Marian Goodman, the director of Multiples. At that time Multiples specialised in publishing multiples of works of art. These prints are essentially multiples of drawings Marden was making using graphite and wax, the wax being applied as a binder and as a ground into which he mixed the graphite. He found that if he used graphite alone it caught the light but if he applied wax he could obtain a quieter surface with a certain body. A drawing which closely corresponds to these prints in which he has employed wax and graphite is 'Untitled' 1968 (repr. Kunstraum, Munich, no.3).

Each print has one screen printed in black marked up with a grid of lines and another screen with a grid of infill. The wax appears to have been applied through the second screen which was metallic and heated. The same screens were used for both prints. The grid is printed black in the first print and grey in the second. According to Baro there were eleven printings including wax and graphite applications.

*28 **Five Threes** 1976–7
Portfolio of 5 etchings with aquatint on Stonehenge paper
Image size: various
Paper size: various
1 copper plate each
Colour: various
Printed by Doris Simmelink at Crown Point Press, Oakland, California and published by Parasol Press, New York
Edition: 25 plus 10 APs
Each inscribed 'B. Marden 76–77' below image b.r and numbered below image b.l.; printer's stamp b.r.
Lit: Margaret Betz, 'New Editions – Brice Marden', *Art News*, vol.76, Sept. 1977, p.[104]

(a) Image size: 53.3 × 75.8 (21 × 29⅞)
Paper size: 83.8 × 101.5 (33 × 40)
Colour: Thalo blue and Graphic Chemical and Ink Co. 327 black
Reproduced in colour on p.67

(b) Image size: 53.2 × 75.6 (21 × 29¾)
Paper size: 83.8 × 101.5 (33 × 40)
Colour: Thalo blue and Graphic Chemical and Ink Co. 327 black
Reproduced in colour on p.68

(c) Image size: 53.3 × 75.5 (21 × 29¾)
Paper size: 83.8 × 101.6 (33 × 40)
Colour: Thalo blue and Graphic Chemical and Ink Co. 327 black
Reproduced in colour on p.69

(d) Image size: 53.3 × 75.5 (21 × 29¾)
Paper size: 83.8 × 100.8 (33 × 39¾)
Colour: Graphic Chemical and Ink Co. 327 black

(e) Image size: 53.3 × 75.4 (21 × 29⅝)
Paper size: 83.8 × 100.2 (33 × 39⁹⁄₁₆)
Colour: Graphic Chemical and Ink Co. 327 black

Marden worked on 'Five Threes' between 26 July and 8 August 1976, spending one further day on the project in January 1977 when he returned to Oakland to work on '12 Views for Caroline Tatyana' (no.29).

The portfolio consists of five prints, each made from one plate divided into three vertical panels. The prints are all landscape format. The panels in the first three prints are subdivided into a number of bands and rectangles which have the appearance of closed doors. Marden had visited tombs in Egypt and had been impressed by doorways blocked off by massive stones. He was also familiar with Greek temple architecture. 'Five Threes' is one of the first statements of the Greek post and lintel theme which Marden was to take further over the next few years, particularly from 1979 onwards (the post and lintel theme had made a rudimentary appearance in 'Watsonville' 1963, no.11) . Additionally, the configurations of the first three prints relate to Roman fresco paintings, especially of the kind found in the Villa of P. Fannius Synistor at Boscoreale, Pompeii (50–40 B.C., late Second Style) on display in the Metropolitan Museum of Art, with their *trompe l'oeil* panelling, columns and friezes (repr. Maxwell L. Anderson, 'Pompeiian Frescoes in the Metropolitan Museum of Art', *Metropolitan Museum of Art Bulletin*, vol.45, Winter 1987–8, particularly pp.23 and 32–3). Marden's interest in Roman painting derives partly from his desire to 'get more space into a painting'. This is achieved by the push–pull effect of contrasting colours. In the etchings it results from the modulation of tone and directional strokes of the needle.

'Five Threes' shows Marden's considerable sensitivity to the basic techniques of etching. In the first two prints he laid down a light aquatint through which he drew lines. By varying the density of the hatching he introduces subtle nuances of light and shade. The lines themselves are delicately veiled by a further light covering of aquatint. In the blue area of the first print the aquatint has been flat-bitten out, to introduce more light, and then drawn over. In the third print the hatching is left revealed. Marden's sensitivity to the efficacy of line to indicate tonal variations of light brings to mind the work of Rembrandt, who was a master of etching in this manner. In the final two prints Marden has drawn columns of hatched lines as in the previous three and covered them with a dense black aquatint so that they only just register and give off a silvery, subtly inflected light.

Working proofs at Crown Point Press and the San Francisco Museum of Art show that Marden did not settle on the compositions and the tones of the first three prints immediately. In the first print the large rectangle on the right was considerably darker at an earlier stage, while in the second image the three narrow bands on the left were not included. The first two bands from the left were unified and were unhatched, while the third stripe from the left simply did not exist. In addition, the lintel above the middle panel was printed in a lighter tone and the second of the wider rectangles from the right began life as a flat aquatint, which Marden subsequently drew over. The proofs also show that he removed areas of foul biting which did not please him.

The compositions in which the plane is divided and subdivided are a development of strategies employed in paintings such as 'To Corfu' 1976 (repr. Whitechapel, p.49), and 'Morada' 1976 (repr. p.38 and Whitechapel, p.20 in col.). They also anticipate the 'Annunciation Series' although they are considerably more intricate.

Marden explained that these prints were related to the three 'Moon' paintings of 1977. The compositions of the last two prints in particular, but also broadly the third print, relate to these paintings and the 'Moon Study' drawings ('Moon I' and 'Moon III' repr. Whitechapel, pp.23 and 24 in col., 'Moon Study I' and 'Moon Study II' repr. Stedelijk, p.39). The fifth print also resembles 'For Hera' 1977 in its configuration of a dark band separating two light ones. The proportions of all the prints are similar to those of the paintings.

Partly as a result of spending so much time in Greece Marden was greatly interested in Greek myth. Being an American citizen he was acutely aware of the short time span of American history and culture when compared with that of Europe. He states that he considers himself a Western painter and that one of the reasons why he was in Greece 'was to study the beginnings of Western culture and where it went wrong'. Reading books by Robert Graves, he established that the cause was the shift from the matriarchal to the patriarchal society. The 'Moon' paintings are celebrations of the matriarch.

Marden explained his choice of blue as being 'more of a moon colour, cool and watery'. He had used blue in an etching once before, in 'Ten Days', although it was of a different tone. 327 is a blue-black but not as blue as Thalo blue. The working proofs show that Marden tried other tones, notably a brown in place of the blue. The ink used was relatively transparent, to give a veiled effect. Before hand-wiping, at the request of the artist the plate was also probably overwiped with a tarlatan to thin the ink.

For further discussion of these prints see pp.37–41.

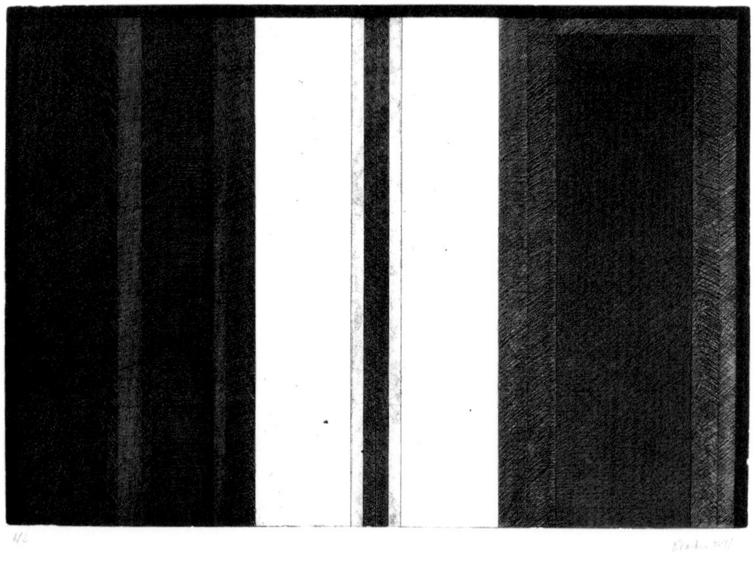

28 (a)

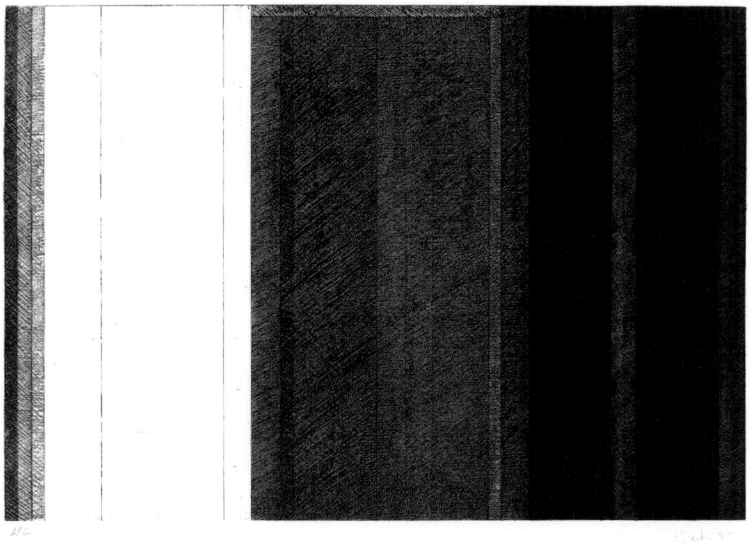

28 (b)

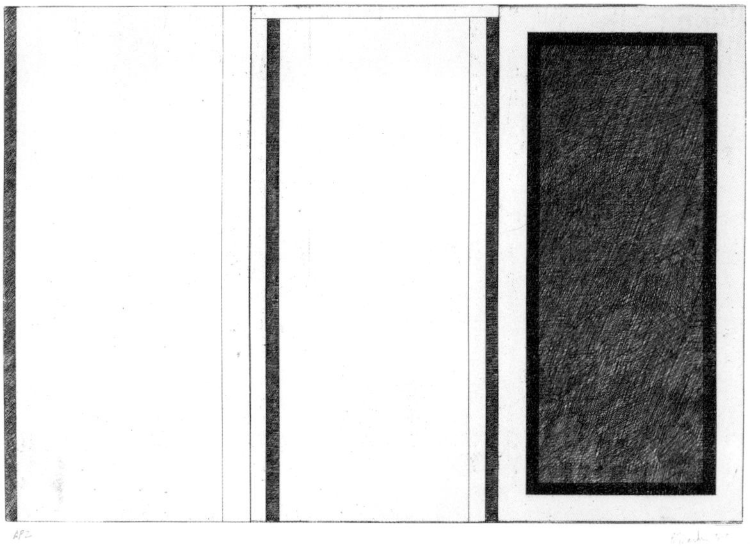

28 (c)

28 (d)

28 (e)

*29 **12 Views for Caroline Tatyana**
1977–9, pub.1989
Portfolio of 12 etchings and aquatint on Arches paper
Image size: (a)–(h) 25 × 17.6 (9⅞ × 7)
(i)–(l) 25 × 35.2 (9⅞ × 14)
Paper size: 67.3 × 51.9 (24⅜ × 18⅜)
(a)–(h) 1 copper plate each
(i)–(l) two copper plates each
Colour: (a)–(h) black
(i)–(l) blue-black
Plates made by Stephen Thomas, assisted by Doris Simmelink and Nancy Anello, at Crown Point Press, Oakland, California 1977–9 and printed by Doris Simmelink in Santa Monica, California 1989; published by Parasol Press, New York
Edition: 50 plus 13 APs and 1 BAT
Each inscribed 'B. Marden' b.r and numbered b.l.
Lit: 'Brice Marden Interviewed by Robin White', *View*, vol.3, no.2, 1980, p.9; Ronny H. Cohen, 'Minimal Prints', *PCN*, vol.21, May–June 1990, p.44
(k) reproduced in colour on p.70

'12 Views for Caroline Tatyana' was started in January 1977 and the plate-making completed in January 1979 (in *View* Marden recalls incorrectly that he began in the summer of 1976). He worked on them initially, therefore, while he finished 'Five Threes' (no.28) and completed them during the course of making 'Tiles' (no.31).

The post and lintel theme was adumbrated in 'Five Threes' but receives a clearer expression in '12 Views for Caroline Tatyana'.

Inspired by ancient Greek architecture, Marden has created a series of prints which play with the contrasts between light and dark and solid and void. These interests arise partly out of his observation of the columnar facades of temples where brilliant light contrasts with mellow shadow, where it can dissolve the material into the immaterial and where, as the viewer moves along and around, the flat plane can change into a labyrinthine depth as layer upon layer of columns are revealed and concealed in turn.

Eight plates were made and printed singly and then paired up and printed again. Thus the doubles are made up as follows: print (i) combines plates (d) and (c); print (j) unites plates (g) and (b); print (k) joins together plates (h) and (a); print (i) marries plate (e) with (f). Broadly speaking, when combined in a double, the two plates are mirror images of each other but with subtle differences. For example in print (i) the two outer white bands of equal tone correspond to two darker bands of varying tone.

The tonal variation is generally achieved through hatching and aquatint which has been flat-bitten out. Marden removed the aquatint because, he said, 'it became clotted.' The cross-hatching was so deep, however, that when scraping and flat-biting it out the lines were unaffected. He then enhanced them by further drawing. In plate (e) the outer columns were aquatint only until flat-bitten. Upon removal of the aquatint Marden shaded them with lines. Earlier proofs show that plate (e) also had two horizontal lines which spanned the two white columns dividing them into thirds. These were removed. Plate (h) in its earlier state consisted of hardground lines to delineate the division of the plane and solid aquatint for shading. The aquatint was then flat-bitten and knocked back (traces of it are still noticeable). The same is true of plate (d). Marden also scraped the plates.

Marden's approach to aquatint is substantially different here from 'Five Plates' (no.23). As Brown states, 'This is much grainier than "Five Plates".' Looking at the earlier proofs she remarked 'This is a fine, even aquatint. This is a beautiful, technically perfect aquatint.' Brown maintains that the proofs show a perfect aquatint from which a beautiful rich colour could have been obtained. 'Maybe that's the reason why he wanted to flat-bite it, because that would have made it imperfect and mess it up.'

Originally Marden experimented with colour printing the plates, trying versions of green and red with black. The BATs were printed in these colours in 1979 at Crown Point Press on a paper handmade by Don Farnsworth which had a green cast. The paper size (in range 61.5–62.5 × 46–47.1 cm,

24¼–24⅝ × 18⅛–18½in) was smaller than the brilliant white paper chosen for the edition ten years later . The BATs consisted of the single plates only, although Marden had previously obtained trial proofs of the doubles. At one stage he was going to print the doubles with one plate in red and the other in green to try to obtain a push-pull effect.

Editioning began at Crown Point Press in 1979 on the handmade paper but was called to a halt halfway through because Feldman felt he would not be able to find a market for the prints. When Feldman offered to publish them in 1989 he and Marden decided to eliminate the hints of colour 'because they didn't read', and to change the paper to a stock, brilliant white. The black chosen had a brownish tint. The only other concession to a contrast of colour was in Marden's choice to print the doubles in blue-black. Doris Simmelink, who had worked on the plates when she was employed at Crown Point Press, was asked to edition the prints because Crown Point Press was by then running its own print publishing programme and no longer took on jobbing work. Simmelink worked from the BATs which Brown lent to her.

In a sketchbook with a reproduction of Picasso's 'Demoiselles d'Avignon' attached to the front is a page headed '8 Views for Caroline Tatyana'. It contains sketches replicating prints (c), (d), (e), (f) and (g). Three other sketches were modified. The density of the hatching in the final prints is only hinted at in the sketches. This sketchbook also contains drawings for 'Thira' 1979–80 (repr. p.43 and Whitechapel, p.32), the 'Annunciation Series' (repr. Whitechapel, pp.27–31) and the three 'Moon' paintings (nos. I and III repr. ibid., pp.23 and 24). Other related works are the drawings entitled 'Thira I–IV' 1975–6 (repr. ibid., p.52), which are an earlier statement of the theme of inside-outside and mirror images, and the 'Hydra Series' of drawings (repr. Stedelijk, pp.42–3 in col.). All these works are on the 'Grecian' theme of which Marden considers '12 Views for Caroline Tatyana' to be the 'summation' and 'a very complete, definitive statement.'

The series was dedicated to Caroline Tatyana Cunliffe, Marden's god-daughter. The word 'views' is meant to imply views through doorways and colonnades. The portfolio was originally published as 'For Caroline' but Marden considers the title as printed here to be correct.

Although there is an internal logic to the series Marden does not demand that the works be hung in any particular order.

In addition to the proofs listed above there are two sets of trial proofs of single plates, two sets of trial proofs of doubles in colour, and one set of four single plates all printed on the handmade paper and held by Crown Point Press.

For further discussion of this portfolio see pp.41–4.

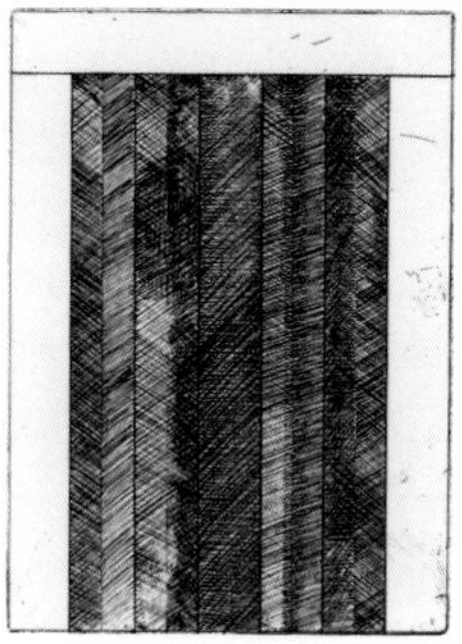

29 (a)

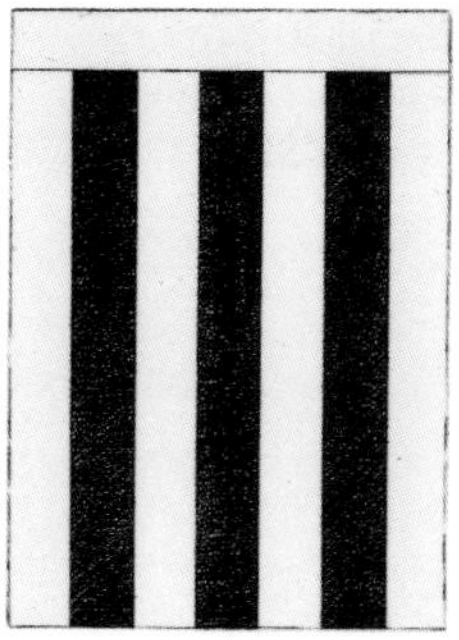

29 (b)

29 (d)

29 (c)

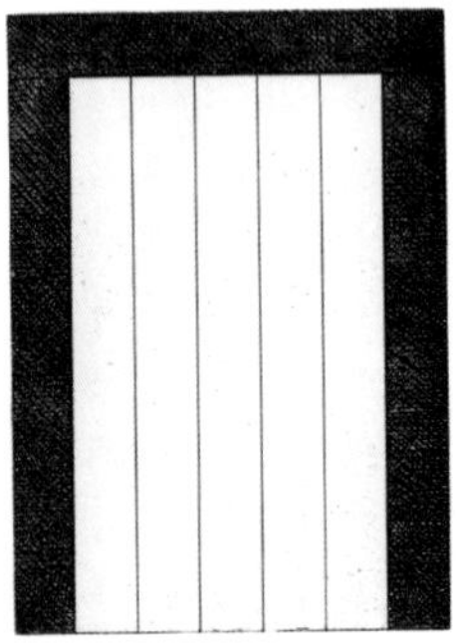

29 (d)

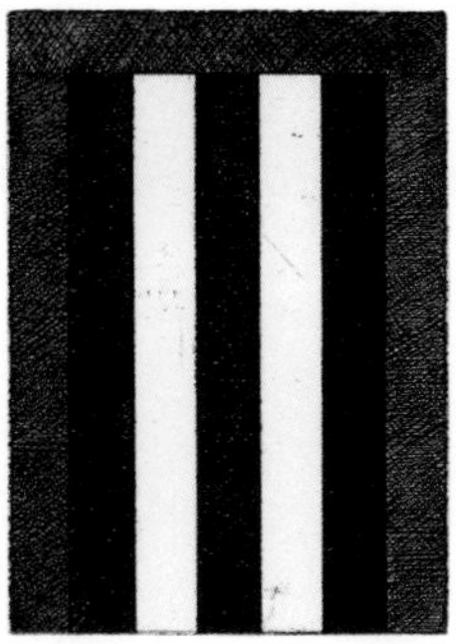

29 (e)

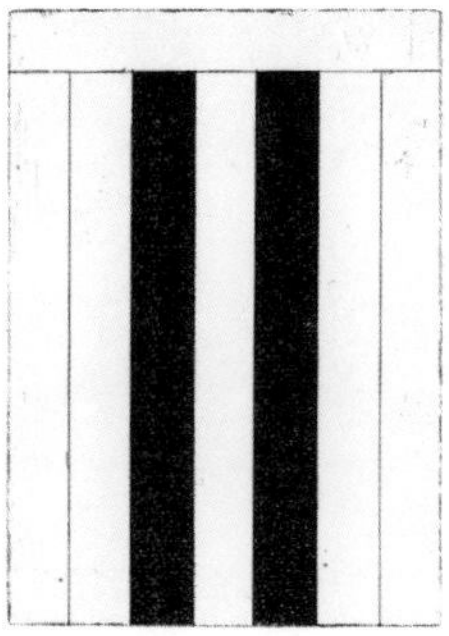

29 (f)

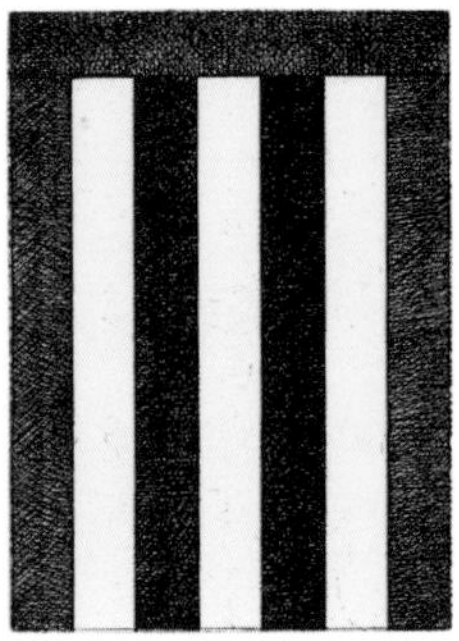

29 (g)

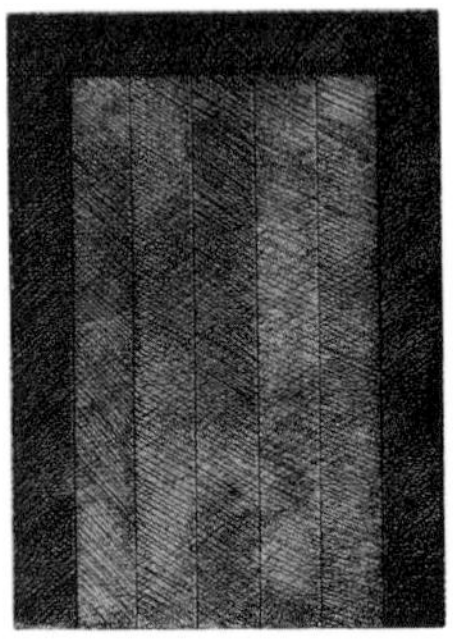

29 (h)

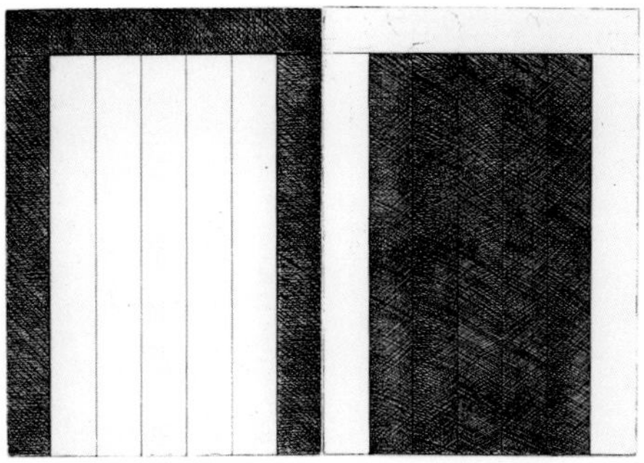

29 (i)

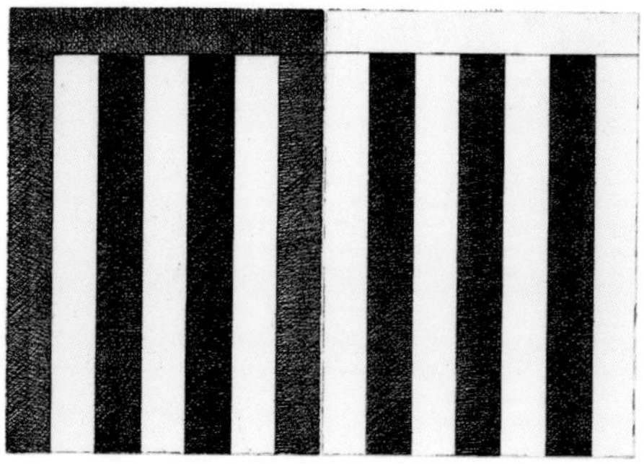

29 (j)

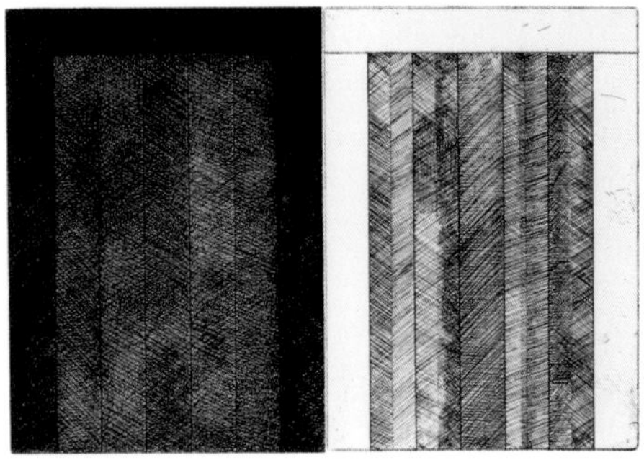

29 (k)

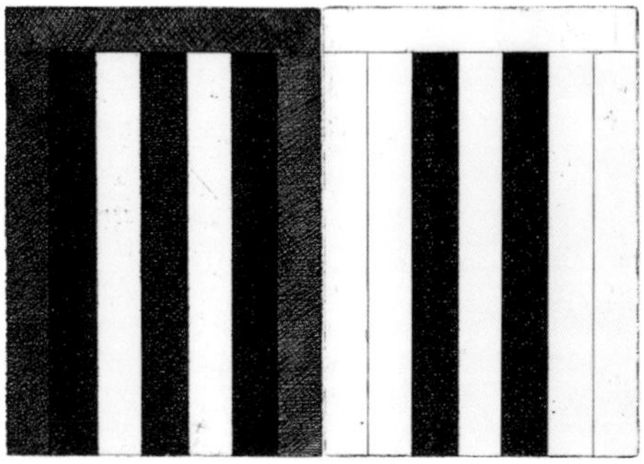

29 (l)

30 Tile I 1979
Etching and sugarlift aquatint on Somerset satin paper
Image size: 20.3 × 20 (8 × 7$\frac{15}{16}$)
Paper size: 75.5 × 57.8 (29$\frac{3}{4}$ × 22$\frac{3}{4}$)
1 copper plate
Colour: black
Printed by Stephen Thomas, assisted by Nancy Anello, at Crown Point Press, Oakland, California and published by Crown Point Press
Edition: 30 plus 10 APs and 1 BAT
Inscribed 'B. Marden 79' below image b.r and numbered below image b.l.
Repr: 'Brice Marden Interviewed by Robin White', *View*, vol.3, no.2, June 1980, p.3

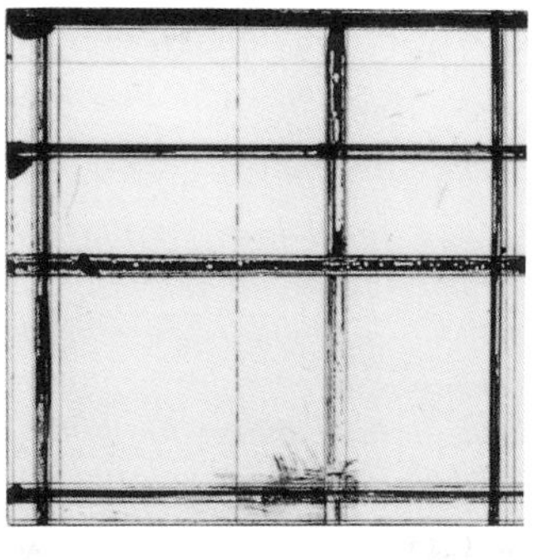

Prior to going out to Oakland to work on '12 Views for Caroline Tatyana' (no.29) Marden had received a letter from Kathan Brown stating that she was about to start a print publishing business which would run alongside the printing business. Having sought Robert Feldman's permission to approach the artists whose works she had printed for him, she asked each of them, including Robert Mangold, Sol LeWitt, Richard Diebenkorn and Brice Marden, whether they would make a print each, which could be given to subscribers to the publishing programme. She felt unable to ask these artists to do larger projects with her because she did not want to 'poach' them from Parasol Press. All the artists agreed.

The 'bonus print' which Marden made was 'Tile I'. He worked on all the 'Tiles' prints at once. 'Tile I' was not necessarily the first of them but was the first to be titled. In addition to the proofs listed above, Crown Point Press hold a trial proof.

For further discussion of 'Tiles' and related works see the entry for no.31 below.

***31 Tiles** 1979
Portfolio of 4 etchings with other media on Somerset satin paper
Image size: 20 × 20 (7⅞ × 7⅞)
Paper size: 75.5 × 56.2 (29¾ × 22¾)
1 copper plate each
Colour: black
Printed by Stephen Thomas, assisted by Nancy Anello, at Crown Point Press, Oakland, California and published by Parasol Press, New York
Edition: 50 plus 12 APs and 1 BAT
Each inscribed 'B. Marden 79' below image b.r. and numbered below image b.l.; printer's stamp b.r.
Lit: 'Prints and Photographs Published', *PCN*, vol.10, Nov.–Dec. 1979, p.162; Robin White, 'Brice Marden Interviewed by Robin White', *View*, vol.3, no.2, June 1980; *The Tate Gallery 1982–84: Illustrated Catalogue of Acquisitions*, 1986, p.413 ((c) repr.)

(a) Etching with sugarlift aquatint
Paper size: 75.5 × 57 (29¾ × 22$\frac{5}{16}$)

(b) Etching with softground etching and sugarlift aquatint
Paper size: 75.5 × 56.7 (29¾ × 22$\frac{5}{16}$)

(c) Etching with sugarlift aquatint
Paper size: 75.5 × 57 (29¾ × 22½)

(d) Etching with aquatint and sugarlift aquatint
Paper size: 75.5 × 57.5 (29¾ × 22⅝)

Marden worked on these plates alongside 'Tile I' (no.30) and '12 Views for Caroline Tatyana' (no.29) in January 1979. Each print is a square on which he has superimposed a grid, the grid being different in each case.

Using sticks dipped in sugar solution he began by drawing directly onto the plate. The results were then proofed and fine lines were added in hard-ground. Constant reimmersion in the acid resulted in the deepening of the foul biting, particularly in the first print.

Spotting in the sugarlift often occurred. Kathan Brown did not help in the plate-making but on examining the prints she outlined a possible explanation of this phenomenon:

> Normally the sugar solution you use to draw doesn't really like to sit very cleanly on the plate. It's something about the resistance of the metal. So we usually put a little bit of gum arabic in it in order to make it smooth and adhere better. But if you put too much in you have trouble lifting the sugar so you have to be careful. We usually underdo it slightly to see, and then if it does draw up like this we add a little more. So I think that's what happened. We would have washed it off at that point. He would have done the line and said, 'Oh, look, it's pulling back' and we would have said, 'Oh, wait a minute. We'll go and put a little more gum in it.' And then we would have taken the plate and washed it and given it back to him clean to start again. But he'd say, 'No, I like that. I think we'd better keep it'.

If this is actually what happened Marden would simply have had to rule in the affected lines again, which would not have been difficult. Indeed it is so widespread that clearly it became an intentional strategy. With other lines he would have used a stronger solution of gum arabic.

Progressive proofs show that Marden had not decided on the number of lines or their disposition from the outset but that the image evolved in stages. On the second print, for example, he originally drew a sugarlift line vertically along the left edge. He subsequently scraped it out, significantly altering the balance of the image. Similarly, the black edge forming the top border in the final state was not included in earlier proofs.

Although these prints are printed with black ink, employing a considerable amount of extender to make it transparent, Marden also experimented with colour. He tried grey-green, blue-black and blue.

The 'Tile' images were of a kind which Marden had been making on paper since 1973. He considers them as experimental prints because this was the first time he had drawn on plates using sticks. He was engaged principally with '12 Views for Caroline Tatyana' but, while awaiting proofs, he worked on 'Tiles' and 'Tile I'. Since there are a number of sheets on which four tiles were printed together in a square, and some of these sheets include 'Tile I', it seems likely that Marden designated which was to be the 'bonus print' only on completion of the project. Neither he nor Brown can remember.

Marden took some of the sheets on which four 'tiles' had been printed and drew over them. There remain three such sheets in three different states, without overdrawing, at Crown Point Press. One which has been overdrawn is 'Study I' 1980 (repr. Whitechapel, p.39), where Marden has intensified the image by drawing further lines and reinforcing those already there. By printing the plates in a square of four Marden could also begin to appreciate how a series of ceramic tiles might look. For further information on the 'Tile' project see pp.44–5.

In addition to the proofs listed above, one unsigned set was sent by Crown Point Press to the artist after publication and there are eleven working proofs at Crown Point Press.

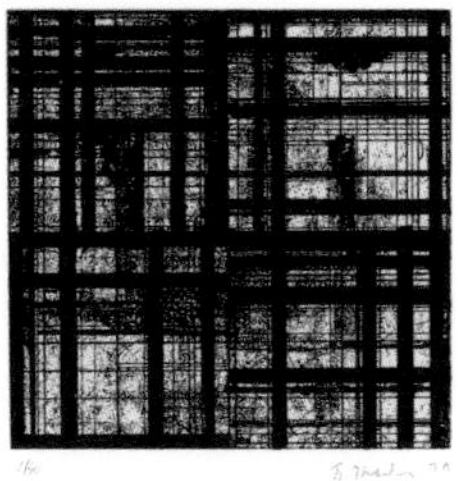

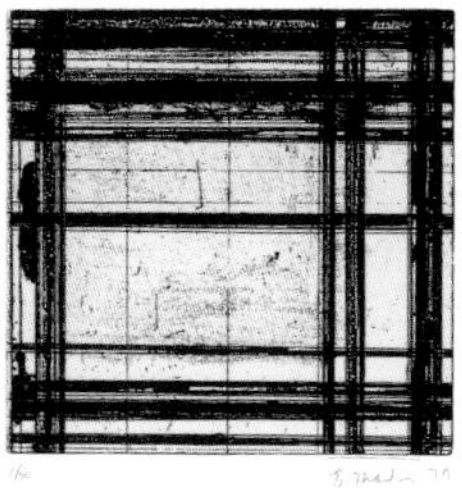

31 (a)

31 (b)

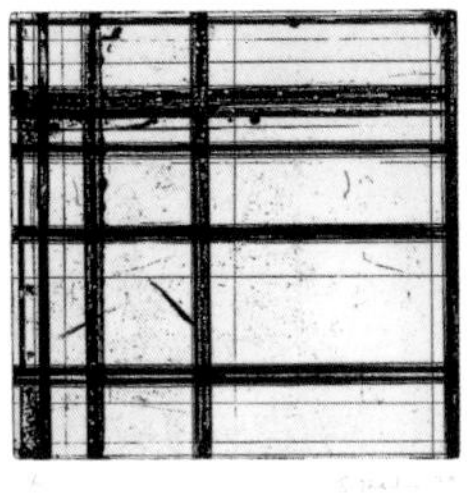

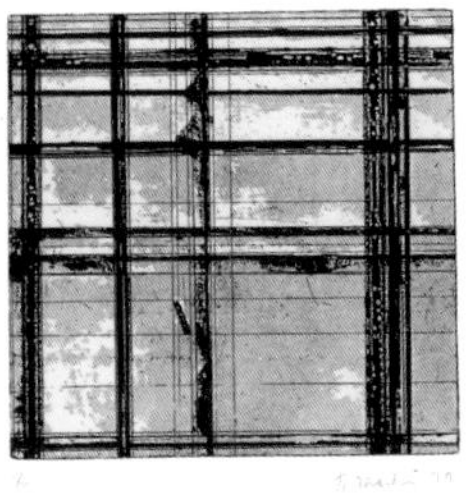

31 (c)

31 (d)

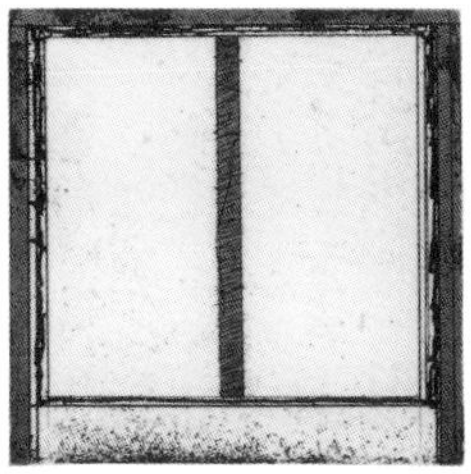

32/I

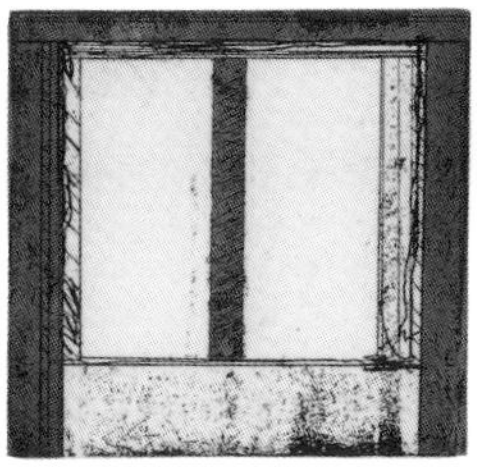

32/II

32 **Focus I–V** 1979
Portfolio of 5 etchings with aquatint on handmade Twinrocker paper
Image size: 10.2 × 10.2 (4 × 4)
Paper size: 39.4 × 27.9 (15½ × 11)
2 copper plates each
Colour: terre verte and blue black
Plates made by Patricia Branstead and printed by Peter Drake at Aero Press, New York; published by Brooke Alexander, New York
Edition: 75 plus 15 APs and 1 BAT
Each inscribed 'B. Marden 79' and numbered bottom centre; printer's stamp b.r
Lit: 'Prints and Photographs Published', *PCN*, vol.11, Mar. – Apr. 1980, p.17 (as 'Untitled')
Repr: Whitechapel, pp.42–3; Deborah C. Phillips, 'Artist and Printer. "A Coincidence of Sympathies"', *Art News*, vol.80, March 1981, p.102

Of all the prints that Marden has made these are the smallest images. They were made at the same time as 'Untitled' 1979 (no.33) and 'The Skowhegan Print' (no.34), after Marden had made '12 Views for Caroline Tatyana' (no.29) and 'Tiles' (no.31).

The theme of the series is related to the themes of '12 Views for Caroline Tatyana' and 'Five Threes' (no.28) in terms of the division of the plane into window and door-like panels. It is also closely connected to Marden's interest in Roman painting. These prints are distinguished from the earlier portfolios by the pronounced sense of depth arising from the juxtaposition of colours and from the division of the plane down the centre. Marden was beginning to feel a sense of crisis in Minimal art, that he could not continue simply to make paintings which asserted the flatness of the plane. He wanted his art to become more complicated and so he began to introduce space in his graphics. He thinks of these images almost as 'theatrical settings'. They are also frames within frames. Marden recalls that he probably chose to print them in green because he had been considering using green in '12 Views for Caroline Tatyana' and 'Tiles'.

In addition to the proofs listed above there are sixteen sets of stage proofs in which Marden tried out other colours as well as different intensities of the green. These have not been seen by the author.

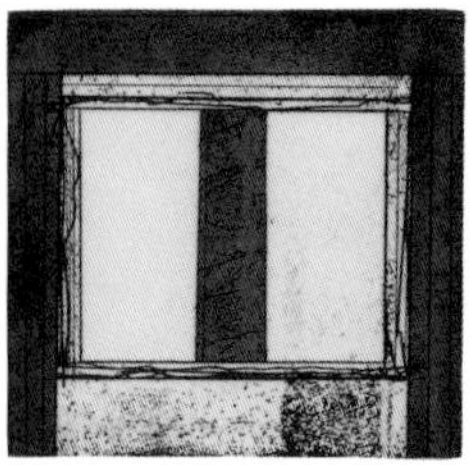

32/III

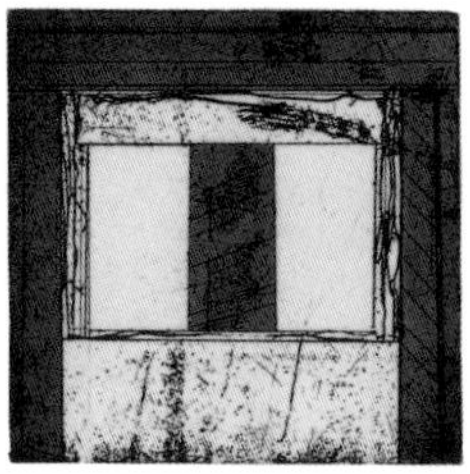

32/IV

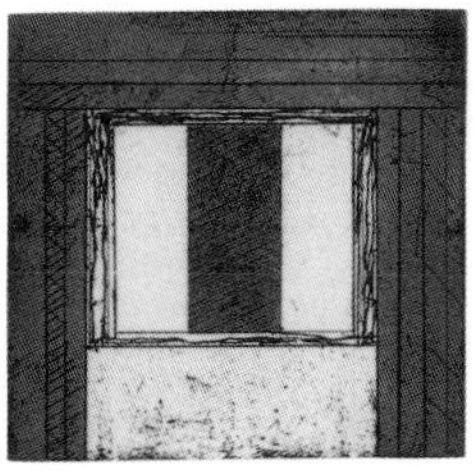

32/V

33 Untitled 1979
Etching and sugarlift aquatint on Rives BFK paper
Image size: 12.6 × 15.2 (5 × 6)
Paper size: 29.8 × 19.8 (11¾ × 7¾)
1 copper plate
Colour: black
Plates made by Patricia Branstead and printed by Peter Drake at Aero Press, New York; published in a special edition of *Brice Marden: Zeichnungen Drawings 1964 – 1978*, exh. cat., Kunstraum, Munich 1979
Edition: 45 of which 35 were distributed with the special edition of the catalogue and 10 were retained by the artist plus 10 APs and 1 BAT
Inscribed 'B. Marden 79' below image b.r. and numbered below image b.l.; printer's stamp b.r.
Repr: Kunstraum, Munich, no.52

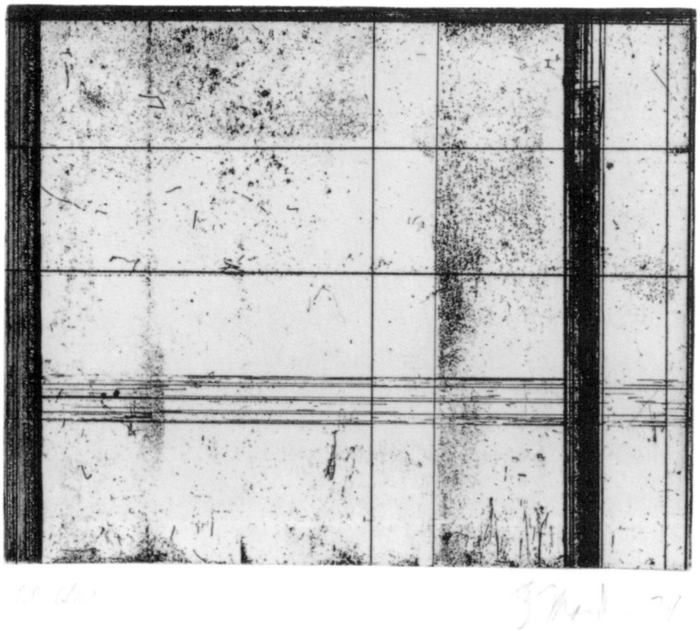

This print was made for a special edition of the catalogue to Marden's exhibition at Kunstraum München, Munich, in 1979 (also seen in Nuremburg). It was made after 'Tiles' and is of a different proportion, being smaller overall and wider than it is tall. It was made alongside 'The Skowhegan Print' (no.34).

For further discussion of this kind of image see entry for 'Tiles' (no.31) above.

34 **The Skowhegan Print** 1979
Etching and sugarlift aquatint on Rives BFK paper
Image size: 15 × 12.6 (5⅞ × 5)
Paper size: 46 × 35.4 (18 × 13⅞)
1 copper plate
Colour: black
Plates made by Patricia Branstead and printed by Peter Drake at Aero Press, New York; published by the Junior Committee of the Skowhegan School of Painting and Sculpture
Edition: 40 plus 10 APs and 1 BAT
Inscribed 'B. Marden 79' below image b.r. and numbered below image b.l.; printer's stamp b.r.

This print was made for the benefit of the Skowhegan Scholarship Fund. Marden was on the Board of Governors of the Skowhegan School of Painting and Sculpture. It was made alongside 'Untitled' (no.33).

The image is smaller overall than 'Tiles' (no.31) and the vertical dimension is greater than the horizontal.

For further remarks on this kind of image see entry for 'Tiles' (no.31) above.

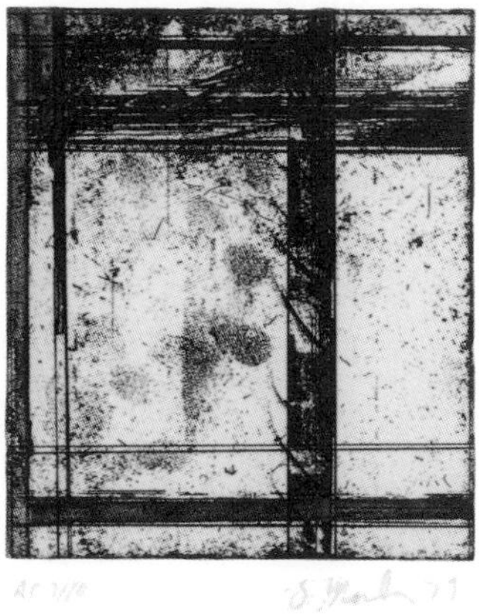

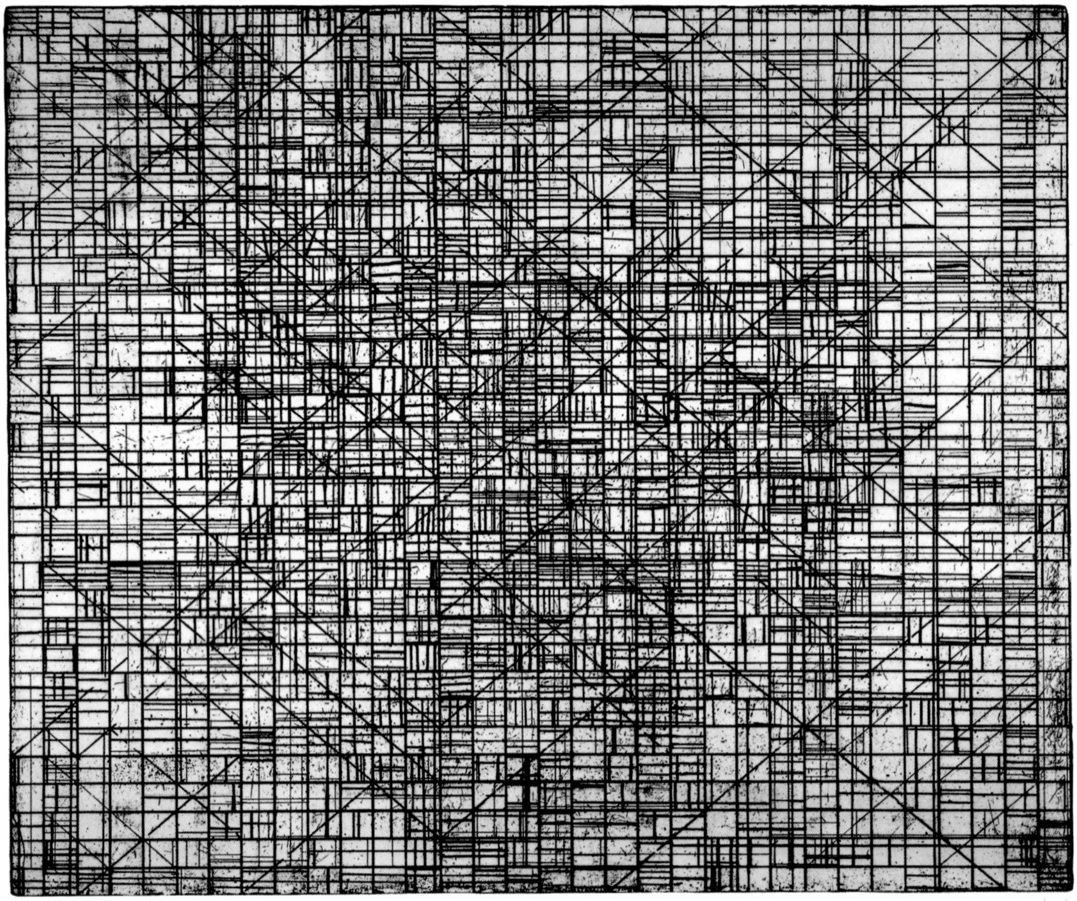

*35 **Untitled** 1973–9, pub. 1988
Etching on paper
Image size: 60.5 × 72
(23 13/16 × 28 3/8)
Paper size: 81.2 × 91.5
(32 × 36 1/8)
1 copper plate
Colour: black
Printed by Stephen Thomas at Crown Point Press, Oakland, California and published by Parasol Press, New York
Edition: 5 plus 5 APs
Inscribed 'B. Marden 79' below image b.r and numbered below image b.l.; printer's stamp b.r.

The basis of this print is the plate Marden used for print (f) of 'Adriatics' (no.22). The print was never officially published. Marden intended to edition it in three states, of which this is one, but the additional two states have never been executed.

Taking the large grid as a basis, Marden inserted horizontal, vertical and diagonal lines into the individual rectangles in freehand and added longer diagonal lines which cross from rectangle to rectangle. These latter were ruled. Marden relates the grids within the grid – the lines within the rectangles – to 'Tiles': 'I figured each one of these little things is a tile.'

Marden worked on this plate each time he visited Crown Point Press between the completion of 'Adriatics' and that of 'Tiles'. He has not worked on it since then because he has not returned to Crown Point Press. It was decided to issue the print in its current state in a small edition in October 1988.

Crown Point Press hold at least two proofs in earlier states as well as the plate.

For further discussion of this print see p.45.

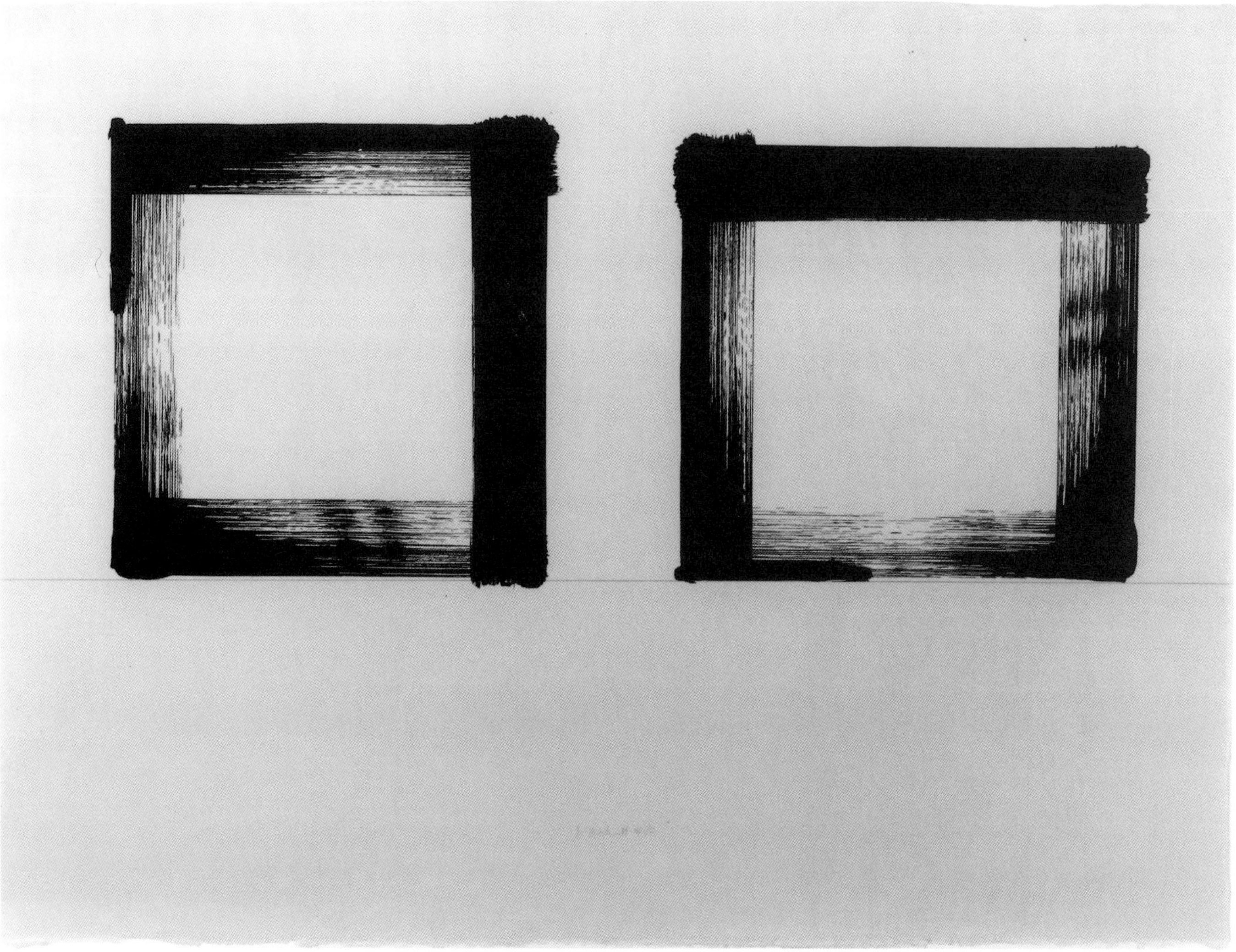

36 **Untitled** 1983
Screenprint on Japanese handmade Kurotani Kozo paper
Image size: 96.5 × 127 (38 × 50)
Paper size: 99.3 × 127.6 (39 × 50½)
2 screens
Colour: three kinds of black
Printed by Hiroshe Kawanishi at Simca Print Artists, New York and published by them and the artist
Edition: 15 plus 4 APs, 2 PPs, 1 BAT and 2 *hors commerce* proofs
Inscribed 'B. Marden 83' and numbered above bottom centre

Marden made this print on 11 May 1983, four years after his previous prints. It had been nine years since he had last executed screenprints and ten years since he had worked with Kawanishi (see nos.24 and 25). Marden recalls that Pace Gallery, his agents at the time, asked him to make some prints which they would publish. Marden agreed to do it and suggested working with Kawanishi. He set to work but, in the event, Kawanishi could not agree terms with Pace and Marden suggested that he and Kawanishi should co-publish them. This applies to nos.36, 37 and 38.

The print consists of two black squares alongside each other but separated by a margin. They are joined by a fine line at the bottom which extends horizontally across the sheet from edge to edge.

Marden drew on the first screen with tusche and printed it twice. On the second occasion it was turned through ninety degrees anti-clockwise. Thus both squares are the same image but with a different orientation. The image was brushed on swiftly. The second screen was hand-cut to print the fine line.

In comparison with his paintings of the period, this and nos.36 and 37 are relatively simple designs. Marden suggested that he was 'in an oriental, Zenish mood' when he made them.

37 **I, II, III** 1983
Series of 3 screenprints on Rives papier de lin
Image size: 76.7 × 58.6 (30 × 22)
Paper size: 97.8 × 60.8 (30½ × 23⅞)
2 screens each
Colour: orange and blue
Printed by Hiroshe Kawanishi at Simca Print Artists, New York and published by them and the artist
Edition: 35 plus 6 APs, 2 PPs, 1 BAT and 1 *hors commerce* proof
Each inscribed 'B. Marden 83' and titled and numbered bottom centre

Marden made these screenprints on 13 May 1983. These are the only screenprints which Marden executed that year which included a colour other than black. Each of the three images is a variation on a rectangle just larger in one dimension than a square. The way in which the rectangle is divided down the middle recalls 'Focus I–V' (no.32), as well as drawings Marden made in Greece in 1979 entitled 'The Hydra Series' (repr. Stedelijk, pp.42–3 in col.).

Both screens were drawn with tusche. The first screen was printed in orange and the second screen in blue. Marden stated that he 'liked the idea of having a colour underneath and then altering it by printing another colour over it, so making two colours look like three.'

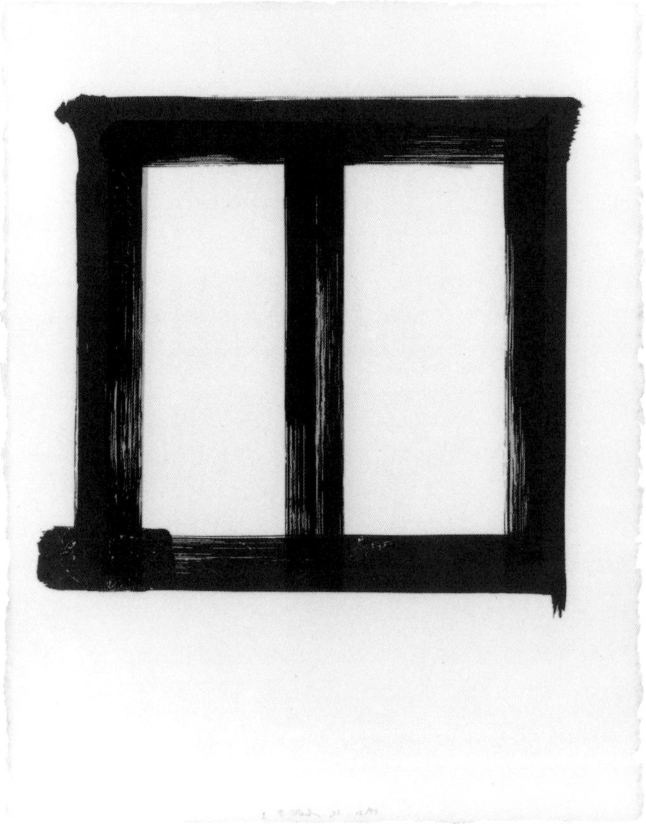

37/I

37/II

37/III

38 1,2,3,4 1983
Series of 4 screenprints on Japanese handmade Mino Kozo Kizuki paper
Image size: 73.7 × 83.3 (29 × 37¾)
Paper size: 97 × 73.7 (38¼ × 29)
3 screens each
Colour: transparent black and black
Printed by Hiroshe Kawanishi at Simca Print Artists and published by them and the artist
Edition: 32 plus 5 APs, 2 PPs, 1 BAT and 1 *hors commerce* proof
Each inscribed 'B. Marden', titled, dated and numbered below image at centre

Each image depicts a square with extended sides within a square within a rectangle of tone. Each image is slightly different.

The three screens were made as follows: Marden drew on the first screen with lacquer and printed it in transparent black; the second screen was executed in tusche and printed in black; the third screen was a photographic silkscreen and printed in black (the fine line). The square with thick sides in each case was applied swiftly with a brush.

This and nos.36 and 37 rclate to a series of works on paper Marden made in 1979 entitled 'The Hydra Series' (repr. Stedelijk, pp.42–3 in col.) and to drawings he had executed in Greece during the summer of 1983. For these latter he had used paper which Kawanishi had given to him as a sample.

This group is reminiscent of a painting by Franz Kline entitled 'Wotan' 1950 (repr. *Franz Kline: A Retrospective Exhibition*, exh. cat., Whitechapel Art Gallery, 1964, no.5). Although Marden was not actually thinking of Kline at the time he certainly knew this image.

38/1

38/2

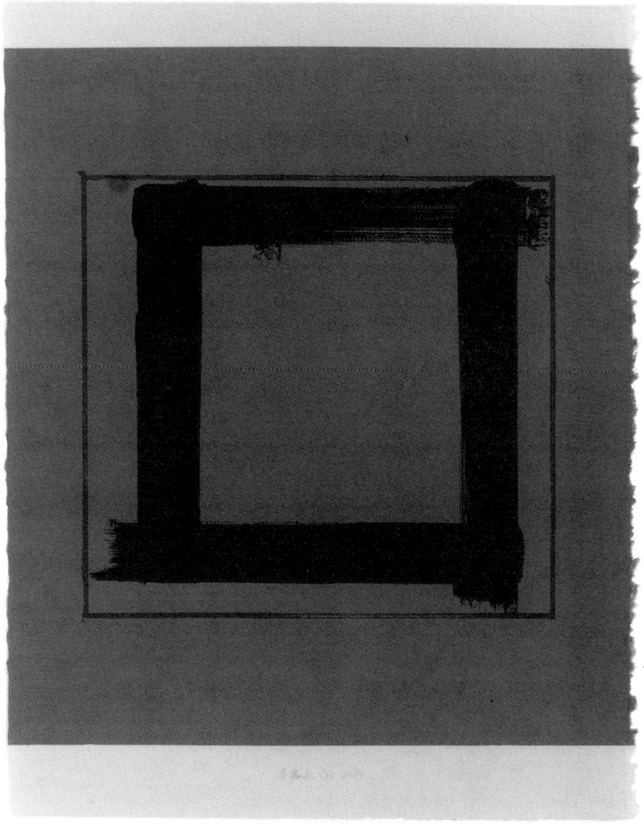

38/3

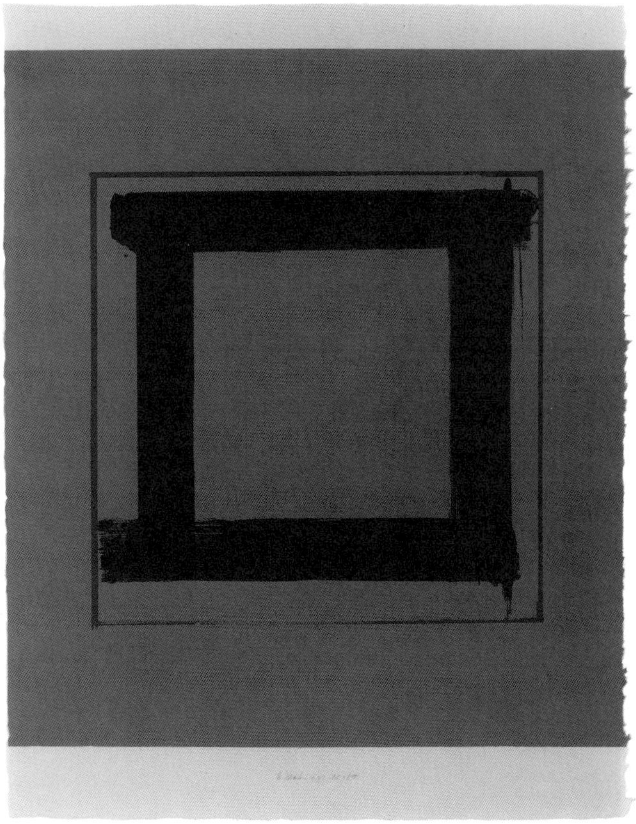

38/4

*39 **Etching for *Parkett*** 1985
Etching with spitbite aquatint and sugarlift aquatint on Rives BFK paper
Image size: 20.3 × 16.5 (8 × 6½)
Paper size: 25.4 × 20.8 (10 × 8⅛)
1 copper plate
Colour: black
Printed by Jennifer Melby, New York and published by Parkett Verlag, Zürich
Edition: 100 plus 10 APs numbered in Roman numerals
Inscribed 'B. Marden' below image b.r and numbered below image b.l.
Repr: *Parkett*, p.21

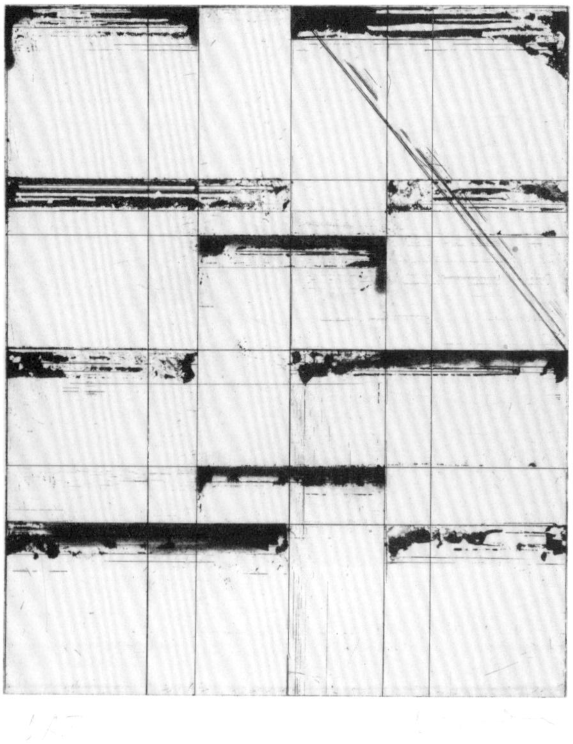

This print was published as part of the deluxe edition of *Parkett*, number 7, 1986. It depicts a grid ruled vertically and horizontally in hardground and wide bands drawn horizontally with sticks using sugar solution and spitbite. The print is the last in a sequence of seven graphic images – the others were drawings – reproduced in a fold-out in *Parkett*. It is, broadly speaking, the mirror image of the sixth drawing, although the quality of the mark is entirely different, the etching being sharper and more physical. The sequence becomes more complex as it proceeds. It begins with a rectangle divided horizontally and vertically by two fine lines, the quadrant at the top right being flanked top and bottom by a broad band of ink applied with a stick and cut diagonally by a fine line. The second drawing is divided into nine rectangles. In the third drawing the central, vertical column of rectangles is divided in half, while in the fourth the whole image is sectioned into sixteen quadrants. The fifth and the sixth works return to the basic format of the third, although one inch either side of the central column Marden has marked off another vertical line. The series is therefore an investigation into dividing the rectangle into factors of two and three. Although there appears to be a logic to the sequence, in fact there is not.

The images relate closely to Marden's drawings for the windows of Basle cathedral (repr. *Parkett*, pp.45 and 47 in col.). He stated that 'the windows were based on a grid that was made up by dividing the rectangle [of the window] in thirds and the grid into fourths superimposed on each other, four being the idea of earth and three being the idea of a Trinity or more divine number. So these became combinations of those elements.' The colours of the windows were related to the Elements. Marden was thinking in terms of notions connected with alchemy and consulted a table of correspondences (see p.56, n.66) which has an appendix of trigrams and hexagrams representing 'divination and spiritual meaning' among other things. The corresponding figures are parallel bars in various lengths. Seeing these may have encouraged him to change to this kind of imagery.

In October 1985 Marden began drawing on three or four plates in Melby's studio using hardground and then spitbite. He gradually eliminated the plates with which he was unhappy. He did not bring the drawings with him but had them in mind. He had not used spitbite much before and was unhappy with the result so he went back over it with sugar solution. For the spitbite he used a stick and for the sugar solution a brush. The grid was not altered after the first marking but the diagonal line was a late addition.

At one time Marden considered printing it in colour – red and green – and when he was unhappy with that he experimented with *chine collé*. Ultimately he felt it did not work and printed it in black.

For further discussion of this print see pp.47–8.

***40 Etchings to Rexroth** 1986
Portfolio of 25 etchings with other media on Rives BFK paper
Image size: 20.3 × 17.8 (8 × 7)
Paper size: 49.7 × 40.5 (19⅝ × 16)
1 copper plate each
Colour: black
Printed by Jennifer Melby, New York and published by Peter Blum Editions, New York
Edition: 45 plus 10 APs numbered in Roman numerals
Each inscribed 'B. Marden 86' b.r., numbered b.l. and numbered in sequence bottom centre
Lit: 'Prints and Photographs Published', *PCN*, vol.17, Jan.–Feb. 1987, p.216; Tu Fu, *Thirty-six Poems*. Translated by Kenneth Rexroth with twenty-five etchings by Brice Marden, New York 1987 (all repr.); John Yau, 'Brice Marden: A Vision of the Unsayable', *Brice Marden: Recent Paintings and Drawings*, exh. cat., Anthony d'Offay Gallery, 1988, pp.[14–15]; Susan Tallman, 'The Other Biennial', *Arts Magazine*, vol.64, Feb. 1990, p.18.
Also repr: Barry Walker, *Projects and Portfolios: The 25th National Print Exhibition*, exh. cat., Brooklyn Museum, New York 1989, no.53 (all repr.)

1–4 Etching and sugarlift aquatint
5 Sugarlift aquatint
6–15 Etching and sugarlift aquatint
16 Etching, sugarlift aquatint and aquatint
17–19 Etching and sugarlift aquatint
20 Sugarlift aquatint
21–24 Etching and sugarlift aquatint
25 Etching, sugarlift aquatint and aquatint

The following prints from this series are included in the exhibition: 1, 2, 6, 7, 9, 11, 15, 16, 17, 18, 21 and 25

Print 16 reproduced in colour on cover
Print 18 reproduced in colour on p.71

This portfolio was made at the time when Marden's art was undergoing a radical change of direction (see p.46). Having reached a crisis point in his life and a state of dissatisfaction with the prospect of continuing to produce paintings which consisted of flat, rectangular colour panels joined in different configurations, Marden decided to unite his graphic and painting activities. He had been making drawings from nature with sticks and had become very interested in oriental calligraphy. These two aspects were brought together in all the media in which he was working. This change of approach was first seen in his exhibition of paintings held at Mary Boone Gallery, New York in March 1987. The paintings for this exhibition were worked alongside the 'Rexroth' etchings.

The 'Rexroth' etchings consist of variations on triangular shapes, which might loosely be called ideographs, arranged in vertical columns. Unlike ideographs, however, they do not have specific connotations. In the first five prints the forms remain relatively separate but from the sixth image onwards Marden began to link them up. By the end of the series he appears to have abandoned the grid in favour of an all-over composition. The initial prints were sugarlift aquatint only but, as the series progressed, he introduced further media and worked the plates more intensively. The last print in the series is the most heavily worked with considerable scraping and rebiting.

Having successfully collaborated with Melby on 'Etching for *Parkett*' (no.39), Marden was happy to continue working with her on the new series of prints commissioned by Peter Blum. He initially made plates along the lines of the earlier print and in a larger size. As Melby recalls, 'after working quite a while with these images, he brought in some notebooks with a lot of drawings he had done in Greece. Pen and ink drawings.' She suggested that he could make similar kinds of images on copper plates using sugarlift and so he tried it out using sticks to apply the solution. Taking one of the larger prints as a guide, he decided to work on a plate half the size. This was to become the size for the whole set. Having previously worked with a grid it was natural for him to fit the images into such a format. The grid was marked up very lightly on the edge of each plate but not etched into it. Marden began each plate in the top right corner and worked vertically downwards before moving horizontally along the plate to the next column.

Once the series was underway he worked on groups of about four plates. He rarely returned to an earlier group once he had moved on to the next one. In addition to sugarlift Marden used hardground etching, employing razor blades to cut through the ground. Razor blades make a thicker line than a needle. Towards the end of the series, for example in nos.15, 16 and 25, the plates were extensively flat-bitten to provide a velvety tone in contrast to the bolder aquatint. Marden also scraped many of the plates to enliven the texture and used roulette in nos.9, 14, 16 and 19.

When the plates were completed he experimented with colour printing and with doubling up the plates on one sheet. Not only did he print some of the plates in colour but he also printed plates either side of a solid tone, colour plate. Blues and greens were tried on a number of them. He also tried *chine collé* but disliked it.

He worked on the series from January to June 1986, attending Melby's workshop twice a week. After completing the series Marden began to work on some larger prints on the same theme but has never published them.

Marden named the prints 'Etchings to Rexroth', meaning to the accompaniment of Rexroth. He had been reading Kenneth Rexroth's translations of poems by the Chinese poet Tu Fu (eighth-century Tang dynasty). He has always had a strong interest in poetry and his new-found regard for oriental art and life encouraged him to read oriental verse. As well as a translator, Kenneth Rexroth (1905–82) was a poet whose work was influenced by Chinese poetry. He described Tu Fu's poems as:

> saturated with the exile's nostalgia and the abiding sense of pathos of glory and power. In addition he shares with Baudelaire and Sappho, his only competitors in the West, an exceptionally exacerbated sensibility, acute past belief. You feel that Tu Fu brings to each poetic situation, each

experienced complex of sensations and values, a completely open nervous system. (Quoted in a biographical note on Tu Fu in the Tu Fu book mentioned above, p.[5])

Although Marden's images are not illustrations of Tu Fu's poems they have a sharpness and a delicacy which Rexroth noted in the lyrics.

Marden had embarked on the series before he discovered the Rexroth translations. At that time he was reading *Cathay* by the poet Ezra Pound (1875–1972), himself a learned orientalist, which consisted for the most part of translations of poems by the Chinese poet Rihaku. Peter Blum had given Marden a first edition of *Cathay* halfway through the project and Marden asserts that the prints had more to do with Pound than with Rexroth's translations.

Although the prints are numbered in a sequence which broadly represents the order in which they were made, they do not have to be displayed in a line but can be banked.

For further discussion of this portfolio see pp.48–50.

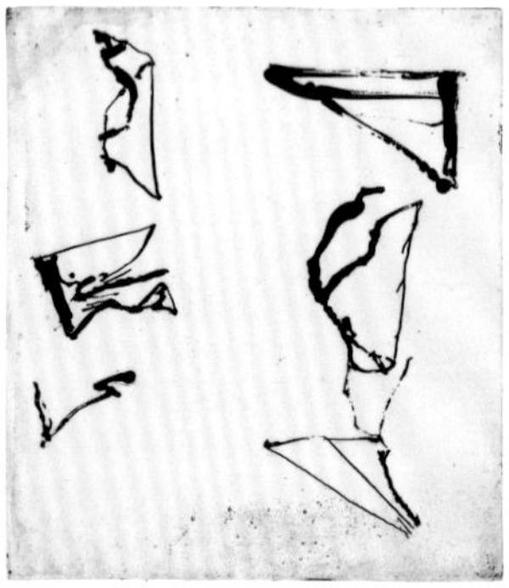

40/I

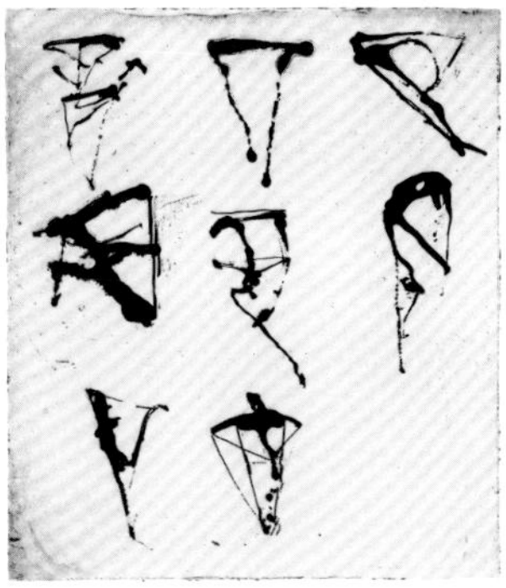

40/2

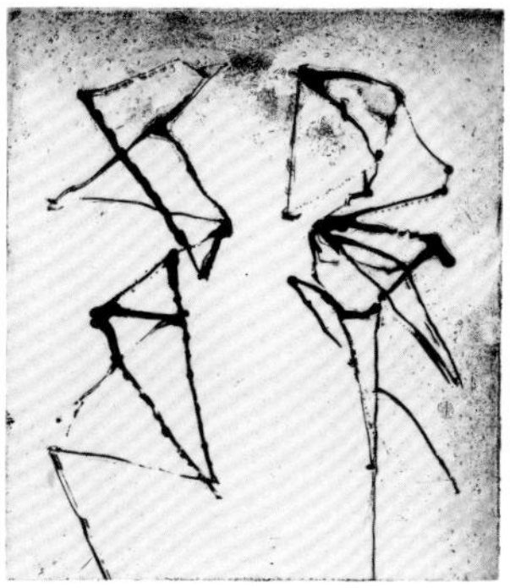

40/3

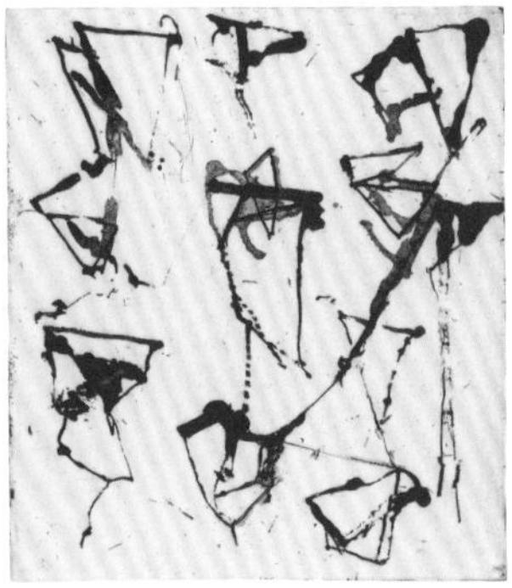

40/4

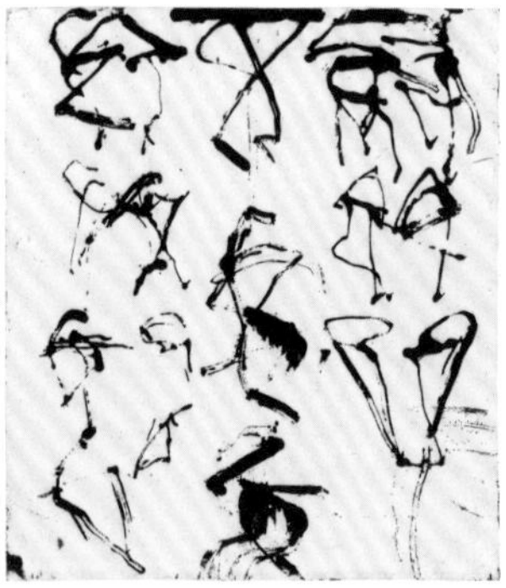

40/5

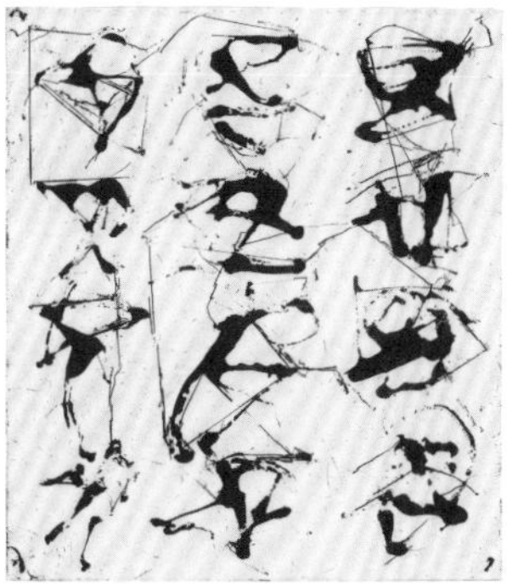

40/6

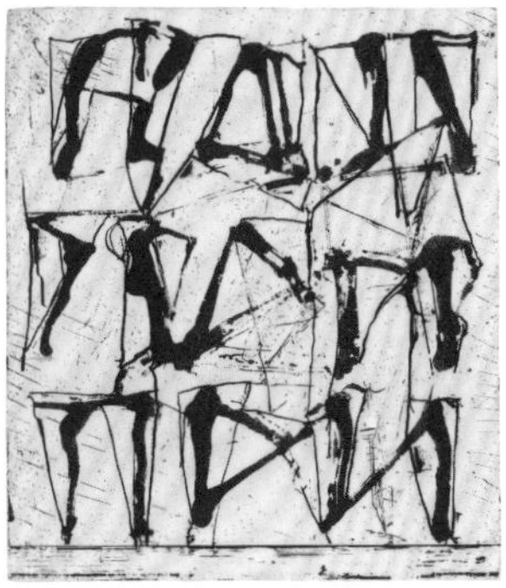

40/7

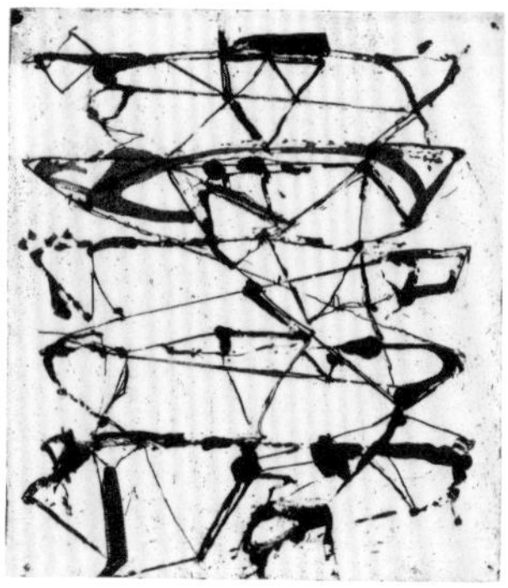

40/8

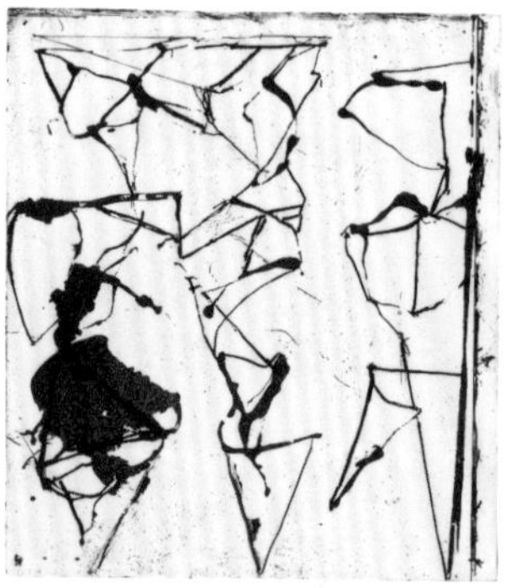

40/9

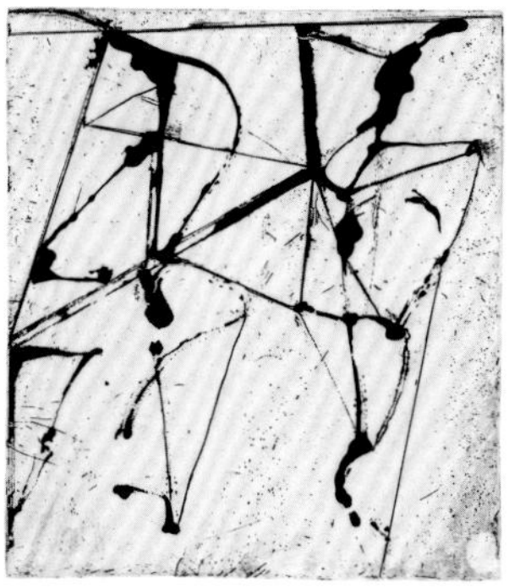

40/10

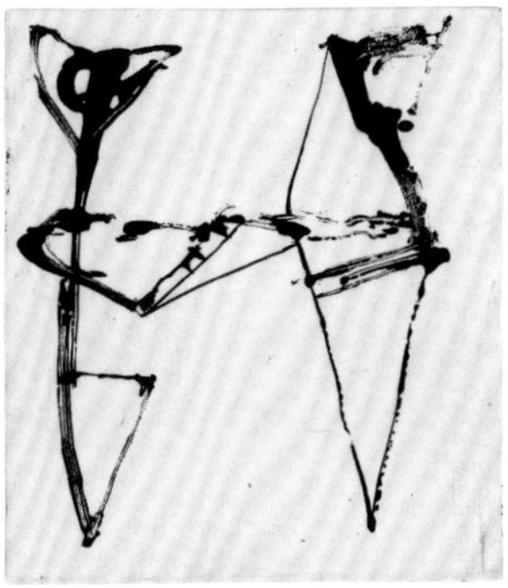

40/11

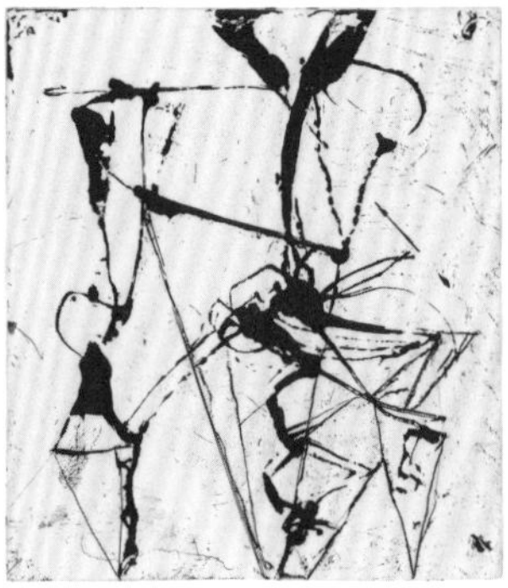

40/12

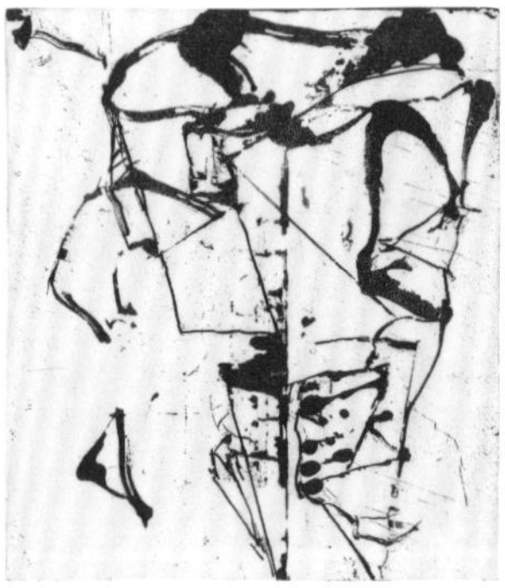

40/13

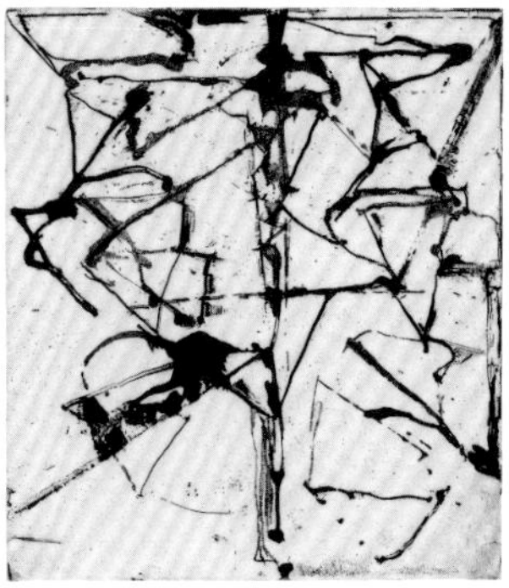

40/14

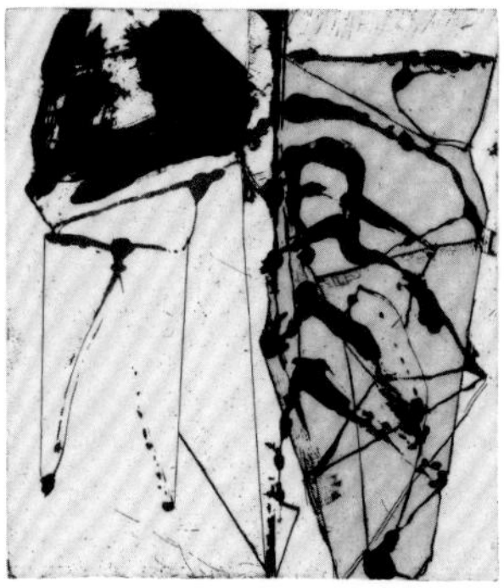

40/15

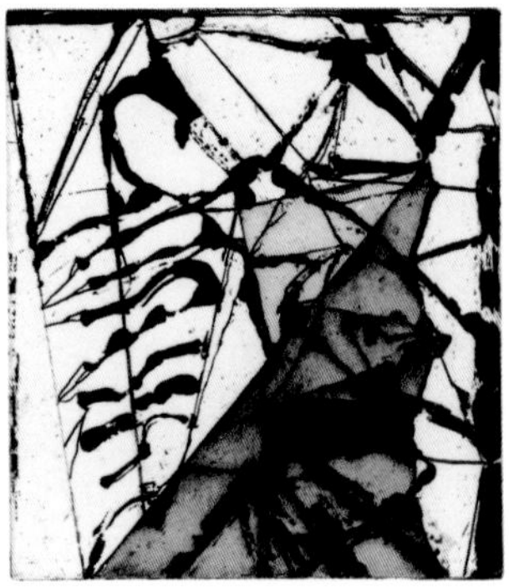

40/16

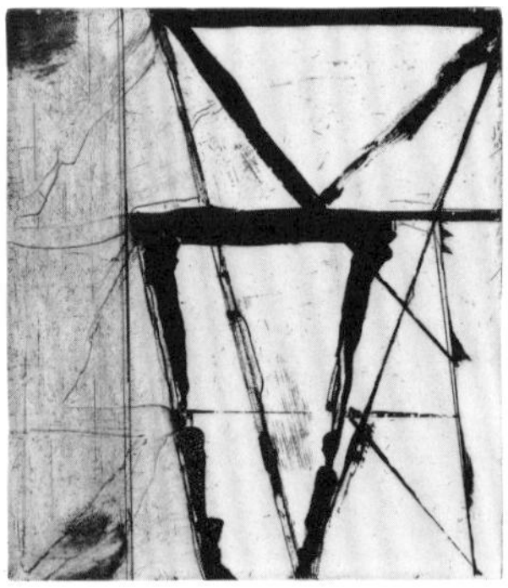

40/17

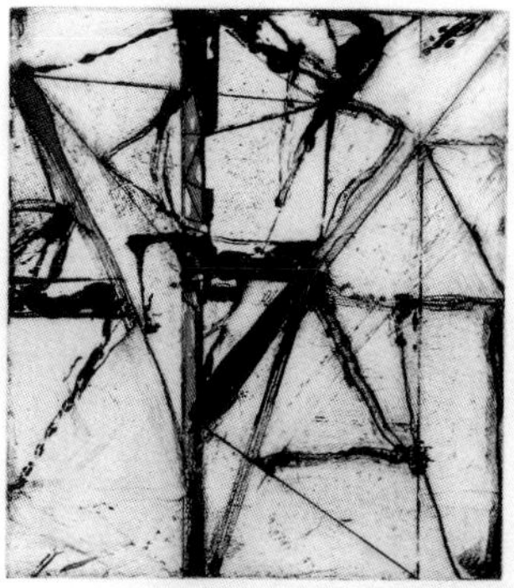

40/18

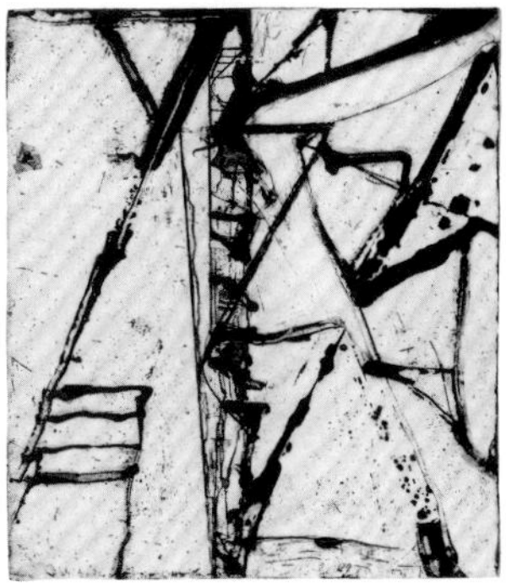

40/19

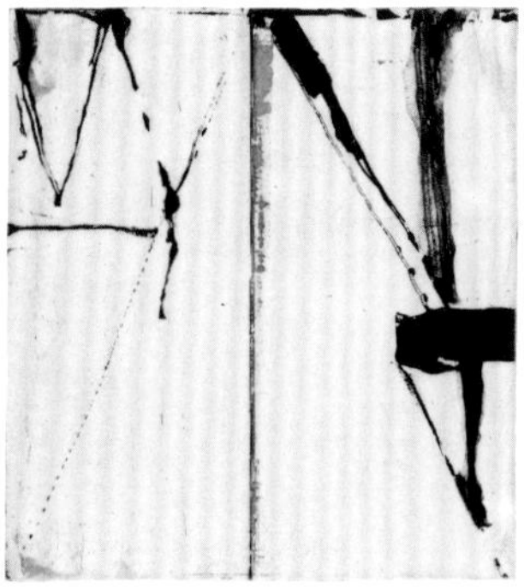

40/20

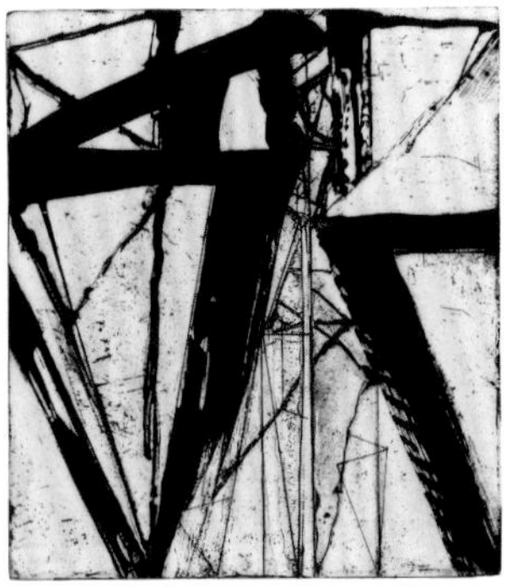

40/21

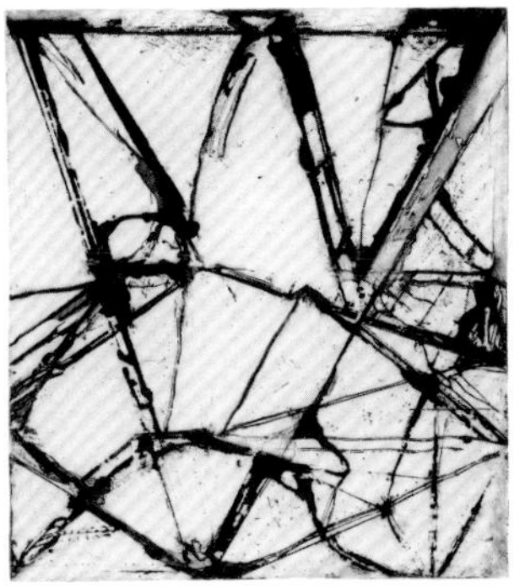

40/22

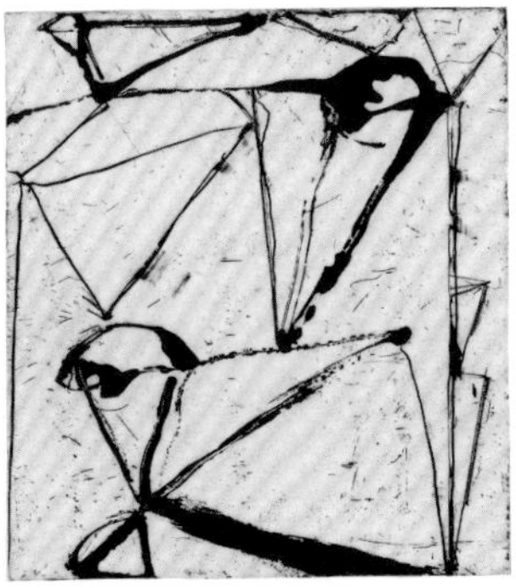

40/23

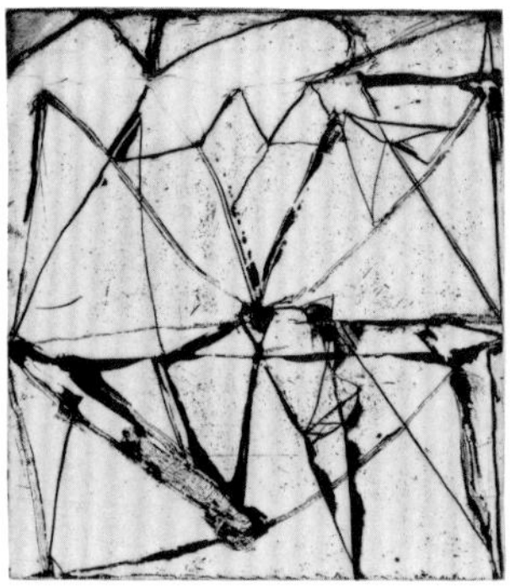

40/24

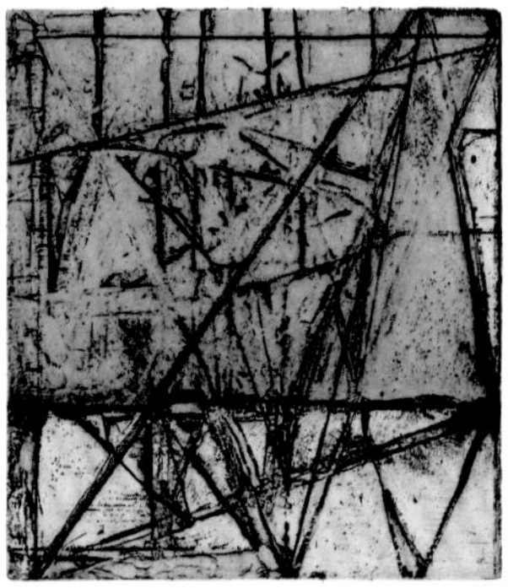

40/25

***41 Tu Fu** 1987
Etching and sugarlift aquatint on Rives BFK paper
Image size: 12 × 10 (6¾ × 4⅞)
Paper size: 24.1 × 17.7 (9½ × 7)
1 copper plate
Colour: black
Printed by Jennifer Melby, New York and published by Peter Blum Editions, New York
Edition: 140 plus 2 PPs and 1 BAT
Inscribed 'B. Marden 87' below image b.r. and numbered below image b.l.

This print was made to accompany the special edition of the book of *Thirty-six Poems* by Tu Fu translated by Kenneth Rexroth with twenty-five etchings by Brice Marden, published by Peter Blum Editions, New York in 1987. In addition to the poems and reproductions of the 'Rexroth' etchings (no.40) the book contains a preface by Peter Blum, an 'Introduction to the Poems' by Bradford Morrow, Kenneth Rexroth's literary executor, and an 'Introduction to the Etchings' by the poet John Yau. The 'Tu Fu' etching itself is not reproduced in the book.

Marden liked the idea of collecting all Rexroth's Tu Fu translations in one book because previously they were published in a number of different sources. At the time he was less happy about the concept of the accompanying essays, although he has now come to like it. He was also unhappy with the quality of the reproductions of the 'Rexroth' etchings.

The 'Tu Fu' print, which is structured in three columns of three characters, feels more open than many of the 'Rexroth' etchings. The forms trickle down the paper like a series of small waterfalls. After biting Marden scraped back the puddles to admit light.

Marden has overdrawn at least four proofs of this print (see reproduction p.52). At least three of these drawings were made over an earlier state before the aquatint was so heavily scraped.

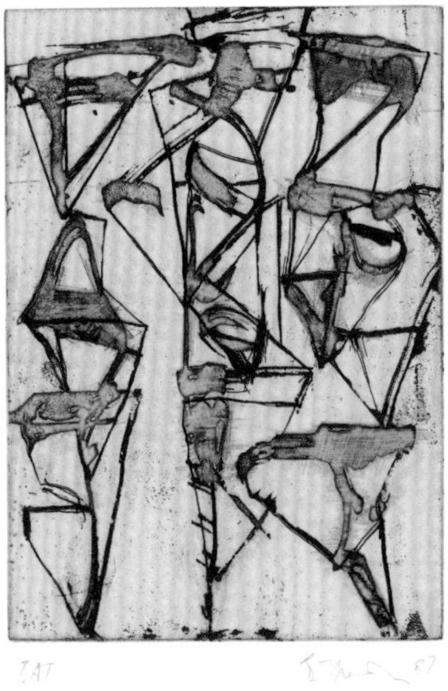

*42 **Cold Mountain Series, Zen Studies 1–6 (Early State)** 1990
Series of six etchings with other media on Whatman paper
Image size: 52.5 × 68.6 (20⅝ × 27)
Paper size: 69.5 × 89.5 (27¼ × 35¼)
1 copper plate each
Colour: black
Printed by Jennifer Melby, New York and published by the artist
Edition: 3 plus 2 APs
Each inscribed 'B. Marden 90' below image b.r. and numbered below image b.l.
Repr: *Brice Marden: Recent Drawings and Etchings*, exh. cat., Matthew Marks, New York 1990, nos.28–33 (later states)

1–2 Etching with sugarlift aquatint

3 Etching with spitbite aquatint and sugarlift aquatint

4–6 Etching with sugarlift aquatint

See entry for no.43 below.

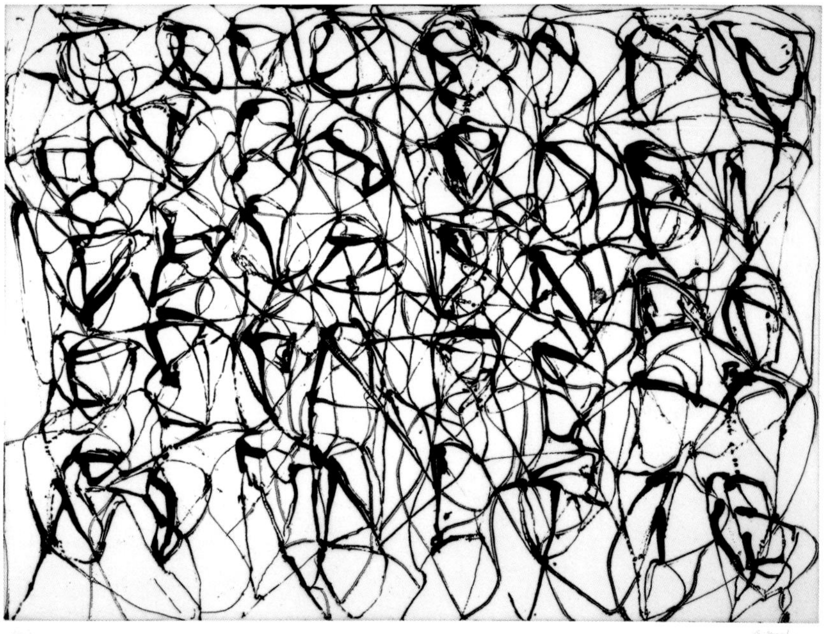

42/1

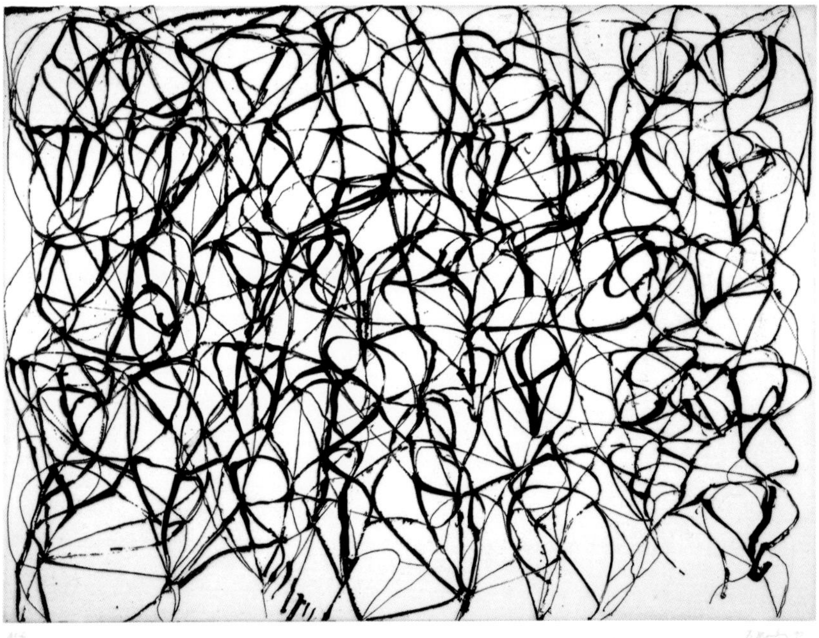

42/2

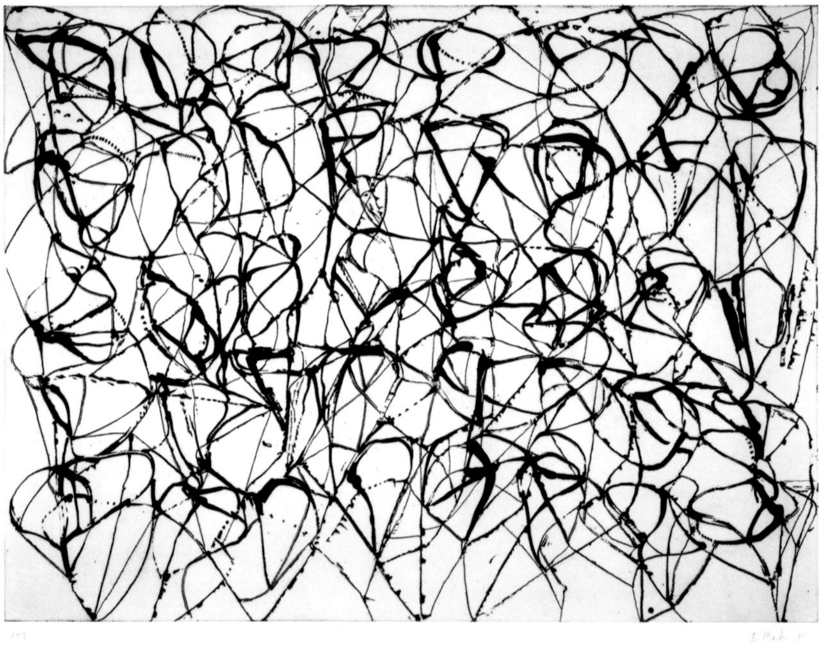

42/3

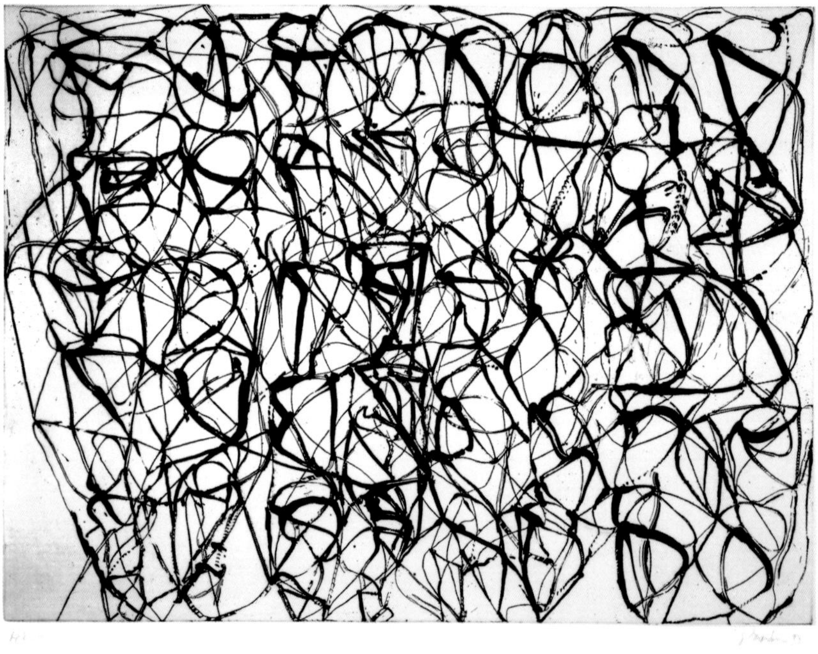

42/4

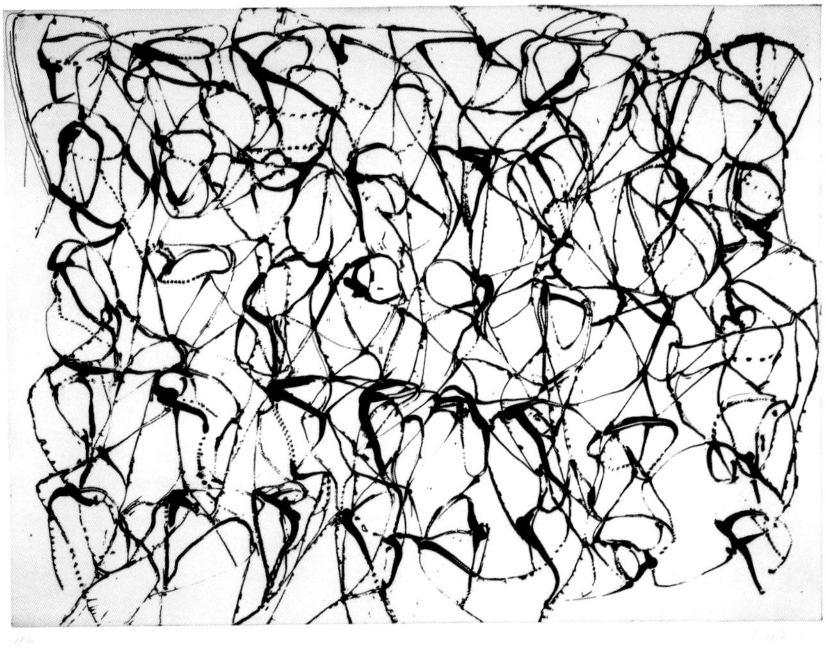

42/5

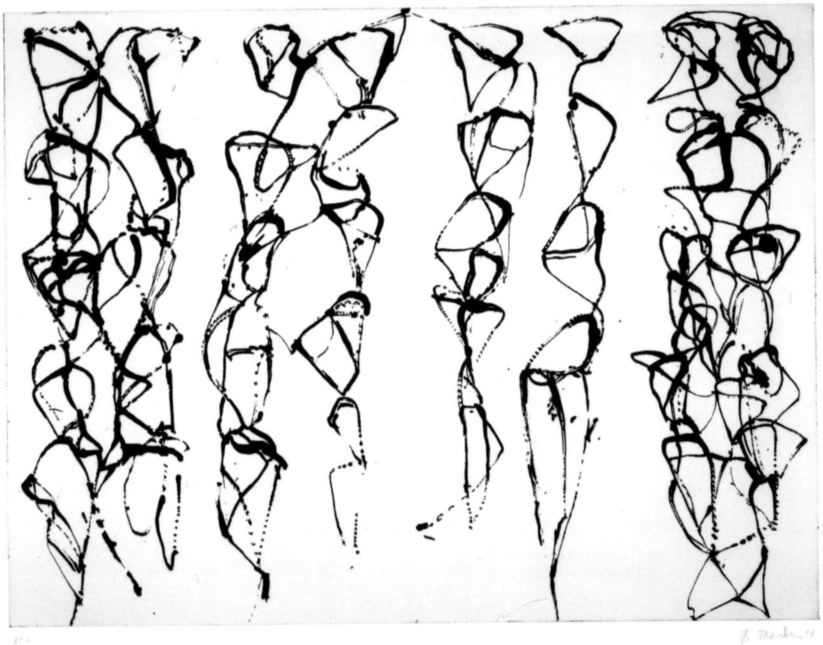

42/6

***43 Cold Mountain Series, Zen Studies 1–6** 1991
Series of six etchings with other media on Whatman paper
Image size: 52.5 × 68.6 (20⅝ × 27)
Paper size: 69.5 × 89.5 (27¼ × 35¼)
Copper plates
Colour: various
Printed by Jennifer Melby, New York and published by the artist
Edition: 35 plus 15 APs numbered in Roman numerals
Each inscribed 'B. Marden 91' below image b.r. and numbered below image b.l.
Repr: *Brice Marden: Recent Drawings and Etchings*, exh. cat., Matthew Marks, New York 1991, nos.28–33 (earlier states)

1 Etching with sugarlift aquatint and aquatint
2 plates
Colour: white and black
Detail reproduced on endpapers

2 Etching with sugarlift aquatint and aquatint
2 plates
Colour: white and black

3 Etching with spitbite aquatint, sugarlift aquatint and aquatint
1 plate
Colour: black

4 Etching with sugarlift aquatint
1 plate
Colour: black
Reproduced in colour on p.72

5 Etching with sugarlift aquatint and aquatint
1 plate
Colour: black

6 Etching with sugarlift aquatint and aquatint
2 plates
Colour: white and black

The 'Cold Mountain' prints, named after the celebrated Chinese poet of the Tang dynasty, are composed of four couplets of five characters each, arranged vertically on the page. This structure follows that of the poems in the original Chinese as reprinted in *The Collected Songs of Cold Mountain Translated from the Chinese by Red Pine*, Port Townsend, Washington 1983.

Marden measured out a grid and marked it lightly on the edge of the plates with a pen. He began all the prints except the third by drawing with a stick dipped in sugar solution. The table on which the plate lay was tilted at a slight angle so that he could stand back and work on it at a distance, as he was accustomed to doing with his drawings. However he was careful to avoid accidental runs.

To take the second print as an example of his working method, he began by drawing the characters individually and keeping them separate but in the second states he linked up the two sides of the couplets. Often small droplets of sugar solution would fall onto the plate but Marden worked them into the drawing at a later stage. In the third state he began to join the couplets together using sugarlift to complicate the image. The fourth state saw the addition of lines etched in hardground and sugar solution, adding to the interlaced appearance of the print. Between the fourth and the final state Marden continued to draw with sugar solution and in the final state itself he decided to print a flat white aquatint from a separate plate before printing the drawn plate on top. The prints published in an edition of three (no.42) were of the fourth state.

Marden began the third plate using spitbite but disliked it and refrained from working with it again. He went over the spitbite in hardground etching. He made marks in the ground using razor blades, the side of a burnisher and a broken palette knife among other instruments. He often encountered resistance from the aquatint when doing this and did not always score right through it. He also added a flat grey aquatint to the whole of the plate. Plates four and five also had areas of flat aquatint, but Marden felt that they described strong forms and decided to scrape them out in the final state. In the fifth print Melby did this using a stick of etcher's rouge but Marden scraped the aquatint off the fourth plate himself. Evidence of the aquatint remains and differentiates the tone of the image from the margins of the paper.

Marden began these prints in January 1990 and carried on through to June, coming in once or twice a week. He worked on all the plates simultaneously and Melby proofed them between each session. He returned in January 1991 and continued at irregular intervals until he completed them in August 1991.

Marden had the idea to print white as an undertone in nos.1, 2 and 6 after seeing some prints by Andrew Spence in Melby's studio in which white was printed as a colour. Melby normally uses Charbonnel inks but Charbonnel white tends to oxidise. She eventually discovered that T.N. Lawrence white was relatively stable. Whatman paper was chosen because it is brilliant white. The paper was trimmed to have a deckle edge. Some early proofs were printed on handmade paper but Marden considered it to be too heavy.

His initial idea was to make six prints the size of the present series and one print one and a half times the size. He has not made the latter.

The prints were made in tandem with the series of six 'Cold Mountain' paintings recently exhibited at Dia Center for the Arts, New York. The compositions of the paintings are closely related. The first painting and sixth print are the least complex of all the images, the couplets remaining separate from each other (repr. *Brice Marden*, exh. cat., Michael Werner, Cologne 1989, pp.[12–13] in col.), while the other paintings and prints consist of cursive webs. Interconnectedness appears to be one of the themes of these images.

Unlike many of the related drawings but like the paintings, the prints are generally worked to the edge and then tend to loop back inwards in a movement of renewed and contained energy. This characteristic is also found in the work of Pollock, whom Marden admires above all other artists of the mid-century.

For further discussion of these prints see pp.51–4.

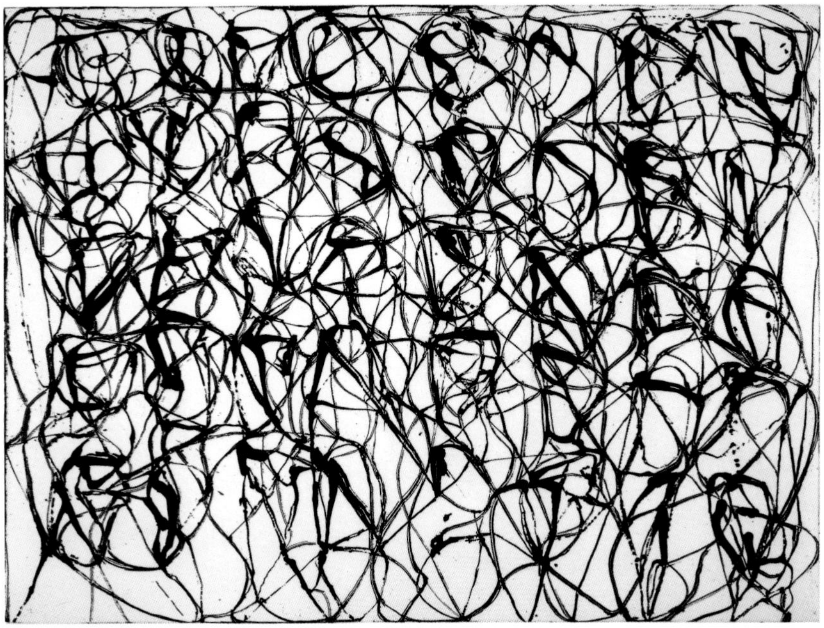

43/1

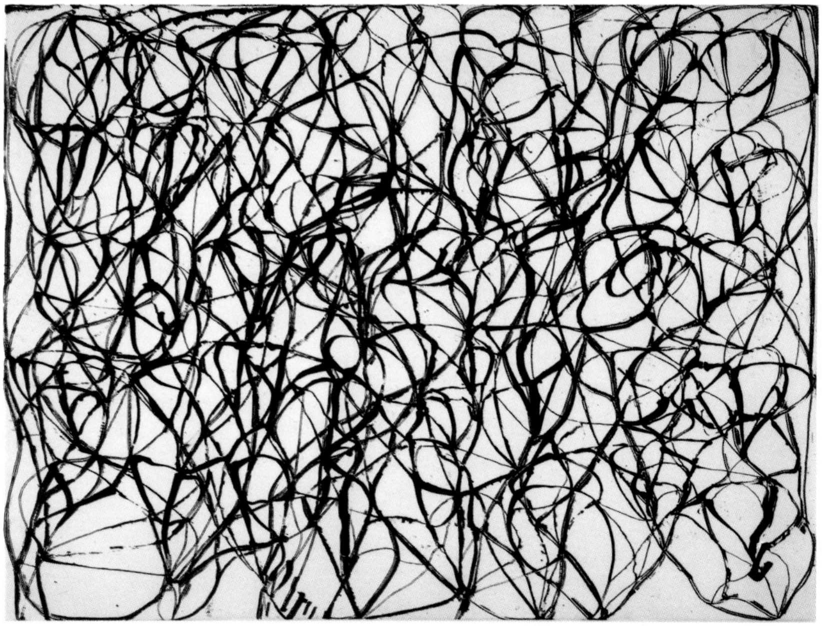

43/2

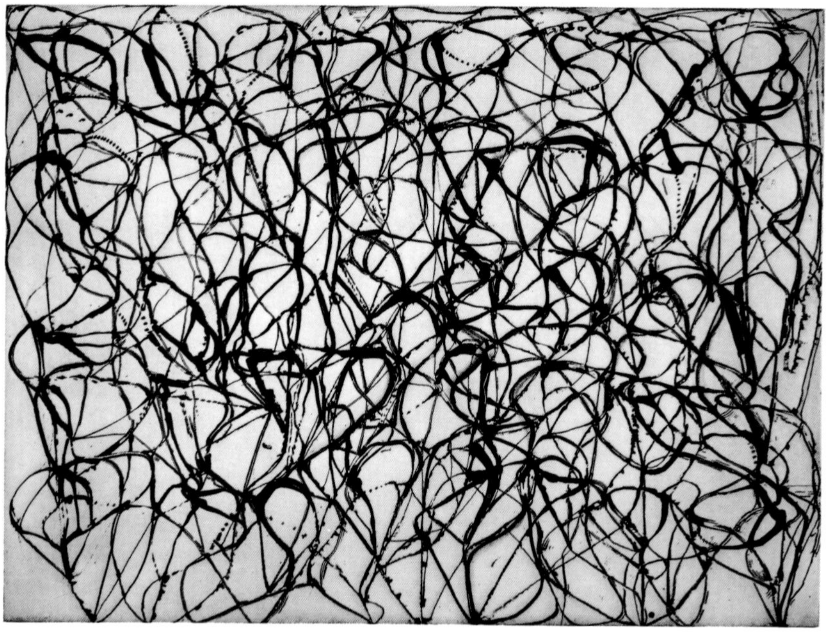

43/3

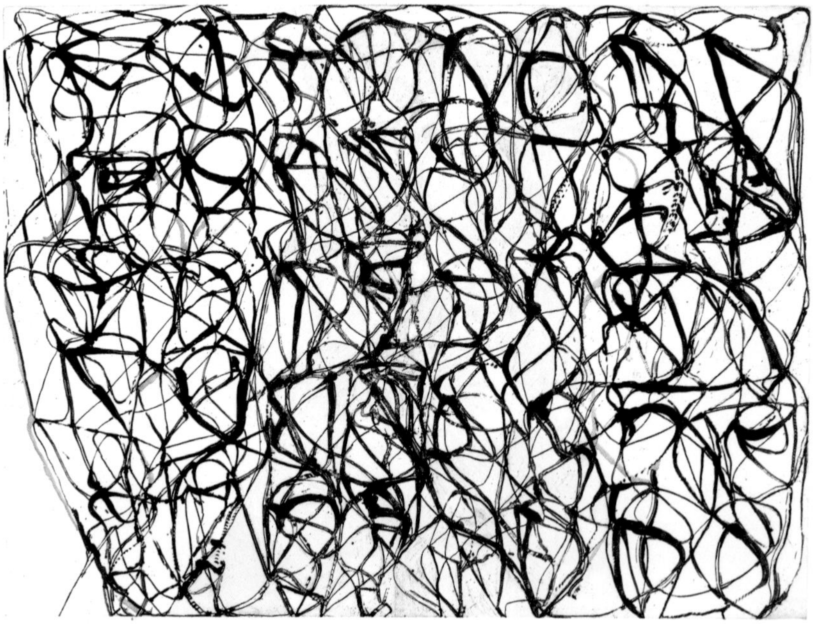

43/4

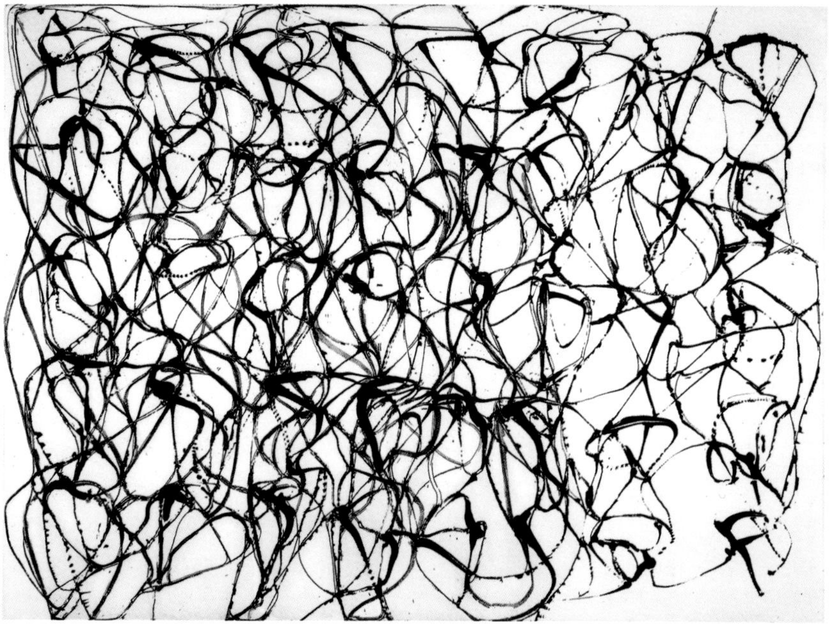

43/5

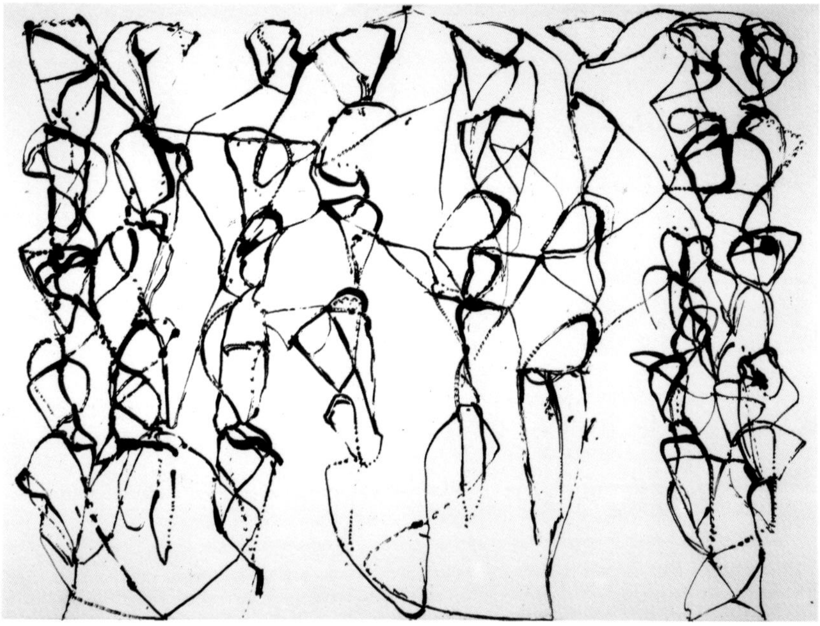

43/6

Bibliography

This is a very selective bibliography of material specifically relating to the prints of Brice Marden. A more comprehensive bibliography on all aspects of the artist's work may be consulted in the Tate Gallery Library.

Book

Tu Fu. *Thirty-six poems*. Translated by Kenneth Rexroth; with 25 etchings by Brice Marden. New York: Peter Blum, 1987. 'Etchings to Rexroth'.

Exhibition catalogues

In date order. The number of works in parentheses refers to the number of prints or print suites in the exhibition.

Wadsworth Atheneum, Hartford (Conn.). *Prints from the Untitled Press, Captiva, Florida*. Oct.–Nov. 1973. (1 work). Texts by Jack Cowart and James Elliott, pp.5–6, 20–5. 'BM 72' *or* 'Untitled Press Series 1972'.

Arts Council of Great Britain, London. *Order and experience*. 1975. Travelling to 10 U.K. venues. (3 works). Text by N. Lynton. 'Untitled, 1971' illus., 'Ten Days', 'Adriatics'.

Solomon R. Guggenheim Museum, New York. *Brice Marden*. Mar.–Apr. 1975. Text by L. Shearer.

Städtisches Museum, Mönchengladbach. *Mel Bochner, Sol LeWitt, Robert Mangold, Brice Marden, Agnes Martin, Edda Renouf, Dorothea Rockburne: Graphiken aus der Edition der Parasol Press, New York*. Mar.–Apr. 1975. Text by J. Cladders, C. Weyergraf.

Davison Art Center, Wesleyan University, Middletown (Conn.). *Recent American etching*. Oct.–Nov. 1975. (1 work). Travelling exhibition organised by the National Collection of Fine Arts, Smithsonian Institution, Washington, D.C. Text by R.S. Field. 'Five Plates', illus.

Art Gallery of Ontario, Toronto. *Prints: Bochner, LeWitt, Mangold, Marden, Martin, Renouf, Rockburne, Ryman*. Dec. 1975–Jan. 1976. (2 works). Introduction by N. Tousley. Artist's statement. pp.31–5. 'Adriatics', 'Five Plates'.

Kestner-Gesellschaft, Hanover. *Minimal Druckgraphik*. Dec. 1976–Jan. 1977. (3 works). Texts by N. Lynton, K. Brown, N. Tousley. pp.40–5, 5 illus. 'Ten Days', 'Five Plates', 'Adriatics'.

Kunstraum München, Munich. *Brice Marden: Zeichnungen/drawings, 1964–1978*. Sept.–Oct. 1979. Travelling to Institut für moderne Kunst, Nürnberg. Texts by H. Kern and K. Kertess. 'Untitled 1979' published in a special edition of the catalogue, and illus. on p.52 of the catalogue itself.

Stedelijk Museum, Amsterdam. *Brice Marden: schilderijen, tekeningen, etsen/ paintings, drawings and etchings, 1975–1980*. Mar.–Apr. 1981. (2 works). Travelling to Whitechapel Art Gallery. Texts by R. Smith, S. Bann. Parallel Dutch/English text. 'Five Threes', 'Focus I–V'; illus. from 'Focus I–V'.

Whitechapel Art Gallery, London. *Brice Marden: paintings, drawings and prints, 1975–1980*. May–June 1981. (2 works). Travelling from Stedelijk Museum, Amsterdam. Texts by N. Serota, S. Bann, R. Smith. 'Five Threes', 'Focus I–V'; illus. from 'Focus I–V'.

Davison Art Center, Wesleyan University, Middletown (Conn.). *No title: the collection of Sol LeWitt*. Oct.–Dec. 1981. (3 works). Ed. by J.T. Paoletti; text on Marden by J.B. Ravenal. pp.77–9. 'Ten Days', 'Five Plates'.

Tate Gallery, London. *American art: minimal expression*. July–Aug. 1984. (2 works). Text by J. Lewison. 'Five Plates'. 'Tile 1'; illus. from 'Five Plates'.

Nigel Greenwood Gallery, London. *New edition prints*: [by various artists including Brice Marden]. Mar. 1987. (1 work). 'Etchings for Rexroth'.

Anthony d'Offay Gallery, London. *Brice Marden: recent paintings and drawings*. Apr.–May 1988. (1 work). Introduction by John Yau. Cover title: Brice Marden: a vision of the unsayable, by John Yau. 'Etchings to Rexroth'.

Matthew Marks, New York. *Brice Marden: recent drawings and etchings*. May–June 1990.

Serial Articles

In date order. *PCN* is the *Print Collector's Newsletter*.

Brice Marden [cat.no.] 38 a–h 'Ten Days', 1971. In Selection III: contemporary graphics from the Museum's collection. *Bulletin of Rhode Island School of Design, Museum Notes*, vol.59, no.6, Apr. 1973, pp.[62–3], illus.

Brice Marden, 'Ten Days' (1972). In Prints & portfolios published. *PCN*, vol.3, no.4, Sept.–Oct. 1972, p.85.

Brice Marden, 'BM 72' (1972). In Prints & portfolios published. *PCN*, vol.4, no.2, May–June 1973, p.37. 'Untitled Press Series 1972' (cat.no.21).

H. Herrera. David Novros, Brice Marden (Bykert downtown). In Reviews and previews. *Art News*, vol.73, no.4, Apr. 1974, pp.97–8. 'Five Plates'.

Brice Marden, 'Adriatics' (1974). In Prints & portfolios published. *PCN*, vol.5, no.2, May–June 1974, p.41.

P. Larson. Minneapolis: Brice Marden at Locksley/Shea. In Arts reviews. *Arts Magazine*, vol.49, no.5, Jan. 1975, p.23.

Brice Marden, 'Etchings & Aquatints' (1973–74). In Prints & portfolios published. *PCN*, vol.5, no.6, Jan.–Feb. 1975, p.151. 'Five Plates'.

A Ellenzweig. Brice Marden, Knoedler Contemporary Prints, [New York]. In Arts reviews. *Arts Magazine*, vol.49, no.7, Mar. 1975, p.12. Review of exhibition of 'Adriatics' and 'Five Plates'.

F. Crichton. Brice Marden at Hester Royen: [exhibition review]. In London. *Art International*, vol.19, no.4, Apr.1975, pp.39–40. 'Adriatics', 'Five Plates'.

S. Bann. Adriatics: à propos of Brice Marden. *20th Century Studies*, no.15–16, 1976, pp.116–29.

P. Larson. Aquatints again. *PCN*, vol.8, no.3, July–Aug. 1977, pp.61–5. 'Ten Days', 'Five Plates', 'Adriatics'; illus. 'Untitled' from 'Ten Days'.

M. Betz. Brice Marden: ['Five Threes']. In New editions. *Art News*, vol.76, no.7, Sept. 1977, p.104. 'Five Threes'.

Brice Marden, 'Five Threes' (1976–77). In Prints & photographs published. *PCN*, vol.8, no.5, Nov.–Dec. 1977, p.145.

Brice Marden, 'Tiles' (1979). In Prints & photographs published. *PCN*, vol.10, no.5, Nov.–Dec. 1979, p.162. 'Tiles'.

Brice Marden, 'Untitled' (1979–80). In Prints & photographs published. *PCN*, vol.11, no.1, Mar.–Apr. 1980, p.17. 'Focus I–V'.

R. White. Brice Marden: interview. *View*, vol.3, no.2, June 1980, whole issue. '12 Views for Caroline Tatyana', 'Tiles'.

Brice Marden, 'Untitled' (1983). In Prints & photographs published. *PCN*, vol.14, no.4, Sept.–Oct. 1983, p.144.

Parkett, no.7, Jan. 1986. Includes 3 articles on Marden: Drawings/Brice Marden, pp.1, 3–4; Brice Marden: the Duse of minimalism = die Duse der Minimal art, by Lisa Liebmann, pp.37–44; For Brice Marden: twelve fragments on surface (and some after thoughts) by Francesco Pellizzi, pp.50–63; and a print 'Etching for Parkett 1985', as a 6p. foldout at p.21.

Brice Marden, 'Etchings to Rexroth' (1986). In Prints & photographs published. *PCN*, vol.17, no.6, Jan–Feb. 1987, p.216.

S.Tallman. The other biennial: [the Brooklyn Museum's 'National Print Exhibition']. *Arts Magazine*, vol.64, no.6, Feb. 1990, pp.17–18. 'Etchings to Rexroth'.

R.H. Cohen. Minimal prints. *PCN*, vol.21, no.2, May–June 1990, pp.42–6. 'Adriatics', 'Five Plates', '12 Views for Caroline Tatyana'; illus. 'Untitled Press Series 1972', p.44.

M. Kimmelman. Matthew Marks, New York: recent drawings and etchings. *New York Times*, 24 May 1991, p.C26.

Matthew Marks, New York: recent drawings and etchings. *New Yorker*, 3 June 1991, p.14.

K. Larson. Matthew Marks, New York: recent drawings and etchings. *New York*, 10 June 1991.

List of Exhibited Works

The following catalogue raisonné numbers are the prints included in the exhibition. They have been lent by the artist and Matthew Marks Gallery, New York, and are marked with an asterisk by each catalogue entry:
2, 5, 9, 10, 11, 12, 13, 14, 15, 16, 20 (a–h), 21 (#1, #2, #3, #4), 22 (a, b, c, f), 23 (a–e), 24, 25, 28 (a–e), 29 (a–l), 31 (a–d), 35, 39, 40 (nos 1, 2, 6, 7, 9, 11, 15–18, 21, 25), 41, 42 (nos.1–6), 43 (nos.1–6)

The following works are also included in the exhibition:

Untitled 1966
Graphite on paper
27.9 × 34.9 (11 × 13¾)
The artist

The work is a study for 'Four' (no.12)

Untitled 1966
Charcoal and graphite on screenprint on paper
50.8 × 60.3 (20 × 23¾)
Matthew Marks Gallery, New York

The basis of this work is 'Four' (no.12)

Untitled 1971
Proof for print (b) from 'Ten Days' (no.20)
Etching on Arches paper
Image size: 55 × 27 (21⅝ × 10⅝)
Paper size: 76 × 56.3 (30 × 22⅛)
The artist

Untitled 1971
Proof for print (b) from 'Ten Days' (no.20)
Etching on Arches paper
Image size: 55 × 27 (21⅝ × 10⅝)
Paper size: 76 × 56.3 (30 × 22⅛)
The artist

Untitled 1971
Proof for print (b) from 'Ten Days' (no.20)
Etching and aquatint on Arches paper
Image size: 55 × 27 (21⅝ × 10⅝)
Paper size: 76 × 56.3 (30 × 22⅛)
The artist

Untitled 1971
Proof for print (b) from 'Ten Days' (no.20)
Etching and aquatint on Arches paper
Image size: 55 × 27 (21⅝ × 10⅝)
Paper size: 76 × 56.3 (30 × 22⅛)
The artist

Plate for print (b) from 'Ten Days' (no.20) 1971
Zinc plate
55 × 27 (21⅝ × 10⅝)
Crown Point Press, San Francisco

Mosaic Study no.2 1978
Ink and graphite over etching and aquatint on paper
76.2 × 55.8 (30 × 22)
Arnold and Mildred Glimcher
Reproduced on p.26

The basis of this work is print (d) from 'Ten days' (no.20)

Painting Study I 1980
Ink over screenprint on paper
49.9 × 60.3 (19$^{11}/_{16}$ × 23¾)
Private Collection
Reproduced on p.19

The basis of this work is 'Lana' (no.13)

Painting Study II 1980
Ink over screenprint on paper
49.9 × 60.3 (19$^{11}/_{16}$ × 23¾)
Mirabelle Marden

The basis of this work is 'Lana' (no.13)

Untitled 1980
Ink over etching and aquatint on paper
75.5 × 56.2 (29¾ × 22¾)
The artist

The basis of this work is 'Tiles' (no.31)

Drawing for *Parkett* Laparello 1985
Ink on 6 sheets of coated layout paper joined together
each sheet 25.4 × 20.8 (10 × 8⅛)
The artist

Tu Fu Dog 1 1986–91
Ink over etching and aquatint on paper
24.1 × 18.2 (9½ × 7⅛)
Richard Brown Baker, New York
Reproduced on p.52

The basis of this work is 'Tu Fu' (no.41)

Untitled 1987
Ink over etching and aquatint on paper
24.1 × 17.7 (9½ × 7)
Private Collection; Courtesy Matthew Marks Gallery, New York

The basis of this work is 'Tu Fu' (no.41)

Cold Mountain Series, Zen Study 4 (State 1) 1990
Sugerlift aquatint on paper
Image size: 52.5 × 68.6 (20⅝ × 27)
Paper size: 69.5 × 89.5 (27¼ × 35¼)
The artist

Cold Mountain Series, Zen Study 4 (State 3) 1990
Etching with sugarlift aquatint on paper
Image size: 52.5 × 68.6 (20⅝ × 27)
Paper size: 69.5 × 89.5 (27¼ × 35¼)
The artist

Cold Mountain Series, Zen Study 4 (State 7) 1990–1
Etching with sugarlift aquatint and aquatint on paper
Image size: 52.5 × 68.6 (20⅝ × 27)
Paper size: 69.5 × 89.5 (27¼ × 35¼)
The artist

Cold Mountain Series, Zen Study 4 (State 9) 1990–1
Etching with sugarlift aquatint and aquatint on paper
Image size: 52.5 × 68.6 (20⅝ × 27)
Paper size: 69.5 × 89.5 (27¼ × 35¼)
The artist

The Friends of the Tate Gallery

Since their formation in 1958, the Friends of the Tate Gallery have helped to buy major works of art for the Tate Gallery Collection, from Stubbs to Hockney.

Members are entitled to immediate and unlimited free admission to Tate Gallery exhibitions with a guest, invitations to previews of Tate Gallery exhibitions, opportunities to visit the Gallery when closed to the public, a discount of 10 per cent in the Tate Gallery shop, special events, *Friends Events* and *Tate Preview* magazines mailed three times a year, free admission to exhibitions at Tate Gallery Liverpool, and use of the new Friends Room at the Tate Gallery, supported by Lloyd's of London.

Three categories of higher level memberships, Associate Fellow at £100, Deputy Fellow at £250, and Fellow at £500, entitle members to a range of extra benefits including guest cards, and invitations to exclusive special events.

The Friends of the Tate Gallery are supported by Tate & Lyle PLC.

Further details on the Friends and Supporters may be obtained from:

Friends of the Tate Gallery
Tate Gallery
Millbank
London SW1P 4RG

Tel: 071-821 1313 or 071-834 2742

Tate Gallery Liverpool Supporters

The Tate Gallery Liverpool Supporters were established in 1989 to promote the Gallery and help raise funds for its exhibitions and other projects.

Members are entitled to unlimited free admission to Tate Gallery Liverpool and London exhibitions, invitations to private previews of Tate Gallery Liverpool exhibitions, a discount of 10 per cent on Tate Gallery Liverpool catalogues and on goods in the Tate Gallery London Shop, special events, invitations to the Supporters' annual party, regular information on all Tate Gallery Liverpool activities and *Tate Preview* magazine mailed three times a year.

Patrons of the Tate Gallery

The Patrons of British Art support British painting and sculpture from the Elizabethan period through to the early twentieth century in the Tate Gallery's Collection. They encourage knowledge and awareness of British Art by providing an opportunity to study Britain's cultural heritage.

The Patrons of New Art support contemporary art in the Tate Gallery's Collection. They promote a lively and informed interest in contemporary art and are associated with the Turner Prize, one of the most prestigious awards for the visual arts.

Annual membership ranges from £350 to £750, and funds the purchase of works of art for the Tate Gallery Collection. Benefits for both groups include invitations to Tate Gallery receptions, an opportunity to sit on the Patrons' acquisitions committees, special events including visits to private and corporate collections and complimentary catalogues of Tate Gallery exhibitions.

Further details on the Patrons of the Tate Gallery can be obtained from:

The Development Office
Tate Gallery
Millbank
London SW1P 4RG

Tel: 071 821 1313

Sponsorship

Tate Gallery, London – Sponsorships since 1989

Agfa Graphic Systems Group
1991, *Turner: The Fifth Decade* exhibition
Barclays Bank plc
1991, *Constable* exhibition
Beck's
1992, *Otto Dix* exhibition
British Gas plc
1989, Education study sheets
British Gas plc
1989, *Colour into Line: Turner and the Art of Engraving* exhibition
The British Land Company plc
1990, *Joseph Wright of Derby* exhibition
The British Petroleum Co plc
1989, *Paul Klee* exhibition
1990–93, *New Displays*
British Steel plc
1989, *William Coldstream* exhibition
Carroll, Dempsey & Thirkell
1990, *Anish Kapoor* exhibition
Channel 4 Television
1991–93, The Turner Prize
Clifton Nurseries
1989–91, Sponsorship in kind
Daimler Benz
1991, *Max Ernst* exhibition
Debenham Tewson & Chinnocks
1990, Turner *Painting and Poetry* exhibition
Digital Equipment Co Ltd
1991, *From Turner's Studio* touring exhibition
Drivers Jonas
1989, *Turner and Architecture* exhibition
Erco Lighting
1989, Sponsorship in kind
The German Government
1992, *Otto Dix* exhibition
The Independent
1992, *Otto Dix* exhibition
KPMG Management Consulting
1991, *Anthony Caro: Sculpture towards Architecture* exhibition
Linklaters & Paines
1989, Japanese Guide to Turner Bequest
Lin Pac Plastics
1989, Sponsorship in kind
Olympia & York
1990, Frameworkers Conference
PA Consulting Group
1989, Video projector
Reed International plc
1990, *On Classic Ground* exhibition
SRU Ltd
1989, Market research consultancy
Tate & Lyle PLC
1991–93, Friends relaunch marketing programme
Ulster Television plc
1989, *F.E. McWilliam* exhibition
Volkswagen
1989–92, The Turner Scholarships
Westminster City Council
1989, Trees project
1989, *The Tate Gallery Companion* (New Display Guidebook)

Tate Gallery Liverpool – Sponsorships since 1989

Barclays Bank plc
1989, Sculpture for the visually impaired
BASF
1990, *Lifelines* exhibition
Becks Beer
1990, *Lifelines* exhibition
British Alcan
1991, *Dynamism and Giacometti* exhibitions
British Telecom
1989, Salary for media van
1990, Outreach Programme
Cultural Relations Committee, Department of Foreign Affairs, Ireland
1991, *Strongholds* exhibition
Granada Television
1990, *New North* exhibition
Merseyside Development Corporation
1989, Outreach Programme for two years
Miller & Santhouse plc
1989, Sculpture show for visually impaired
Mobil Oil Company Ltd
1990, *New North* exhibition
Momart plc
1989–92, Artist-in-residence at Tate Gallery Liverpool
NSK Bearings Europe Ltd
1991, *A Cabinet of Signs: Contemporary Art from Post Modern Japan* exhibition

Corporate Membership Programme

Partners
Agfa UK Ltd
Barclays Bank plc
The British Petroleum Co plc
Manpower UK Thorn EMI
Unilever

Associates
Debenham, Tewson & Chinnocks
Ernst & Young
Global Asset Management
Lazard Brothers & Co Ltd
Tate & Lyle PLC

Index

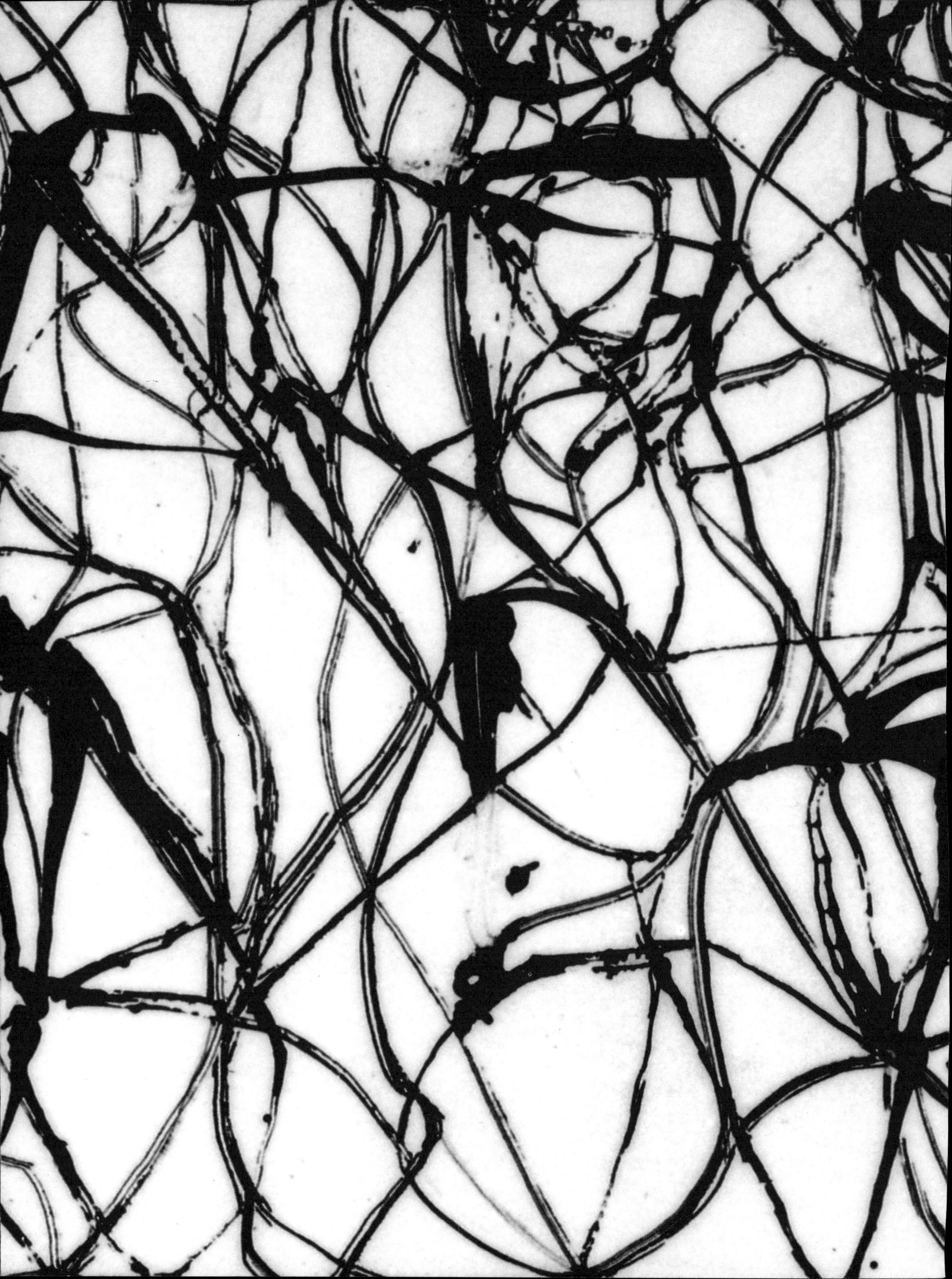